Spiced Pears in Party Dress . . .
P193

Mes Tartes

ALSO BY CHRISTINE FERBER

Mes Confitures: The Jams and Jellies of Christine Ferber

Mes Tartes

The Sweet and Savory Tarts of Christine Ferber

CHRISTINE FERBER

With the collaboration of Gilles and Laurence Laurendon
Translated by Virginia R. Phillips

Michigan State University Press • *East Lansing*

Michigan State University Press
East Lansing, Michigan 48823-5245

Printed and Bound in China

09 08 07 06 05 04 03   1 2 3 4 5 6 7 8 9 10

LIBRARY OF CONGRESS CATALOGING-IN-PUBLICATION DATA
Ferber, Christine.
Mes tartes : the sweet and savory tarts of Christine Ferber / Christine Ferber ; with the
collaboration of Gilles and Laurence Laurendon ; translated by Virginia R. Phillips.
p. cm.
ISBN 0-87013-688-7 (casebind : alk. paper)
1. Pies. 2. Cookery, French. I. Title.
TX773.F39 2003
641.8'652—dc22
2003015599

Cover design by Ariana Grabec-Dingam, New York
Book design by Sharp Designs, Lansing, MI
Photos: Bernhard Winkelmann
Food Styling: Soraya Winkelmann
The photography was done at the Ecomusée d'Ungersheim
© 1998 Editions Payot & Rivages
106 Boulevard Saint-Germain, Paris VIe

Visit Michigan State University Press on the World Wide Web at: *www.msupress.msu.edu*

To Monique Lang

To Léa Linster

To my family

Contents

A Gourmet's Passion

The first time we tasted one of Christine's tarts was in her shop in Niedermorschwir, an enchanted, fairy-tale cottage if ever there was one.

On this particular day Christine was with one of her apprentices, a boy barely sixteen who had just made his first brioche tart and his first almond-paste bear. The bear was looking at us with a woebegone expression. And the tart . . .

"Your bear doesn't look like he's having much fun! Do you really think living in a pastry shop makes somebody that sad?"

Christine came closer and tweaked the bear's ears a little forward. Then she plumped up the little creature's cheeks.

"Look! He's happier already!"

The bear now radiated a wonderful teasing smile and cast a mocking eye at the brioche tart that still didn't dare come out of its pan.

"Tell me what you put in the dough," Christine said.

"Uh, flour, sugar, an egg, milk, salt, butter, that's all, everything there's supposed to be."

Christine burst out laughing.

"How about the yeast—did you leave that under your pillow?"

The boy turned as red as a little Alsatian apple. Yeast! He forgot it!

Christine took some flour and quickly put together a little yeast dough on the work surface:

"I'm going to show you how to make a tart. You know, it's not that hard . You just have to be a little patient, handle the dough the right way . . . and never forget the whole point of pastry is to make somebody happy."

Just then a flock of chattering kids appeared like starlings to perch on the stairs to the shop. They peered in through the tiny basement window.

"We did the same thing when I was little," said Christine. "I loved watching my dad knead his bread, put the plum tarts into the oven, or take kugelhopfs out of the pans. From up there you can see everything. And you had the wonderful bakery smells floating up there through the vent. When we got to school we smelled good, too, like cake."

As she talked, Christine went on making the tart. Her fingers seemed to taste the dough with gourmet discrimination.

"For my eleventh birthday, I was allowed to make my first éclairs and my first little tarts all by myself.

"I'd fill them with sour cherries or wild fruit that I picked near the village. Sometimes my grandmother would bring me the wonderful, rosy peaches that came from the Obermorschwihr vineyards. Someday I'd like to write a book on tarts. I'd like to explain the chemistry of dough, the kind of magic you can do with flan cream and crème anglaise. What I really want is to give people the kind of gourmet stirrings that make them want to create their own new tastes and aromas."

~:~

The last time we tasted one of Christine's tarts was at our own home in Paris. We had been working together for several months on her book about tarts and we were proud of our gourmet plunder.

"What if we added an apricot tart baked with thyme honey," Christine offered.

You can't say no to a good thing. But we were beginning to wonder if this book would ever come to an end. It was at least the tenth "last" recipe that Christine absolutely wanted to add!

"You've already tested this one?" we asked, teasing her a little.

Christine doesn't like being asked this kind of question. As if she needed to test a recipe to know if it would be good! She shrugged:

"No, I haven't tested it, but I'm sure it's delicious!"

She shut her eyes for a second or two and mentally reviewed the ingredients, the proportions and, most important, the balance of tastes and flavors. When she envisions a new cake, she feels the intoxication of a treasure hunter. We wrote the new recipe. Then Christine went to the kitchen. She got out butter, crème fraîche, flour, eggs, and wonderful Bergeron* apricots bought that same morning . . .

Two hours later, enraptured, we were tasting that flavorful apricot tart.

"You're right, it's delicious. It would have been a shame to leave it out."

We had barely finished our second piece when Christine burst out:

"I just had another idea. Could we add just one more tart? It'll be the last, I promise! William pears, fresh walnuts, syrup flavored with cinnamon, vanilla, clove, star anise, and cardamom. I'll call it the Three Pirates Tart."

That night, drunk with satisfaction and exhaustion, Christine murmured,

"If I were listening to myself, I'd think I lived on nothing but tarts!"

Gilles and Laurence Laurendon

*A late summer apricot with one side red, the other yellow.

Techniques and Ingredients

Dispensing with bowl and mixer, Christine Ferber sifts a mound of flour directly on her tabletop. She pokes a hollow in the heap to corral the butter and sugar. With her hands she gradually rubs the outer ring of flour into the fat and sugar until it looks like sand. In the sand pile, she pokes another hole for water. Gathering the outer ring toward the liquid middle again, she uses her sensitive fingertips to press the mixture into flaky pastry dough.

Il faut mettre la main à la pâte—You've got to get your hands in there to know when the mix is right. Not the way most Americans learned to make a pie.

Similarly, French ingredients vary slightly from the baking supplies we usually use.

French flours tend to be a little softer—containing less protein or gluten. Gallic sugar is not packaged in exactly the same fineness or coarseness that we find here. French butters come in various moisture contents, depending on application. Measurements are, like much of the world, metric.

Most differences are easily resolved. These recipes use granulated and confectioners' sugar, except for a few instances in which extra-fine sugar will really help. Butter in this book is American. The pastry dough recipes are grouped at the front of the book and appropriate American flours for them are indicated.

In a few instances, a Gallic item poses a challenge. Though French dairy cheeses and butter are increasingly available here, certain of France's signature dairy products are not. *Crème faîche*, widely used in baking in France, is a staple in French grocery stores. Here you may not find it even in specialty stores. French soft, fresh white cheeses, collectively called *fromage frais*, are not easy to find outside of France. Workable substitutions and sources for hard-to-find items appear below and in the sources list on page 283.

FLOUR

Ferber uses French flour type 45 for flaky pastry, for sweet pastry, and for puff pastry. Type 45 is a bleached flour and a little softer than American bleached all-purpose flour. Flour that is bleached contributes to tenderness of the pastry. The author uses type 55 for bread with yeast and for strudel. Type 55 is an unbleached flour and has a little higher gluten, approaching the gluten level of American bread flour. Flour that is unbleached enhances the dough's capacity to stretch and rise.

For type 45: *Option 1.* Wondra flour (a bleached, rapid-dissolve flour) at 9.8 grams gluten. *Option 2.* Make an equivalent, about 9.9 grams gluten, by blending bleached all-purpose flour and cake flour. Rose Levy Beranbaum, in *The Pie and Pastry Bible*, suggests the following: 4 cups bleached all-purpose flour, measured by dip and sweep, and 2¼ cups cake flour, measured by dip and sweep. Stir the flours lightly before measuring and mix them well after combining to blend them evenly.

For type 55: A national brand, unbleached all-purpose flour such as Pillsbury or Gold Medal, at approximately 11 percent gluten. Flours are all measured by dip and sweep. The dip and sweep method of measuring means dipping the measuring cup into the container and sweeping off the excess with a knife. Flour should be stirred lightly before measuring. Recipes indicate which flour to use.

SUGAR

Ferber uses three types of French sugar, described here for interest since American sugars are used in the book. **Sucre cristallisé**—slightly coarser than American granulated sugar. The American recipes here use granulated in its place. **Sucre semoule**—slightly finer than American granulated sugar. Granulated is usually a good substitute. In a few recipes when finer sugar is important, extra-fine, available in supermarkets, is specified. Extra-fine may also be made by whirling granulated in a food processor or blender for a few minutes to make it finer. Fine sugar is easier to blend in meringues and fillings. **Sucre glace**—very close to confectioners' sugar but does not contain the American version's 3 percent cornstarch. Recipes calling for sucre glace use confectioners.'

DAIRY

Crème fraîche is a cultured (fermented) heavy cream with rich, nutty, slightly tart flavor and a thick silky texture. It is sold in some specialty stores. If it is not easy to find it in your area, make a thick and flavorful approximation by combining heavy cream with a tablespoon or two of sour cream or buttermilk. Allow the mixture to stand at room temperature for 24 hours. Then put it in the refrigerator where it will thicken in the next several hours or overnight and will keep for at least a week. **Crème fraîche liquide** is the French pourable version of crème fraîche. A substitute is whipping cream, though it will lack the French product's slight tang.

Fromage frais simply means young fresh cheese. **Fromage blanc** "white cheese," and **faisselle**, "basket cheese," are types of fromage frais. Fromage blanc is a creamy, white, very fresh, unripened cheese made with little or no salt. It can be made from cow's, goat's, or even ewe's milk or cream and can range from 0 to 40 percent butterfat. Fromage blanc is extremely soft, with a texture like thick sour cream. Faisselle, similar to fromage blanc, is a very young, soft, mild white cheese. It is sold tightly sealed in a plastic, sieve-like container, or basket. Italian basket cheese sometimes appears in markets as well. These two cheeses can be difficult to find.

An authentic fromage blanc is nationally distributed by Vermont Butter & Cheese, makers of specialty European-style creamery products. (800/884-6287; *www.vtgoats.com*). This fromage blanc is nonfat—0 percent butterfat. Ferber specifies 0 percent, 20 percent and 40 percent butterfat, depending on the recipe. For higher butterfat applications, home cooks could enrich the 0 percent fromage blanc by replacing about a third of it with 70–75 percent butterfat mascarpone or with 40 percent butterfat heavy cream. The Ideal Cheese Shop in New York City (800/ 382-0109; *www.idealcheese.com*) will ship an imported 40 percent butterfat fromage blanc anywhere in the United States. If mail-ordering isn't an option, VB&C president Allison Hooper suggests other options. The cheese-maker who learned her art in France says VB&C's Quark, a liquidy-textured, spreadable fresh white cheese at 11 percent butterfat, can be drained through a cheesecloth-lined sieve for an hour or two, until it resembles the thick sour cream texture of fromage blanc. She notes, "Eleven percent butterfat gives a much creamier taste than 0 percent fromage blanc and is more forgiving in baking." Quark can be drained further as a substitute for the firmer faisselle. In a pinch, Hooper suggests, whole milk yogurt, usually about 5 percent butterfat, can be drained to the texture required. A pinch of sugar will soften the yogurt's tartness.

BUTTER

Some pastry chefs prefer French Plugrá butter, available in specialty markets, because of its lower moisture content—especially for puff pastry in which lower moisture content gives a better soft butter consistency and less steam. Ferber likes Charentes butter for its lower moisture. Other professional bakers say that it makes no big difference. Butter in these recipes is the unsalted supermarket variety.

PRODUCE

Farmers' markets and farm stands are always the gold standard. Of course France's local produce includes varieties we don't grow here. But our own locally grown fruits and vegetables are bursting with seasonal freshness and flavor—not to mention the intensification they will receive under Christine's artistry. French varieties are usually described to aid in creative substitution.

MEASUREMENTS

A home scale that indicates both ounces and grams makes for speedy, accurate measurements and is highly recommended. Recipes indicate both metric and English measures except for these units: French "coffee-spoons" have been converted to teaspoons. A "knifepoint" is about ⅛ teaspoon. A "knob" of butter is 1½ ounces.

Successful Flaky Pastry

The secret to a good tart has to do first and foremost with the quality of ingredients—you must be adamant about this.

FLOUR

For flaky pastry, brioche dough, and bread dough, I advise you to use type 55 flour*. It is also suitable for making certain fillings. For puff pastry or rich flaky pastry, type 45 flour with a little less gluten is perfect.

BUTTER

Butter is used in making all pastry except bread dough. Its flavor is unique! There are no substitutes. Butter can't be compared to any other shortening.

Normandy butter works best for making flaky pastry, rich flaky pastry, sweet pastries, and fillings. Charentes butter, with a little less moisture, is best for puff pastry. Be sure to keep the butter refrigerated and tightly wrapped in plastic wrap. Otherwise it picks up odors.

SUGAR

I use *sucre semoule*,*for flaky pastry, brioche dough, and pastry creams.

For rich flaky pastry and sweet pastry; I prefer using *sucre glace*, confectioners' sugar: It is finer and

* *Slightly finer than American granulated sugar. American sugars are specified in the recipes.*

dissolves more quickly, so the dough can be made without working it too much. It is also good for decorating the tarts.

For some pastry doughs, I use vanilla sugar. I always keep some on hand in my kitchen. I give it the vanilla taste and aroma by combining two pounds of granulated sugar with 8 vanilla beans, and storing it in a glass jar away from the light.

SALT

All pastry calls for salt. You need just a pinch to enhance flavors and balance tastes.

EGGS

Eggs enrich the pastry, adding silkiness and flavor and giving it an attractive golden color. Eggs also bind the ingredients. They give body to pastry creams and fillings. As a finishing touch, I often use beaten egg to "gild" tarts.

Egg whites beaten stiff let you make magnificent meringue tarts.

WATER AND MILK

Both are "binders" for pastry dough. You use milk in many pastry creams. Always use whole milk!

LEAVENING

For raised dough, I use brewer's yeast,* which you can buy at a bakery.

Baking powder is an ingredient in some sweet pastries and rich flaky pastries (scant 1 teaspoon [3 g] of baking powder to 3½ cups [500 g] of flour).

---

* Same as baker's yeast, available in compressed fresh packets at the supermarket.

CREAM

I use light whipping cream for whipped creams and flan creams. I use crème fraîche, which is thicker and a little tangy, for tarts with browned toppings and for savory tarts.

FRUIT

Most of the fruit I use is picked in the orchards and woods or bought at local markets. I use fresh fruit only. It must look wonderful, be very fragrant, and have perfect flavor!

Secret of Good Pastry

Each pastry recipe given makes enough for at least two tarts. You can freeze the dough and use it as your needs dictate.

You can't have a good tart without good pastry!

With a little flour, sugar, butter, egg, and milk, the array of textures you can create is tremendous!

But be careful— "make haste slowly": Pastry is the part of the recipe that demands the most work and patience. You can't be half-hearted about setting aside the time for it. It is the pastry that gives your tart its texture, beautiful golden color, and shape—in other words, all that appeals to the eye and stimulates the appetite.

You can enhance your pastry by flavoring it with spices. It will be more harmonious, more voluptuous, and the pleasure of tasting it can only become more intense.

Before getting started, check to see that you have everything that you'll need—utensils, measured ingredients, and the recipe—within reach.

FOR A GOOD PASTRY SHELL

It is essential to let your pastry rest thoroughly. The first rest is the most important one. After making the pastry, leave it in the refrigerator for at least 3 hours. The best thing is to make it the day before. This rest allows the dough to release some of its elasticity and prevents it from shrinking during baking.

I advise you to take the pastry out of the refrigerator at least 15 minutes before rolling it so that it will be softer and easier to work. Lightly flour your work surface so that the pastry won't stick. Be careful: Too much flour affects the quality. If you have a marble board, that's perfect. The cool stone prevents the dough from softening.

Roll the pastry with a rolling pin, working it gently. Your pastry circle must always be larger than the size of the pan. Roll the pastry around the rolling pin and lift it above the pan. Unroll it carefully so that it is less likely to tear. If your dough is just too fragile, you can roll it between two sheets of plastic wrap.

Now lift the edge of the pastry and ease it toward the bottom of the pan, pressing it gently with your fingertips against the bottom and sides of the pan. Roll the rolling pin across the top edge of the pan to cut off the excess pastry.

Always remember to prick the pastry with a fork so that the bottom won't puff up.

It is imperative at this point to let the pastry rest, refrigerated and covered with plastic wrap, for about 30 minutes before filling and baking it. This prevents it from shrinking when baked.

BLIND-BAKING A PASTRY SHELL

Often a tart shell is prebaked without the filling—"baking without browning." The dough is first pricked with a fork, then covered with parchment and filled with dried beans or rice. This keeps the bottom of the shell from puffing up and the sides from shrinking away from the sides of the pan during baking.

Do it this way: Cut a circle of parchment paper larger than the diameter of the pan. Fold it in quarters and snip a fringe into the curved edge about ½ inch (2 cm) deep so that the paper will conform more easily to the shape of the pan. Unfold it and place it in the bottom of the tart pan. Fill it with a layer of dried beans or rice up to the rim of the pan.

After the rest period indicated in the recipes, bake the shell for about 12 minutes at 350° F [175° C]. Then remove the dried beans or rice and carefully remove the parchment paper.

FLAKY PASTRY

Light, tender, and crunchy, this dough is the easiest and quickest to make. It is also the most traditional. You can make sweet or savory tarts with it.

> 3½ cups [500 g] national brand, unbleached, all-purpose flour
> 3 Tbsp. [375 g] softened butter
> ¾ tsp. [3 g] salt
> 2½ tsp. [10 g] sugar
> 5 oz. [150 g / 15 cl] cold water

In a bowl, dissolve the salt in the water and set aside. Sift the flour onto your work surface. Make a well and put the butter and then the sugar in the center. Gather the flour little by little toward the center of the well and rub this mixture of butter, flour, and sugar gently between your hands until it has a texture that looks and feels like coarse meal.

Make another hollow and pour the salted water into it. Gather the flour, butter, and sugar mixture toward the center, kneading the dough lightly. Be careful not to work it too much. Now shape the dough into a ball. Wrap it carefully in plastic wrap. Leave it in the refrigerator for at least 3 hours. Ideally, make it the day before and refrigerate it overnight.

FLAKY PASTRY WITH EGG

Adding egg makes your pastry sturdier, perfect for savory tarts.

> 3½ cups [500 g] national brand, unbleached, all-purpose flour
> 3½ oz. [100 g / 10 cl] cold milk
> 3 sticks *plus* 2 Tbsp. / 13.4 oz. [375 g] softened butter
> ¾ tsp. [3 g] salt

2 tsp. [10 g] granulated sugar
2 egg yolks

In a bowl, dissolve the salt in the milk and set aside.

Sift the flour onto your work surface. Make a hollow and put the butter in the center, then the sugar. Gather the flour little by little toward the center of the hollow and rub the flour, butter, and sugar mixture between your hands gently until it looks like coarse meal.

Now make another hollow and pour the salted milk and egg yolks into it. Gather the flour, butter, and sugar mixture toward the center, lightly kneading the dough. Be careful not to work it too much. Now shape the dough into a ball. Wrap it carefully in plastic wrap. Leave it in the refrigerator for at least 3 hours. Ideally, make it the day before and leave it refrigerated overnight.

SWEET PASTRY

Sweet pastry is rich and crunchy. It's used for fresh fruit tarts and jam tarts. With leftover dough you can make delicious little sugar-dusted pastry cookies.

I like to give the flavor a lift with a pinch of cinnamon, cardamom, *pain d'épice** or even a little citrus zest.

3½ cups [500 g] Wondra flour *or* pastry-flour equivalent
1⅓ cups [150 g] confectioners' sugar
2 sticks *plus* 5½ Tbsp. / 10¾ oz. [300 g] softened butter
2 eggs *or* 3½ oz. [100 g] créme fraîche
Scant ½ tsp. [2 g] salt
1½ Tbsp. [20 g] vanilla sugar

A gingerbread spice mixture of anise, cinnamon, and cloves.

Sift the flour onto your work surface. Make a hollow. Sprinkle the salt around the edge of the hollow. Put the butter, confectioners' sugar, and vanilla sugar in the center. Work the butter and the two sugars with your fingertips until you have a smooth cream. Gather the flour little by little into the center of the hollow and rub this mixture lightly between your hands until it has a texture like coarse meal.

Now make another hollow. Beat two eggs *or* crème fraîche in a bowl and pour this liquid into it. Gather the flour, butter, and sugar mixture toward the center, lightly kneading the dough. Be careful not to work it too much. Shape the dough into a ball. Protect it by wrapping it carefully in plastic wrap. Let it rest in the refrigerator for at least 3 hours. Ideally, make it the day before and leave it refrigerated overnight.

RICH FLAKY PASTRY NO. I

Rich flaky pastry is a delicious crunchy dough that melts in your mouth. It contains more butter than sweet pastry, which makes it more crumbly and a little trickier to shape.

> 1½ cups [200 g] **Wondra flour** *or* **pastry-flour equivalent**
> ½ cup [50 g] **confectioners' sugar**
> 1 stick *plus* 3 Tbsp. / 6½ oz. [160 g] **softened butter**
> 2 **egg yolks, hard-boiled**
> Generous ⅓ cup [40 g] **blanched ground almonds**
> Scant ¼ tsp. [1 g] **salt**
> 2½ tsp. [10 g] **vanilla sugar**

Hard-boil the 2 eggs. When they are cool, remove the yolks and mash them thoroughly with a fork.

Sift the flour onto your work surface. Make a hollow. Sprinkle the salt around the edge of the hollow. Put the butter, confectioners' sugar, and vanilla sugar in the center. Work the butter and the two sugars with your fingertips until you have a smooth cream. Add the mashed egg yolk and ground almonds. Mix.

Now gather the flour little by little into the center of the well and rub the mixture gently between your hands until the texture looks like coarse meal. Lightly knead the dough. Be careful not to work it too much. Shape the dough into a ball. Protect it by wrapping it carefully in plastic wrap. Let it rest in the refrigerator for at least 3 hours.

I advise you to let this dough rest at room temperature for at least 20 minutes before rolling it.

You can also make delicious little pastry cookies with this dough. To do so, add a scant ½ teaspoon [2 g] baking powder to the flour.

Alternatively, you can use ground hazelnuts or walnuts instead of the ground almonds. Orange zest is a perfect partner with the hazelnuts, and lemon zest goes beautifully with the walnuts.

RICH FLAKY PASTRY NO. 2

This dough is even more crumbly and fragile than the one before, but it is that much more flavorful because it has more butter. In Alsace we use it a lot at Christmas to make quantities of little cutout sugar cookies.

1⅘ cups [250 g] Wondra flour *or* pastry-flour equivalent
1¼ cups [150 g] confectioners' sugar
2 sticks *less* 2 Tbsp. / 7 oz. [200 g] softened butter
Finely grated zest of ¼ lemon
1 egg white
½ tsp. [2 g] baking powder
Scant ½ tsp. [2 g] salt

Sift the flour onto your work surface. Make a hollow. Sprinkle the salt, baking powder, and finely grated lemon zest around the edges of the hollow. Place the butter and confectioners' sugar in the center. Work the butter and sugar with your fingertips until they become a velvety cream. Gather the flour little by little into the center of the hollow and rub the mixture lightly between your hands until it resembles coarse meal. Make another hollow and pour the egg white into it. Bring the flour, butter, and sugar mixture toward the center, lightly kneading the dough. Be careful not to work it too much.

Now shape the dough into a ball. Protect it by wrapping it carefully in plastic wrap. Leave it in the refrigerator at least 3 hours. Ideally, make it the day before and leave it refrigerated overnight.

I advise you to let this dough rest at room temperature for at least 20 minutes before rolling it.

RICH FLAKY PASTRY WITH PRALINE PASTE AND HAZELNUTS

This dough is perfect for blind-baked (prebaked) tart shells. It has the characteristic of never shrinking as it cooks, so it isn't necessary to fill a parchment liner with dried beans or rice. Just be sure that it fits tightly against the sides and into the angles of the pan.

1⅘ cups [250 g] **Wondra flour** *or* **pastry-flour equivalent**

¾ cup [90 g] **confectioners' sugar**

1 stick *plus* 2¾ Tbsp. / 5⅓ oz. [150 g] **softened butter**

1 **egg**

¼ cup [25 g] **finely ground almonds**

2 Tbsp. [15 g] **praline paste*** *or* **ground caramelized almonds**

Scant ½ tsp. [2 g] **salt**

1 tsp. [5 g] **vanilla sugar**

Sift the flour onto your work surface. Make a hollow. Sprinkle the salt and ground almonds around the edge of the hollow. Place the butter, confectioners' sugar, vanilla sugar, and praline in the center. Work the butter, the two sugars, and the praline with your fingertips until the mixture becomes a velvety cream.

---

* Praline paste, paté pralinée, is a very finely ground preparation of caramelized almonds requiring specialized commercial equipment to make; ground praline, pralin, also made with caramelized almonds, is crunchier and can be made in a food processor. Both can be mail-ordered.

Gather the flour little by little toward the center of the hollow and rub the mixture lightly between your hands until it looks like coarse meal.

Now make another hollow. Beat the egg in a bowl and pour it into the well. Bring the flour, butter, sugar, and praline mixture toward the center, lightly kneading the dough. Be careful not to overwork it. Now shape the dough into a ball. Protect it by wrapping it carefully in plastic wrap. Let it rest in the refrigerator for at least 3 hours. Ideally, make it the day before and leave it refrigerated overnight.

SEMI-PUFF PASTRY

Crunchy and light, and quicker to make than classic puff pastry, this dough is equally well suited to sweet or savory tarts. This recipe is a good warm-up for attempting real puff pastry!

> 3½ cups *plus* 1 Tbsp. [500 g] Wondra flour *or* pastry-flour equivalent
> 2 sticks *plus* 5½ Tbsp. / 10¾ oz. [300 g] cold butter
> 1 tsp. [5 g] salt
> 2 tsp. [10 g] sugar
> ⅔ oz. / 1½ Tbsp. [20 g / 2 cl] cold water

In a bowl, dissolve the salt in the water and set aside.

Cut the butter into small dice. Sift the flour onto your work surface. Toss the bits of butter in the flour, coating without mashing them. Make a well and pour the salted water into it. Add the sugar. Gather the flour, butter, and sugar mixture gradually toward the center, lightly kneading the dough. Take care not to overwork it. The cubes of butter must keep their initial consistency and the dough should keep its lumpy appearance. Now shape the dough into a ball. Protect it by wrapping it carefully in plastic wrap. Let it rest in the refrigerator for about 20 minutes.

On your lightly floured work surface, shape the ball of dough into a rectangle a little more than ½ inch [1.5 cm] thick. Brush off the excess flour with a pastry brush.

Fold the rectangle in thirds, folding the top third down and the bottom third up, as you would a letter. This is the first "turn" for your pastry. Rotate the folded pastry a quarter turn to the right. From here on, you won't change the direction of rotation and you won't turn the dough over. Protect it by wrapping it carefully in plastic wrap. Let it rest in the refrigerator for 10 minutes.

Lightly flour your work surface. Take the dough out of the refrigerator and, keeping it facing in the same direction, roll your dough again, folding it in thirds as before. You've done the second "turn" for your dough. Now rotate the folded packet a quarter turn to the right. Without changing the way it is facing or turning it over, wrap it carefully in plastic wrap and leave it for 10 minutes in the refrigerator.

Flour your work surface again. Take the dough out of the refrigerator, keeping it facing the same direction. Roll it out a third and last time and fold in thirds as before. You've completed the third "turn" for your dough. Wrap it carefully in plastic wrap and this time before rolling it out let it rest in the refrigerator for 30 minutes.

It's essential to work this dough in a cool room and on a cold surface; a marble work surface is ideal. For the best puff pastry, I advise you to wait until the next day to do the third "turn," an hour before you roll out the pastry.

TRUE PUFF PASTRY

Puff pastry is a delicate dough, suitable for sweet or savory tarts. It is light, melt in your mouth, and crunchy all at the same time, but is also the most technically challenging to make. This marvelous dough is more demanding of time and skill than any other.

For the first dough:

¼ cup [40 g] **Wondra flour** *or* **pastry-flour equivalent**
2 sticks *plus* 2 Tbsp. / 9 oz. [250 g] **softened butter**

For the second dough:

1⅘ cups [250 g] **Wondra flour** *or* **pastry-flour equivalent**
2 Tbsp. / 1 oz. [30 g] **softened butter**

1 tsp. [5 g] **salt**

½ cup [125 g / 12.5 cl] **water**

To prepare the first dough: Mix the softened butter with the flour. Shape a flattened round of this dough on a lightly floured work surface. Form a disk a little less than 1 inch [2 cm] thick. Wrap it carefully in plastic wrap and put it in the refrigerator for an hour.

To prepare the second dough: In a bowl, dissolve the salt in the water and set aside. Sift the flour onto your work surface. Make a hollow and place the butter in it. Pour in the salted water. Bring the flour gradually into the center, lightly kneading the dough. Take care not to overwork it (it should look lumpy). Now shape the dough into a ball. Wrap it carefully in plastic wrap. Let it rest in the refrigerator for about 30 minutes.

On the lightly floured work surface, roll the first dough disk out very thin until it is about ⅛ inch [3 mm] thick. On the board next to it, flatten out the second dough ball into a square a little less than 1 inch [2 cm] thick. Put this square on the circle made with the first dough and fold the edges of the circle in toward the center of the square. Roll the new square of dough, making a rectangle a little less than ¾ inch [1.5 cm] thick. Brush off the excess flour with a brush. Fold the two shorter edges of the rectangle toward the center so that they join. Now fold these two parts in two, one over the other. You have given your dough the first "double turn." Now rotate your rectangle a quarter turn to the right. From here on you won't change the direction or turn the dough over. Wrap the dough carefully in plastic wrap and refrigerate it for 30 minutes.

Lightly flour your work surface. Roll your dough a second time into a rectangle a little less than ¾ inch [1.5 cm] thick. Brush off the excess flour with a brush. Fold the two shorter edges of the rectangle to the center so that the edges meet. Now fold these two parts in two, one over the other. You have done your second "double turn." Rotate your rectangle a quarter turn to the right. Without turning it over, wrap it carefully in plastic wrap and let it rest in the refrigerator for 30 minutes.

Flour your table again. Roll your dough a third and last time into a rectangle a little less than ¾ inch

[1.5 cm] thick. Brush off the excess flour with a brush. Fold this rectangle in thirds, bringing the top down and the bottom up, as in folding a letter. This is the last turn, which is a "single turn." Wrap the dough carefully in plastic wrap and refrigerate it for an hour.

It is essential to work with this dough in a cool room and on a cold surface; a marble work surface is ideal.

For the best puff pastry, I advise you not to do the third turn until the following day, about an hour before rolling it.

BRIOCHE DOUGH

I love to work with raised dough because it's "alive" and its swelling curves bespeak the exquisite pleasure it offers. Crusty on the outside and tender in the middle, this dough is flavorful and melts in the mouth. Still, of all the doughs, it contains the least butter!

⅔ cup [100 g] *plus* 2¾ cups [400 g] national brand, unbleached, all-purpose flour
1½ packages compressed fresh yeast,* *or* [25 g] fresh yeast
2 Tbsp. [25 g] sucre semoule
1 egg
1 cup *plus* 1 Tbsp. [250 g / 25 cl] cold whole milk
1⅛ tsp. [7 g] salt
1 stick *plus* 1 tsp. / 4¼ oz. [120 g] softened butter

In a bowl, sift the ¾ cup [100 g] of flour and combine it with the fresh yeast and the milk. You will have a little "sponge." Cover with plastic wrap and let it to rest at room temperature for 15 minutes. Now sift the remaining 2¾ cups of flour on your work surface. Make a hollow and sprinkle the salt and sugar onto the ring of flour.

---

* American compressed fresh yeast comes in packages of 6⁄10 oz., or 17 g. So 1½ cakes of fresh yeast, or 25 g, should replace the above.

Put the sponge and egg, slightly beaten, in the center. Gather the flour gradually into the center of the hollow, kneading it firmly for about 5 minutes. The dough will become a little lighter in color. You will know it is kneaded enough when it comes away from your fingers easily.

Place in a bowl. Add the softened butter and beat it until it is well incorporated. Your dough will now be supple and shiny.

Shape the dough into a ball. Put it into a large bowl. Protect it by covering it with a kitchen towel and let it rest at room temperature, about 68°F [20°C], for 30 minutes. When the dough has almost doubled in size, roll it for a few seconds between your hands. Now cover it again with a kitchen towel and let it rest again at room temperature for 20 minutes. The dough is ready to roll.

You can prepare this dough the day before and put it in the refrigerator, covered in plastic wrap. Take it out and leave it at room temperature for 20 minutes before shaping it.

These creams bring an opulent, silky lightness to your tarts. They coat them generously with their creamy softness and are melting and sweet in the mouth. I adore creams!

FLAN CREAM

In many recipes the fruit and flan cream cook together. The cream combines with the fruit juices and gives a sweet and velvety richness to the tart.

You can flavor your flan creams with finely grated orange or lemon zest, herb infusions, or spices.

There are many flan cream recipes, depending on the kind of fruit filling, and I like to give them as we go along.

PASTRY CREAM

Pastry cream provides richness as well. I use it as a filling in sweet tart shells with fresh fruit fillings. The silky cream contrasts marvelously with the crunchiness of the pastry and the texture of the fruits.

You can enhance cold pastry cream with a little clear liquor or liqueur, or make it even lighter by adding the equivalent of half its volume of whipped cream.

> 2 cups *plus* 2 Tbsp. [500 g / 50 cl] whole milk
> ½ cup *plus* 1 Tbsp. [125 g] extra-fine sugar
> 5 egg yolks

3½ Tbsp. [50 g / 5 cl] **light whipping cream**
5 Tbsp. [40 g] **potato starch** *or* **cornstarch**
1 vanilla bean

Split the vanilla bean lengthwise. In a heavy-bottomed saucepan, heat the milk with half the sugar (scant ⅓ cup [60 g]) and the vanilla bean. Bring it to a simmer. Remove from the heat and cover the pan to let the vanilla infuse.

Meanwhile, in a bowl, mix the remaining sugar with the potato starch or cornstarch. Add the egg yolks and cream. Combine them using a whip. Check to see that there are no lumps in the mixture.

Remove the vanilla bean. Scrape out the seeds with the point of a knife and add them to the milk. Slowly add the milk to the sugar, starch, egg yolk and cream mixture. Pour the mixture into a saucepan and bring to a boil on medium heat, whipping constantly so that doesn't stick on the bottom. Let it simmer on low heat for 10 minutes , stirring constantly. The cream should be thick and smooth.

Pour the cream into a bowl. Place a sheet of plastic wrap on the surface of the cream to prevent formation of a skin. Let it cool, then chill for at least an hour in the refrigerator before using it. Ideally, prepare the cream the day before.

CRÈME ANGLAISE

Sweet rich crème anglaise brings a delicately fresh note. Lightly spiced or enhanced with citrus zest, it happily accompanies crumbly, crunchy tarts.

2 cups *plus* 2 Tbsp. [500 g / 50 cl] **whole milk**
Scant ⅞ cup [180 g] **extra-fine sugar**
6 egg yolks
1 vanilla bean
7 oz. [200 g / 20 cl] **whipping cream**

Split the vanilla bean lengthwise. In a heavy-bottomed saucepan, heat the milk, half of the sugar and the vanilla bean. Bring to a simmer. Remove from the heat and cover the pan to let the vanilla infuse.

Meanwhile, in a bowl, combine the remaining sugar and egg yolks. Beat with whip until the mixture becomes light and slightly foamy.

Remove the vanilla bean. Scrape out the seeds with the point of a knife and add them to the milk. Slowly add the milk to the sugar and egg yolk mixture, stirring constantly. Pour this mixture into a saucepan and let it cook on low heat, stirring constantly with a whip until the cream thickens. Check to see if your cream is "à la nappe" by dipping a wooden spatula into it. It has reached the proper point when it will coat the spatula.

Pour the cream into a bowl. Beat it again for about 2 minutes. Place a piece of plastic wrap on the surface of the cream to prevent formation of a skin. Let the cream cool, then chill it for at least an hour in the refrigerator before using it. Add the light whipping cream. Your cream will only be silkier! You can make this cream the day before if you wish.

You can flavor your crème anglaise with spices by replacing the vanilla bean in the milk with ½ cinnamon stick, or 2 star anise, or ¼ teaspoon of ground cardamom, or ¼ teaspoon of ground gingerbread spice, or the finely grated zest of ½ lemon, or even ½ teaspoon of freshly grated ginger.

ALMOND CREAM

This delicately flavored cream goes well with stone fruits. Almond cream also protects the bottom of the tart. As the tart bakes, the cream absorbs the fruit juices and keeps the crust crunchier. It is also good to know that an almond cream-filled tart keeps its flavor and velvety texture for 2 days.

1 stick *plus* 3 Tbsp. / 5½ oz. [150 g] softened butter
1 cup [120 g] confectioners' sugar
1⅓ cups [150 g] finely ground blanched almonds

7 Tbsp. [60 g] flour

3 eggs

In a bowl, combine the butter and sugar. Beat until the mixture is lighter in color and silky smooth. Add the eggs and continue beating for a few minutes.

Mix the flour and ground almonds with your fingertips. Pour the flour and almond mixture in a stream into the bowl with the butter, sugar, and egg mixture, stirring gently with a wooden spatula.

You might also flavor this cream with the finely grated zest of ½ orange or lemon, or a few drops of bitter almond extract or essence of orange blossom.

HAZELNUT CREAM

1 cup [100 g] finely ground hazelnuts

7 Tbsp. / 3½ oz. [100 g] softened butter

⅔ cup *plus* 1 Tbsp. [80 g] confectioners' sugar

3½ Tbsp. [40 g] flour

2 eggs

3½ oz. [100 g / 10 cl] whipping cream

In a bowl, combine the butter and sugar. Beat until the mixture is a little lighter in color and silky smooth. Add the eggs and continue beating for a few minutes.

Combine the flour and the ground hazelnuts with your fingertips. Sprinkle them into the bowl with the butter, sugar, and eggs, stirring gently with a wooden spatula. Add the cream and stir gently.

You can flavor this cream with the finely grated zest of ½ orange, or with 2 ounces [50 g] of grated bitter dark chocolate, or 2 tablespoons [25 g] candied, diced orange or lemon peel.

Glazing and Finishing Tarts

A jelly or gelatin glaze is recommended for fresh fruit fillings. The finish coat makes the tart even more glistening and appealing. An irresistible temptation for the eyes!

The glaze also preserves the bright flavor and freshness of either cooked or uncooked fruit. It prevents fruit from darkening, particularly peach, apricot, or apple tarts.

Apple jelly enlivens the color of yellow fruits. Raspberry or red currant jelly is a better match for tarts filled with red fruits: strawberries, raspberries, blueberries, black currants, and other garden or forest berries. Personally, I use jellies lightly flavored with lemon. The hint of acidity enhances the fruits' fragrance and flavor. Be sure that the jellies you are using have enough body.

APPLE JELLY

3⅓ lbs. [1.5 kg] apples
6⅓ cups [1.5 kg / 150 cl] water
4⅔ cups [1 kg] granulated sugar
Juice of 1 lemon

The day before, rinse the apples with cold water. Remove the stems and quarter the fruit without peeling it. Place the apples in a preserving pan and cover them with water.

Bring the apples to a boil and let them simmer on low heat for 30 minutes. The apples should be soft to the touch. Collect the juice by pouring this preparation into a fine chinois sieve and pressing lightly on the fruit with the back of a skimmer. Now filter the juice a second time in a piece of cheesecloth that you have previously wet and wrung out. Let the juice run freely. It is best to leave it overnight in the refrigerator.

The next day, measure 4¼ cups [1 kg] of the juice collected, leaving behind the sediment formed during the night. Pour the juice into a preserving pan with the sugar and lemon juice. Bring the mixture to a boil and boil for 5 minutes. Skim carefully. Check the set.* Put into jars immediately and seal.

Note: Choose genuinely green apples—as in unripe—preferably at the beginning of July before the fruit has had time to ripen. If under-ripe apples are not available use very tart greenings. You can make a purée with the apple quarters by putting them through a food mill with a coarse disk. Sweeten and flavor with spices to your liking.

RASPBERRY JELLY

> **3⅓ lbs. [1.5 kg] raspberries**
> **7 oz. [200 g / 20 cl] water**
> **4⅔ cups [1 kg] granulated sugar**
> **Juice of 1 lemon**

Pour the raspberries and water into a preserving pan and bring the contents to a boil. Cover the pan and let the fruits soften on low heat for 5 minutes. Collect the juice by pouring the mixture into a fine chinois strainer. For clear jelly, do not press the fruit. Filter it a second time by pouring it through a piece of cheesecloth that has been wet and wrung out.

Pour the collected juice (4⅘ cups [1 kg]) into a copper pan with the lemon juice and sugar. Bring the mixture to a boil and boil for 5 minutes. Skim carefully. Check the set. Return to a boil. Pour into jars immediately and seal.

* To check the set: Jam has to reach 22°F [105°C] on a candy thermometer. If you don't have a candy thermometer, put a few drops of jam on a chilled plate and check the consistency. It should not run and should wrinkle slightly when pushed with the fingertip.

RED CURRANT JELLY

3¾ lbs. [1.7 kg] red currants, *or* **about 3⅓ lbs. [1.5 kg] net**

7 oz. [200 g / 20 cl] water

4⅔ cups [1 kg] granulated sugar

Juice of 1 lemon

Rinse the currant bunches in cold water, drain them, and strip the berries from the stems. In a preserving pan bring them to a boil with the water. Cover the pan and let the berries soften on low heat for 5 minutes.

Collect the juice by pouring this mixture into a chinois strainer. Then filter it by pouring it through a piece of cheesecloth previously soaked and wrung out. Pour the juice collected into a copper pan with the lemon juice and granulated sugar. Bring the juice to a boil and boil 5 minutes. Skim carefully. Pour into jars immediately and seal.

FINISHING TECHNIQUES

A glaze of syrup, confectioners' sugar, vanilla sugar, or honey is another finish for some tarts after they are baked.

Sometimes I top my tarts before baking them by crisscrossing strips of dough over them or by decorating them with pastry shapes cut with a cookie-cutter. I paint the cutouts with beaten egg so they will have a beautiful golden color when they come out of the oven.

If you use just the egg yolk, it is a good idea to dilute it with half water. Otherwise your pastry may brown too quickly.

I like to sprinkle my tarts with a thin layer of confectioners' sugar or top them with a cloud of meringue. What I love best is to cover them with streusel, crunchy ground almonds, or caramelized dried fruit.

The confectioners' sugar is magic! It contrasts wonderfully with the crunchy and velvety tastes of the tart. It makes me think of the sweets of my childhood. This simple little finishing touch provides something celebratory for all your pastries.

Equipment and Utensils

WORK SURFACE

I always prepare my pastry on a table topped with stainless steel or smooth marble. A slab of marble is ideal for rolling pastry. Its cool temperature prevents the pastry from softening. If you don't have marble you can roll your pastry on a wooden board, taking care to cover it with a sheet of heavy plastic wrap.

It is important to prepare your tarts in a kitchen where the ambient temperature is 62°F [15°C] to 75°F [18°C]. When pastry warms up, it sticks and tears.

THE MAJOR ESSENTIALS

Without these, the job won't get done. You need:

- an oven
- a refrigerator for chilling your doughs, creams, and certain basic ingredients such as crème fraîche, milk and butter.
- a freezer for storing dough wrapped in plastic wrap, then wrapped again in aluminum foil. Pastry wrapped this way will keep for a month. Beyond that it dries out.

PANS

Pans lend their appealing forms to your gourmet creations:

- a tinned steel or dark metal or nonstick tart pan, with a removable bottom if you wish, and a plain (not fluted) rim, 10 inches [26 cm] in diameter and 1 inch [3 cm] deep. Dark metal absorbs the heat better and browns the pastry perfectly.

- A nonstick pan, 10 inches [26 cm] in diameter and 2 inches [5 cm] deep, that can go into the oven and on the range top, for making Tarte Tatin.
- A ceramic pan with a fluted rim, 10 inches [26 cm] in diameter and a little more than 1½ inches [4 cm] high for making clafoutis.
- A dozen tartlet pans, 4 inches [10 cm] in diameter and 1¾ inches [2 cm] deep.
- A heavy black steel baking sheet.

LARGE UTENSILS

Basic equipment includes the following:
- A copper pan for making glazes and fruit jellies
- Two stainless steel saucepans for heating syrups and glazes
- One nonstick skillet
- A food processor* or electric mixer for beating egg whites and possibly for making some pastries
- Bowls and dishes of various sizes and materials—stainless steel, glass and ceramic—for holding prepared fruits, preparing cream mixtures, and storing preparations in the refrigerator.

SMALL UTENSILS

These let you do precise work and refine the finishing touches:
- A kitchen scale for weighing ingredients
- A measuring cup
- A cutting board
- A steel or wood pastry rolling pin
- A sifter for flour, ground dried fruit powder or confectioners' sugar.
- A steel spatula for spreading creams in a pastry shell

*Some large food processors have a whip attachment.

- A pastry bag with a plain metal tip for piping cream evenly into tart shells and a fluted tip for decorative piping of cream and meringues
- Two whips, a medium-sized and a small one, for mixing and beating creams
- Several wooden spoons
- A footed strainer for rinsing and draining fruits
- A juicer
- A zester or paring knife
- A table knife
- A small ladle
- Spoons
- A fork
- An apple corer
- A nutcracker
- A candy thermometer
- A roller for cutting pastry
- Cookie-cutters for small pastry cutouts to decorate certain tarts
- A set of round or fluted-edge cookie-cutters for cutting bottoms for tartlets
- Plastic wrap for protecting refrigerated doughs
- Sheets of parchment paper for covering baking sheets or for blind-baking pastry shells
- Dried beans or rice for filling blind-baked pastry shells
- A natural bristle pastry brush for painting egg on pastries or for coating and glazing tarts
- Pastry racks in various sizes for cooling tarts
- A sugar shaker for sprinkling tarts with sugar

Spring

Asparagus and Fennel Tart

---

11 oz. [300 g] flaky pastry with egg (*see recipe page 15*)

1¾ lbs. [800 g] green asparagus, *or* 1 lb. [450 g] net

4 small fennel bulbs

1½ Tbsp. [20 g] butter

1½ Tbsp. [20 g / 2 cl] peanut oil

Salt

Freshly ground black pepper

Granulated sugar

To make the egg custard:

5 oz. [150 g / 15 cl] crème fraîche

7 oz. [200 g / 15 cl] whole milk

4 eggs

Salt

Freshly ground black pepper

To glaze:

1 egg

To bake:

A tart pan with plain rim, 10 inches [26 cm] in diameter and 1 inch [3 cm] deep

The day before, prepare your flaky pastry with egg.

The next day, roll your pastry on a lightly floured work surface into a circle a little more than 1/16 inch [2 mm] thick and 13 inches [34 cm] in diameter.

Butter your pan and carefully place the pastry in it, pressing it lightly with the fingertips against the bottom and sides. Roll the rolling pin across the top edge of the pan to cut off the small amount of excess dough. Prick the bottom of the tart with a fork and refrigerate it for 30 minutes, covered with plastic wrap.

Preheat the oven to 350°F [180°C].

Blind-bake your pastry shell (*see page 14*) for 15 minutes. Then brush the pastry with a little beaten egg and continue baking for about 5 minutes more. This way, the bottom will be more moisture-proof. It will be slightly colored and will keep its crunch.

Meanwhile, prepare your vegetables: Rinse the asparagus in cold water. Peel the stems, carefully removing the fibrous, unappealing outer layer. Cut them into thick rounds, then pour them into a saucepan. Add 1½ tablespoons of butter [20 g],* a pinch of salt, 2 grinds of black pepper, and 3 pinches of sugar, then cover with cold water. Bring to a boil and continue cooking on low heat, covered. The asparagus should be a little crisp and the water should be almost completely evaporated. Turn into a bowl and set aside.

Rinse the fennel bulbs in cold water. Remove the outer leaves. Trim the bottoms of the stalks and slice them thinly. In a skillet, heat the oil. Add 2 tablespoons [30 g] of butter. Add the fennel, a pinch of salt, 2 grinds of black pepper, 3 pinches of sugar and about 1 cup [250 g] of water. Steam them on low heat, stirring carefully. The fennel slices should be slightly translucent and covered with a delicate butter coating. Pour into a bowl and set aside.

Prepare your custard: In a bowl, combine the thick crème fraîche, milk, eggs, 2 pinches of salt, and 2 grinds of black pepper. Beat the mixture for a few seconds with a whip. Place the asparagus and fennel slices on the bottom of the pastry shell, being careful not to pour in any of the cooking juice. Cover with the custard. The custard should coat the vegetables.

Bake for about 40 minutes. The edges of your tart should be well browned and your custard colored and set. Remove your tart from the pan and serve immediately.

* A "knob" or "noix" of butter in the French here, is described as 1½ tablespoons. That is what will be used in this translation.

Carrot, Orange and Cinnamon Tart

11 oz. [300 g] rich flaky pastry No. 1 (*see recipe page 17*)

1¾ cups [400 g] almond cream (*see recipe page 27*)

3½ Tbsp. [50 g] crème fraîche

1 lb. [450 g] carrots, *or* ⅔ lb. [300 g] net

¼ tsp. ground cinnamon

Juice of 1 orange

Zest of 1 orange, finely grated

To decorate:

⅓ cup [50 g] confectioners' sugar

To bake:

A tart pan with plain rim, 10 inches [26 cm] in diameter and 1 inch [3 cm] deep

Roll your pastry on a lightly floured work surface into a circle a little less than ⅛ inch [2.5 mm] thick and 13 inches [34 cm] in diameter.

Butter your pan and carefully place the pastry in it, pressing the pastry lightly with your fingertips against the bottom and sides. Roll the rolling pin across the top edge of your pan to cut off the small amount of excess pastry. Prick the bottom of the tart with a fork and refrigerate it for 30 minutes, covered with plastic wrap.

Preheat the oven to 350°F [180°C].

Wash and zest 1 orange. Squeeze it for the juice. Wash and peel the carrots, being careful to remove any green parts of the core, which are hard and bitter. Grate the carrots on a fine grater.

Prepare your almond cream. Add the crème fraîche, grated carrots, ground cinnamon, and the orange zest and juice and stir gently with a wooden spatula. Fill the tart with this mixture. Smooth the cream with the back of a spoon. Bake for about 45 minutes. The edges of the tart should be browned and the almond cream lightly colored and puffed. Unmold the tart onto a rack and let it cool. Sprinkle confectioners' sugar over the top.

~:~

This tart can be prepared perfectly well the day before—it will only improve! You can serve it with a crème anglaise flavored with finely grated orange zest.

Flaky Pastry Galettes with Carrots, Orange and Cardamom

---

11 oz. [300 g] rich flaky pastry No. 2 (*see recipe page 18*)

For the jam filling:

2 cups [400 g] granulated sugar

1½ lbs. [650 g] carrots, *or* 1 lb. 2 oz. [500 g] net

½ cup [125 g] orange juice, juice of about 4 oranges

Juice of ½ lemon

Finely grated zest of ½ orange

⅛ tsp. ground cardamom

For the decoration:

Generous ⅓ cup [50 g] confectioners' sugar

Zest of 1 orange, slivered finely

For baking:

2 baking sheets covered with parchment paper

The day before, make your rich flaky pastry and your carrot, orange, and cardamom jam. Wash and peel the carrots, being careful to remove any green part of the core, which is hard and bitter. Grate the carrots on a fine grater. In a preserving pan, combine the carrots, sugar, orange zest, orange juice, lemon juice, and cardamom. Bring to a simmer. Pour this mixture into a bowl. Cover with parchment paper and refrigerate overnight.

The next day, bring this mixture to a boil in your preserving pan and cook at a boil for about 10 minutes, stirring gently. Skim carefully. Mix very thoroughly until smooth and purée-like. Return to a boil, pour into a bowl and set aside.

Roll your pastry on a lightly floured work surface to a little less than ⅛ inch [2.5 mm] thick.

With a fluted cookie-cutter, cut 20 small pastry rounds, 4 inches [10 cm] in diameter. Cover the 2 baking sheets with parchment paper. Place 10 pastry rounds on each baking sheet spaced a little more than 1 inch [3 cm] apart so they bake evenly and don't stick to each other. Prick them with a fork and refrigerate them covered with plastic wrap for about 15 minutes.

Preheat the oven to 350°F [180°C]. Bake the pastry rounds for about 8 minutes or until they are golden. Remove them from the baking sheet and let them cool on a rack.

Fill 10 of the rounds with a small spoonful of carrot, orange, and cardamom jam, and cover them with the remaining 10 rounds. Lightly sprinkle your galettes with confectioners' sugar, then put some finely slivered orange zest in the center of each.

∾:∾

Try these galettes with an orange crème brûlée.

Spring Carrot and Little May Onion Tart

---

1 lb. 6 oz. [600 g] semi-puff pastry (*see recipe page 20*)

2¼ lbs. [1 kg] new carrots, *or* 1¾ lbs. [750 g] net

1 bunch of little May onions

1 clove of garlic, very finely chopped

1½ Tbsp. [¾ oz. / 20 g] butter

1½ Tbsp. [20 g / 2 cl] peanut oil

¼ tsp. curry powder

Salt

Freshly ground black pepper

Granulated sugar

For the egg wash:

1 egg

To bake:

A tart pan with plain rim, 10 inches [26 cm] in diameter and 1 inch [3 cm] deep

The day before, prepare your semi-puff pastry.

The next day, roll 12 ounces [350 g] of pastry dough on a lightly floured work surface into a circle a little more than 1⁄16 inch [2 mm] thick and 13 inches [34 cm] in diameter.

Butter your pan and carefully place the pastry into it, press it lightly with your fingertips against the bottom and sides of the pan. Roll the rolling pin across the top edge of your pan to trim off the small amount of excess pastry. Prick the bottom of the tart with a fork and refrigerate it for 30 minutes, covered with plastic wrap.

Roll the remaining pastry on a lightly floured work surface to a little more than ¹⁄₁₆ inch [2 mm] thick. Roll it around a rolling pin and lift it above a baking sheet covered with parchment paper. Unroll it gently. This allows your pastry to relax and prevents it from shrinking when it is cut. Refrigerate it for 30 minutes, covered with plastic wrap.

Preheat the oven to 400°F [200°C].

Bake your tart shell blind (*see page 14*) for 10 minutes and let it cool.

Meanwhile, prepare your vegetables: Rinse the carrots in cold water. Scrape them with a knife to remove their thin skins. Cut them into round slices, then put them in a saucepan. Add 1½ tablespoons [¾ g] of butter, a pinch of salt, 2 grinds of pepper, and 3 pinches of sugar, then cover with cold water. Bring to a boil and continue cooking, covered on low heat, stirring occasionally. The carrots should be tender and the water almost entirely evaporated. Turn into a bowl and set aside.

Rinse the onions in cold water. Cut off the green portion halfway down, discard top, and slice the remaining green portion into thin rounds. Remove the outer skins of the onions and quarter them. In a skillet, heat the oil. Add the butter. Add finely chopped garlic, chopped onion greens, onions, curry, a pinch of salt, 5 grinds of pepper, and 3 pinches of sugar. Let this mixture sweat on low heat for a few minutes, stirring gently. Add ½ cup [100 g / 10 cl] water and let the mixture steam. The onions should be slightly caramelized, with a light butter coating. Turn into a bowl and set aside.

Spoon the carrots and onions into the tart shell, being careful not to include any of the cooking liquid. Using the refrigerated dough, cut strips about 1 inch [3 cm] wide and 11 inches [28 cm] long. Using a pastry brush dipped in cold water, moisten the edges of your tart. Now use the pastry strips to make an evenly spaced lattice across the entire surface. Using a pastry brush, paint the top of the tart with a little beaten egg.

When ready to bake the tart, lower the temperature to 350°F [180°C]. Bake the tart for about 30 minutes. The edges of your tart and the lattice should be nicely golden brown. Remove your tart from the pan and serve immediately.

White Cherry and Raspberry Tart

11 oz. [300 g] rich flaky pastry No. 1 (*see recipe page 17*)

2 cups *plus* 2 Tbsp. [500 g] almond cream (*see recipe page 27*)

1½ lbs. [700 g] white cherries, *or* 1¼ lbs. [550 g] net

To decorate:

3 Tbsp. [25 g] confectioners' sugar

1½ cups [150 g] raspberries

To bake:

A tart pan with plain rim, 10 inches [26 cm] in diameter and 1 inch [3 cm] deep
with removable bottom

Roll your dough on a lightly floured work surface into a circle a little less than ⅛ inch [2.5 mm] thick and 13 inches [34 cm] in diameter.

Butter your pan and carefully place the dough in it, pressing it gently against the bottom and sides with your fingertips. Roll the rolling pin across the top edge of the pan to trim off the small amount of excess pastry. Prick the bottom of the tart with a fork and refrigerate it for 30 minutes covered with plastic wrap.

Preheat the oven to 350°F [180°C].

Prepare your almond cream.

Rinse the cherries in cold water and dry them in a kitchen towel. Stem them and cut them in half to remove the pits. Fill the tart with an even layer of almond cream, perhaps with the help of a pastry bag with a plain tip. Arrange the cherries in a circle on the cream filling, cut surfaces turned toward the center of the tart.

Continue arranging them this way, making concentric circles to the center of the tart.

Bake the tart for about 45 minutes. The edges of the tart should be browned and the almond cream slightly colored and puffed. Unmold your tart onto a rack and let it cool. Dust the raspberries generously with confectioners' sugar and arrange them on top of the tart.

White Cherry and Rose Tart

11 oz. [300 g] sweet pastry (*see recipe page 16*)

2 cups *plus* 2 Tbsp. [500 g] almond cream (*see recipe page 27*)

3½ Tbsp. [50 g] crème fraîche

½ cup [50 g] ground almonds

1 lb. 2 oz. [500 g] white cherries, *or* 15 oz. [400 g] net

2 Tbsp. [30 g / 3 cl] rose water

For decoration:

A few untreated rose petals

½ cup [100 g] apple jelly (*see recipe page 29*)

To bake:

A tart pan with plain rim, 10 inches [26 cm] in diameter and 1 inch [3 cm] deep, with removable bottom

Roll your pastry on a lightly floured work surface into a circle a little less than ⅛ inch [2.5 mm] thick and 13 inches [34 cm] in diameter.

Butter your pan and carefully place the pastry into it. Press it lightly with your fingertips against the bottom and sides. Now roll the rolling pin across the top edge of the pan to cut off the small amount of excess dough. Prick the bottom of the tart with a fork and refrigerate it for 30 minutes, covered with plastic wrap.

Preheat the oven to 350°F [180°C].

Prepare your almond cream. Add the crème fraîche and rose water and mix gently with a wooden spatula.

Rinse the cherries in cold water and dry them in a kitchen towel. Stem them and cut them in half to remove the pits. Fill the bottom of the tart with an even layer of almond cream. You might want to use a pastry bag with a plain tip for this. Sprinkle the ground almonds on top of the cream. Arrange the cherries in a circle on the cream filling, cut surface turned up. Continue arranging them this way, making concentric circles to the center of the tart.

Bake for about 45 minutes. Edges of the tart should be golden brown and the cream lightly colored and puffed. Remove your tart from the pan onto a rack and let it cool. In a small saucepan, heat the apple jelly with the rose water and coat your cherries with it. Sprinkle your tart with rose petals.

Kugelhopf Pain Perdu Tart with Black Cherry Jam

---

1 10-oz. [300 g] purchased kugelhopf,* cut into 12 slices

7 Tbsp. [100 g] softened butter

1 cup *plus* 1 Tbsp. [250 g / 25 cl] whipping cream

1 cup *plus* 1 Tbsp. [250 g / 25 cl] whole milk

7 eggs

⅔ cup [150 g] extra-fine sugar

Finely grated zest of 1 orange

1⅓ cups [150 g] ground almonds

For the jam:

2¾ lbs. [1.25 kg] black cherries, *or* 2¼ lbs. [1 kg] net

1 cup [200 g] granulated sugar

1 cup *plus* 1 Tbsp. [250 g / 25 cl] Pinot Noir

For baking:

A ceramic tart pan with a fluted rim, 10 inches [26 cm] in diameter and a little
more than 1½ inches [4 cm] deep

The day before, prepare the jam: Rinse the cherries in cold water and dry them in a kitchen towel. Stem and pit them. In a bowl, combine them with the sugar and Pinot Noir. Let them macerate for an hour,

* Light yeast cake.

then turn this mixture into a preserving pan and bring it to a simmer. Pour the preparation into a bowl and set aside.

The next day, set your oven to broil. Butter the kugelhopf slices and brown them under the broiler for a few minutes on each side. Let them cool.

Lower your oven setting to 325°F [160°C].

Prepare the flan cream: In a bowl, combine the light whipping cream, milk, eggs, sugar and finely grated orange zest and beat briefly with a whip. Lay the grilled kugelhopf slices in the ceramic tart pan, overlapping them slightly. Cover the slices with your flan cream and sprinkle with all of the ground almonds.

Bake for approximately 45 minutes. The flan is done when the custard is set and has a beautiful golden yellow color.

~:~

The cherry jam gets a little lift with a pinch of cinnamon or cardamom. Serve it very cool and the tart just a little warm.

You can also bake the flan cream without the cake slices in the ceramic tart pan. At the last minute, stand the slices of still-warm, toasted kugelhopf on it.

If you don't have kugelhopf to make this tart, use a butter brioche*. It will be just as delicious!

* *Light yeast bread, rich with butter and eggs.*

Grandfather's Tart

11 oz. [300 g] rich flaky pastry with praline powder and hazelnuts (*see recipe page 19*), chilled 3 hours in the refrigerator or overnight

2 cups *plus* 2 Tbsp. [500 g] almond cream (*see recipe page 27*)

3½ Tbsp. [50 g / 5 cl] whipping cream

2 Tbsp. [30 g / 3 cl] Kirsch

For the jam:

1½ lbs. [700 g] black cherries, *or* 1¼ lbs. [550 g] net

2 Tbsp. [30 g / 3 cl] Kirsch

1 cup *plus* 1 Tbsp. [250 g] raspberry jelly (*see recipe page 30*)

For garnish:

Some fresh raspberries

3 Tbsp. [25 g] confectioners' sugar

To bake:

A tart pan with plain rim, 10 inches [26 cm] in diameter and 1 inch [3 cm] deep, with removable bottom

The day before, prepare the jam: Rinse the cherries in cold water and dry them in a kitchen towel. Stem and pit them, being careful to keep your cherries nice and round. In a preserving pan, combine the raspberry jelly and black cherries and bring it to a simmer. Pour this preparation into a bowl and refrigerate overnight.

The next day, add the Kirsch to the black cherry jam.

Roll your pastry on a lightly floured work surface into a circle a little less than ⅛ inch [2.5 mm] thick and 13 inches [34 cm] in diameter. Butter your pan and carefully place the pastry in it, pressing it lightly with your fingertips against the bottom and sides. Run a rolling pin across the top edge of the tart pan to trim off the small amount of excess dough. Prick the bottom of the tart with a fork and refrigerate it for 30 minutes, covered with plastic wrap.

Preheat the oven to 350°F [180°C]. Bake your tart blind (*see page 14*) for 10 minutes and let it cool.

Meanwhile, prepare your almond cream. Add the cream and Kirsch, folding them in lightly with a wooden spatula. Fill the bottom of the tart with an even layer of almond cream. It might be helpful to use a pastry bag with a plain tip for this.

Bake for about 15 minutes. The edges of the tart should be golden and the almond cream slightly colored and puffed. Remove your tart from the pan onto a rack and let it cool. Cover your tart with black cherry jam. Dust the fresh raspberries generously with confectioners' sugar and put them on your tart.

~:~

This tart is delicious served with thick crème fraîche or with a small oval-shaped scoop of vanilla ice cream.

Black Cherry Clafoutis with Fresh Mint

For the flan cream:

> 1 cup *plus* 1 Tbsp. [250 g / 25 cl] whipping cream
>
> 1 cup *plus* 1 Tbsp. [250 g / 25 cl] whole milk
>
> 6 eggs
>
> 5 egg yolks
>
> ⅔ cup [150 g] granulated sugar
>
> A few mint leaves
>
> 2 lbs. [900 g] black cherries, *or* 1½ lbs. [700 g] net

To decorate:

> A few fresh mint leaves
>
> 1 egg white
>
> 1½ Tbsp. [20 g] granulated sugar

To bake:

> A ceramic tart pan with a fluted rim, 10 inches [26 cm] in diameter and a little
> more than 1½ inches [4 cm] deep

Preheat the oven to 325°F [160°C].

In a heavy-bottomed saucepan, bring the milk to a boil. Remove from the heat. Add the mint leaves and let them infuse for 10 minutes.

Rinse the cherries in cold water and dry them in a kitchen towel. Stem and pit them, being careful to keep them nice and round.

Remove the mint leaves from the pan of milk.

Prepare the flan cream: In a bowl, combine the cream, milk, eggs, egg yolks, and sugar and beat briefly with a whip. Now arrange the black cherries in the ceramic tart pan. Cover them with the custard.

Bake for about 40 minutes. The clafoutis is done when the flan cream is just barely firm and has a nice golden yellow color.

Dip the fresh mint leaves into the beaten egg white, then cover them with granulated sugar. Let them dry on a plate. The leaves will look as if they are beautifully frosted. When the clafoutis is cool, arrange the crystallized mint leaves on top.

~:~

You can accentuate the delicate mint flavor by snipping the leaves for both the infusion and the decoration. You could also use cinnamon rather than mint. Infuse a cinnamon stick in the milk and sprinkle the top of the tart with granulated sugar mixed with a little ground cinnamon.

Morello Cherry Tart with Crunchy Almonds

---

11 oz. [300 g] flaky pastry (*see recipe page 15*)

2 cups *plus* 2 Tbsp. [500 g] almond cream (*see recipe page 27*)

1¾ lbs. [750 g] Morello cherries, *or* 1¼ lbs. [550 g] net

For the crunchy almonds:

1 scant cup [100 g] slivered almonds

¾ cup [100 g] confectioners' sugar

1 egg white

To decorate:

3 Tbsp. [25 g] confectioners' sugar

A few cherries with stems

To bake:

A tart pan with plain rim, 10 inches [26 cm] in diameter and 1 inch [3 cm] deep, with removable bottom

The day before, prepare your flaky pastry.

The next day, roll it on a lightly floured work surface into a circle a little more than ¹⁄₁₆ inch [2 mm] thick and 13 inches [34 cm] in diameter.

Butter your pan and carefully place the pastry in it, pressing it lightly with your fingertips against the bottom and sides. The pastry should extend beyond the edge of the pan a little less than ½ inch [1 cm] to make a border. Pinch this border between the thumb and index finger to flute it. Prick the bottom of the tart with a fork and refrigerate it for 30 minutes, covered with plastic wrap.

Preheat the oven to 350°F [180°C].

Bake your tart shell blind (*see page 14*) for 15 minutes and let it cool. Meanwhile, rinse the cherries in cold water and dry them in a kitchen towel. Stem and pit them, being careful to keep them round.

Prepare the almond cream, then fill the bottom of the tart with an even layer. It might be helpful to use a pastry bag with a plain tip for this. Arrange the cherries in a circle on the filling, pressing them lightly into the cream.

In a bowl, gently mix the slivered almonds, the confectioners' sugar, and the egg white with your fingertips. Distribute the coated almonds on your tart.

Bake for about 45 minutes. The edges of the tart will be attractively browned and the almonds crunchy and lightly meringued. Unmold your tart onto a rack and let it cool. Sprinkle it generously with confectioners' sugar and decorate with a few whole cherries.

~:~

Almonds, sugared and frosted with egg white, make perfect harmony with the cherry flavor. You can also accentuate this slight almond taste by adding a few drops of Kirsch to the cream.

You could also replace the crunchy almonds with a meringue sprinkled with slivered almonds. If so, proceed with the tart as directed for the meringue-topped rhubarb with spice (see page 85).

Morello Cherry Tart with Apple and Lemon Zest

11 oz. [300 g] flaky pastry (*see recipe page 15*)

1 lb. 2 oz. [500 g] Morello cherries, *or* about 1 lb. [400 g] net

4 Ida Red apples

For the flan cream:

5 oz. [150 g / 15 cl] whipping cream

3½ oz. [100 g] whole milk

3 eggs

5 egg yolks

⅔ cup [150 g] granulated sugar

Finely grated zest of 1 lemon

For decorating:

3 Tbsp. [25 g] confectioners' sugar

For baking:

A tart pan with plain rim, 10 inches [26 cm] in diameter and 1 inch [3 cm] deep

The day before, prepare your flaky pastry.

The next day, roll it on a lightly floured work surface into a circle a little more than ¹⁄₁₆ inch [2 mm] thick and 13 inches [34 cm] in diameter.

Butter your pan and carefully place the pastry in it, pressing it lightly with the fingertips against the bottom and sides. The dough should extend beyond the edge of the pan by a little less than ½ inch [1 cm] to make a border. Pinch this border between the thumb and index finger to flute it. Prick the bottom of the tart with a fork and refrigerate it for 30 minutes, covered with plastic wrap.

Preheat the oven to 350°F [180°C].

Bake your tart shell blind (*see page 14*) for 15 minutes. Then, using a pastry brush, paint it with a little beaten egg and continue baking for about 5 minutes. This makes the pastry more "moisture-proof"; it will also have a pretty golden color and will keep its crunch.

Meanwhile, prepare the flan cream: In a bowl, combine the whipping cream, milk, eggs, sugar, and finely grated lemon zest and stir with a whip for a few seconds. Rinse the Morello cherries in cold water and dry them in a kitchen towel. Stem and pit them, being careful to keep them round.

Peel the apples, stem and core them, and cut them into thin slices. In a bowl, mix the cherries and apples. Fill the tart shell with them. Pour in the flan cream, which will partly cover the fruit.

Bake for about 45 minutes. The edges of your tart should be nicely browned and the flan cream colored and set. Remove the tart from the pan and place onto a rack to cool. Sprinkle confectioners' sugar around the outer edge with your fingertips.

Morello Cherry Tart with Fromage Blanc

11 oz. [300 g] flaky pastry (see recipe page 15)

1 lb. 2 oz. [500 g] Morello cherries, or about 1 lb. [400 g] net

½ cup less 1 Tbsp. [100 g] crème fraîche

1¼ cups [300 g] faisselle, 0% butterfat*

5 egg yolks

⅔ cup [150 g] granulated sugar

6 Tbsp. [50 g] cornstarch

Zest and juice of 1 lemon

To decorate:

3 Tbsp. [25 g] confectioners' sugar

To bake:

A tart pan with plain rim, 10 inches [26 cm] in diameter and 1 inch [3 cm] deep

The day before, prepare your flaky pastry.

The next day, roll the pastry on a lightly floured work surface into a circle a little more than ¹⁄₁₆ inch [2 mm] thick and 13 inches [34 cm] in diameter.

Butter your pan and carefully place the pastry in it, pressing it lightly with your fingertips against the bottom and sides. The dough should extend beyond the edge of the pan a little less than ½ inch [1 cm] to make a border. Pinch this border between the thumb and index finger to flute it. Prick the bottom of the tart with a fork and refrigerate it for 30 minutes, covered with plastic wrap.

* A fresh white cheese. See Techniques and Ingredients, page 7.

Preheat the oven to 350°F [180°C].

Bake your tart shell blind (*see page 14*) for 15 minutes. Then, using a pastry brush, paint it with a little beaten egg and continue baking for about 5 minutes more. Doing this makes the shell more "moisture-proof"; it will also have a nice golden color and will keep its crunch.

Meanwhile, prepare the fromage blanc custard: In a bowl, mix the faisselle, crème fraîche, sugar, egg yolks, cornstarch, lemon zest, and juice gently with a whip. Rinse the cherries in cold water and dry them in a kitchen towel. Stem and pit them, being careful to keep them round. In a bowl, combine the cherries and the fromage blanc custard. Fill the tart shell with this mixture.

Bake for about 45 minutes. The edges of your tart should be well browned and the cream golden and set. Remove your tart from the pan onto a rack to cool. Sprinkle it generously with confectioners' sugar.

Brioche Tart with Morello Cherries and Crème Fraîche, Served Slightly Warm

---

14 oz. [400 g] brioche dough (*see recipe page 23*)

1 lb. 2 oz. [500 g] Morello cherries, *or* about 1 lb. [400 g] net

1 cup *plus* 1 Tbsp. [250 g] crème fraîche

¼ cup [50 g] granulated sugar

5 egg yolks

1 cup [100 g] ground almonds

For the egg wash:

1 egg

To decorate:

⅓ cup [50 g] granulated sugar

To bake:

A tart pan with plain rim, 10 inches [26 cm] in diameter and 1 inch [3 cm] deep

Prepare your brioche dough. Roll it on a lightly floured work surface into a circle a little more than ⅛ inch [2.5 mm] thick and 15 inches [38 cm] in diameter.

Butter and flour your pan and place the dough carefully in it, pressing it lightly with your fingertips against the bottom and sides. The dough should extend a little less than 1 inch [2 cm] beyond the edge of the pan to make a border. Cover with plastic wrap and let it rest at room temperature for 10 minutes.

Preheat the oven to 400°F [200°C].

Meanwhile, rinse the cherries in cold water and dry them in a kitchen towel. Stem and pit them, being careful to keep them round.

Using a pastry brush in cold water, paint the edges of your tart. Fold the edges of the pastry toward the inside, as if making a hem. Cover with plastic wrap and let it rest again at room temperature for 10 minutes. Prick the bottom of the tart lightly with a fork. Sprinkle the ground almonds over the bottom of the tart and fill with the cherries.

Prepare your custard cream: In a bowl, combine the crème fraîche, sugar and egg yolks. Using a spoon, coat your cherries with the crème fraîche mixture. Using a pastry brush, paint the edges of your tart with beaten egg.

When you put the tart into the oven, remember to lower the temperature to 350°F [180°C]. Bake for approximately 45 minutes. The edges of your tart will be puffed and nicely browned and the custard cream will be lightly caramelized and crunchy. Remove your tart from the pan and put it on a rack to cool. Before serving, sprinkle it generously with granulated sugar. It is also delicious served a little warm.

Little Cabbage Tarts with Sautéed Salt Pork and Cabecou Goat Cheese

8 large slices of sourdough bread

8 Cabecou* goat cheeses, soft in the center

12 kale leaves

8 slices of salted, fresh pork breast**

¼ tsp. grated fresh ginger

1½ Tbsp. [20 g / 2 cl] peanut oil)

1½ Tbsp. [20 g] butter

Salt

Freshly ground black pepper

To bake:

A baking sheet covered with parchment paper

Preheat the oven to 395°F [200°C].

Detach 12 nice-looking leaves of kale. Rinse them carefully in cold water. Then trim out the stem and chop the leaves into strips a little less than ¾ inch [2 cm] wide. In a saucepan, bring 1 quart [1 liter] of salted water to a boil. Add the kale and blanch it for 1 minute. Remove the strips with a skimmer, drain them and set them aside in a bowl.

Cut the pork into small lardons. In a skillet, heat the oil, then add the butter. On high heat, fry the

---

* *Cabecou cheeses are small, flat disks, that are soft to hard, rindless, and made from goat's or ewe's milk. They are about the size of a silver dollar and twice as thick. A signature cheese of southwest France.*

** *This is unsmoked salt-cured pork. Use salt pork, available from butchers, or pancetta, an Italian unsmoked bacon, available in specialty markets.*

lardons. Then remove them with a skimmer and set them aside. In the same skillet, brown the kale strips for a few minutes on low heat, stirring gently. Add a pinch of salt, 3 grinds of pepper, and the grated ginger. The kale should be lightly caramelized. Remove it with a skimmer, mix it with the lardons, and set aside.

Set your oven to broil. Toast the bread on one side and let it cool. On the baking sheet, arrange the kale and lardons on the untoasted side of the bread. Slice the goat cheeses in half widthwise and place them on the toasts. Place them under the broiler long enough for the cheese to melt and color, then serve immediately.

Spinach Tart with Salmon and Soft Goat Cheese

---

12 oz. [350 g] flaky pastry with egg (*see recipe page 15*)

1 lb. 2 oz. [500 g] fresh salmon fillet

Scant 1 lb. [400 g] whole spinach leaves

3 small, fresh goat cheese crottins*

Salt

Freshly ground black pepper

For the egg custard:

5 oz. [150 g / 15 cl] whipping cream

4 eggs

For the egg wash:

1 egg

To bake:

A tart pan with plain rim, 10 inches [26 cm] in diameter and 1 inch [3 cm] deep

The day before, prepare your flaky pastry with egg.

The next day, roll the pastry on a lightly floured work surface into a circle a little more than 1/16 inch [2 mm] thick and 13 inches [34 cm] in diameter.

Butter your pan and carefully place the pastry in it, pressing it lightly with your fingertips against the

---

* Crottins are 2-inch disks of goat cheese, 1½ inches thick, with a fairly assertive flavor.

bottom and sides. Roll a rolling pin across the top edge of your pan to cut off the small amount of excess dough. Prick the bottom of the tart with a fork and refrigerate it for 30 minutes, covered with plastic wrap.

Preheat the oven to 350°F [180°C].

Bake your tart shell blind (*see page 14*) for 15 minutes. Then, using a pastry brush, paint the crust with a little beaten egg and continue baking for about 5 minutes. Doing this makes the shell more "moisture-proof"; it will also have a nice golden color and will keep its crunch.

Meanwhile, prepare your spinach: Rinse it in cold water, drain it, and remove the stems and ribs. In a nonreactive pot, bring 2 quarts [2 liters] of salted water to a boil. Add the spinach and stir gently with a wooden spatula. Boil for 3 minutes. Turn the spinach into a strainer and let it drain.

Cut the salmon filets into thin, narrow strips. Salt and pepper them lightly.

Prepare your egg custard: In a bowl, combine the cream, milk, eggs, 2 pinches of salt, and 2 grinds of pepper. Beat briefly with a whip.

Arrange the salmon and spinach in your tart shell. Crumble the goat cheese crottins with your fingertips and sprinkle the cheese over the filling. Cover with the custard mixture. Bake approximately 45 minutes. The edges of your tart will be golden brown and your custard colored and set. Remove the tart from the pan and serve immediately.

Strawberry Tart with Fresh Mint

---

11 oz. [300 g] rich flaky pastry with praline paste and hazelnuts (*see recipe page 19*)

1¾ cups [400 g] almond cream (*see recipe page 27*)

1 cup *plus* 1 Tbsp. [250 g] pastry cream (*see recipe page 25*)

1 lb. 2 oz. [500 g] Gariguette* strawberries, *or* 1 lb. 1 oz. [450 g] net

To decorate:

A few fresh mint leaves

3 Tbsp. [25 g] confectioners' sugar

To bake:

A tart pan with plain rim, 10 inches [26 cm] in diameter and 1 inch [3 cm] deep
with removable bottom

The day before, prepare your rich flaky pastry and pastry cream.

The next day, roll the dough on a lightly floured work surface into a circle a little less than ⅛ inch [about 2.5 mm] thick and 13 inches [34 cm] in diameter.

Butter your pan and carefully place the pastry in it, pressing it lightly with the fingertips against the bottom and sides. Roll the rolling pin across the top edge of the pan to cut off the small amount of excess dough. Prick the bottom of the tart with a fork and refrigerate it for 30 minutes, covered with plastic wrap.

Preheat the oven to 350°F [180°C].

Bake your tart shell blind for 10 minutes (*see page 14*).

Meanwhile, prepare your almond cream. Fill the tart shell half full with an even layer of almond

---

* Gariguette is considered the most flavorful of French strawberries. Substitute home-grown.

cream. It might be helpful to use a pastry bag fitted with a plain tip. Bake for about 10 minutes. The edges of your tart should be golden and the almond cream slightly colored and puffed. Remove your tart onto a rack and let it cool.

Quickly rinse the strawberries in cold water. Dry them carefully in a kitchen towel. Stem them and cut them in half lengthwise. Fill your tart with the pastry cream. It might be helpful to use a pastry bag with a plain tip. Stand the strawberries in a circle, cut surface turned out. Continue arranging them in concentric circles to the center of the tart. Dust the outer edges of the tart surface generously with confectioners' sugar. Finely snip the mint leaves and sprinkle them on your tart.

Rich Flaky Tartlets with Homegrown and Wild Strawberries

11 oz. [300 g] rich flaky pastry No. 1 (*see recipe page 17*)

11 oz. / 1¼ cups *plus* 2 Tbsp. [320 g] crème fraîche

9 oz. [250 g] wild Mara* strawberries, *or* 7 oz. [200 g] net

5½ oz. [160 g] wild strawberries

For the egg wash:

1 egg

To decorate:

¼ cup [50 g] confectioners' sugar

To bake:

8 tartlet pans 4 inches [10 cm] in diameter

The day before, prepare your rich flaky pastry.

The next day, roll your pastry on a lightly floured work surface into a circle a little more than ¹⁄₁₆ inch [about 2 mm] thick. Using a fluted cookie-cutter cut 8 small pastry rounds, 5½ inches [14 cm] in diameter.

Butter the tartlet pans and carefully place the dough in them. Press the pastry lightly with the fingertips against the bottom and sides. Roll the rolling pin across the top edges of the pans to cut off the small

* Use the best available wild and/or homegrown strawberries.

amount of excess dough. Prick the bottoms of the shells with a fork and refrigerate them for 30 minutes, covered with plastic wrap.

Preheat the oven to 350°F [180°C].

Bake your tartlet shells blind (*see page 14*) for 10 minutes. Then, using a pastry brush, paint the pastry with a little beaten egg and continue baking for about 5 to 8 minutes. This will serve to make the shells more "moisture-proof"; they will also have a pretty golden color and will keep their crunch. Remove your tartlet shells onto a rack and let them cool.

Quickly rinse the strawberries in cold water. Dry them carefully in a kitchen towel. Stem them and cut them in half lengthwise. Fill your tartlet shells with a spoonful of crème fraîche. Stand the strawberry halves in a circle around the outer edge. Sprinkle generously with confectioners' sugar.

I advise you to fill these tartlets at the last minute so that your pastry stays crunchy.

Strawberry Tart with Red Currant Jelly

11 oz. [300 g] rich flaky pastry with praline paste and hazelnuts (*see recipe page 19*)

2½ cups [600 g] crème fraîche

¼ cup [50 g] granulated sugar

1½ lbs. [650 g] Gariguette* strawberries, *or* 1¼ lbs. [550 g] net

1 cup *plus* 1 Tbsp. [250 g] red currant jelly (*see recipe page 31*)

For the egg wash:

1 egg

To decorate:

3 strawberries with stems

To bake:

A tart pan with plain rim, 10 inches [26 cm] in diameter and 1 inch [3 cm] deep with removable bottom.

The day before, prepare your rich flaky pastry.

The next day, roll the pastry on a lightly floured work surface into a circle a little less than ⅛ inch [about 2.5 mm] thick and 13 inches [34 cm] in diameter.

Butter your pan and carefully place the pastry in it. Press the dough lightly with the fingertips against the bottom and sides. Roll the rolling pin across the top edge to cut off the small amount of excess dough. Prick the tart shell with a fork and refrigerate it for 30 minutes covered with plastic wrap.

Preheat the oven to 350°F [180°C].

* Gariguette is considered the most flavorful of French strawberries. Substitute home-grown.

Bake your pastry shell blind for 10 minutes (*see page 14*). Then, using a pastry brush, paint it with a little beaten egg and continue baking for 5 to 8 more minutes. This way the shell will be more "moisture-proof"; it will also have a pretty golden color and will keep its crunch. Quickly remove your pastry shell from the pan and place it on a rack to cool.

Quickly rinse the strawberries in cold water. Dry them in a kitchen towel. Leaving 3 whole for the garnish, stem the rest and cut them in quarters lengthwise. In a bowl, combine the quartered strawberries with the red currant jelly. Fill your pastry shell with 1⅞ cups [450 g] of crème fraîche, sprinkle it with granulated sugar, and place the strawberries coated in red currant jelly on top. Using a small spoon, decorate the edges of your tart with little oval-shaped mounds of crème fraîche. Stand the 3 strawberries with stems in the center of the tart.

~:~

You could also arrange the cut strawberries on the cream filling and flick small, random spoonsful of red currant jelly over them.

I would advise you to fill this tart at the last minute so that the pastry stays perfectly crisp.

Using a cookie-cutter, you can cut some small shapes from your leftover pastry. Paint them with beaten egg. Bake them at 350°F [180°C] for about 10 minutes. These delicate, crunchy little morsels go nicely with the velvety cream and meltingly juicy strawberries.

Strawberry Tart with Raspberries and Basil

11 oz. [300 g] rich flaky pastry with praline paste and hazelnuts (*see recipe page 19*)

1¾ cups [400 g] almond cream (*see recipe page 27*)

½ cup [125 g] pastry cream (*see recipe page 25*)

½ cup [125 g / 12.5 cl] whipping cream

9 oz. [250 g] Gariguette* strawberries, *or* 8 oz. [220 g] net

8 oz. [225 g] raspberries

To decorate:

12 small basil leaves

1½ Tbsp. [20 g] granulated sugar

1 egg white

To bake:

A tart pan with plain rim, 10 inches [26 cm] in diameter and 1 inch [3 cm] deep with removable bottom

The day before, prepare your rich flaky pastry and your pastry cream.

The next day, roll your pastry on a lightly floured work surface into a circle a little less than ⅛ inch [about 2.5 mm] thick and 13 inches [34 cm] in diameter.

Butter your pan and carefully place the pastry in it. Press the dough lightly with your fingertips against the bottom and sides. Roll the rolling pin across the top edge of the pan to cut off the small amount of excess dough. Prick the pastry shell with a fork and refrigerate it for 30 minutes covered with plastic wrap.

* *Gariguette is considered the most flavorful of French strawberries. Substitute home-grown.*

Preheat the oven to 350°F [180°C]. Bake your pastry shell blind for 10 minutes (*see page 14*).

Meanwhile, prepare your almond cream. Fill the pastry shell halfway with an even layer of almond cream. It might be helpful to use a pastry bag with a plain tip.

Bake your tart for about 10 minutes. The edges of the tart should be golden and the almond cream slightly colored and puffed. Remove your tart from the pan onto a rack and let it cool.

In a bowl, smooth out the pastry cream by mixing it lightly with a whip. In another bowl, chilled in the refrigerator for 15 minutes, whip the cream. Lighten the pastry cream by gently incorporating the whipped cream into it.

Quickly rinse the strawberries in cold water. Dry them gently in a kitchen towel. Stem them and cut them in half lengthwise. Fill the tart with the lightened pastry cream. You might want to use a pastry bag with a plain tip for this. Stand a row of strawberries around the outer edge, cut surface turned up. Now arrange a row of raspberries, then a strawberry row, then a raspberry row until you reach the center.

Dip the basil leaves in egg white, then cover them with granulated sugar. Let them dry on a plate. The leaves will have a pretty frosted look. Decorate the center of your tart with a few frosted basil leaves. Snip the rest of the leaves and scatter them over your tart.

Custard Tart with Spring Fruit

1 lb. [450 g] flaky pastry (*see recipe page 15*)

1 cup *plus* 1 Tbsp. [250 g] almond cream (*see recipe page 27*)

1 cup *plus* 1 Tbsp. [250 g] pastry cream (*see recipe page 25*)

1 cup *plus* 1 Tbsp. [250 g / 30 cl] whipping cream

2 oranges

1 Granny Smith apple

7 oz. [200 g] strawberries, *or* 5 oz. [150 g] net

5 oz. [50 g] raspberries

3½ oz. [100 g] cherries with stems

1 stalk of rhubarb

To decorate:

½ cup *less* 1 Tbsp. [100 g] apple jelly (*see recipe page 29*)

3 Tbsp. [20 g] confectioners' sugar

To bake:

A tart pan with plain rim, 10 inches [26 cm] in diameter and 1 inch [3 cm] deep

The day before, prepare your flaky pastry.

The next day, roll 12 ounces [350 g] of pastry on a lightly floured work surface into a circle a little more than ¹⁄₁₆ inch [about 2 mm] thick and 13 inches [34 cm] in diameter.

Butter your pan and carefully place the pastry in it, pressing it lightly with the fingertips against the bottom and sides. Roll the rolling pin across the top edge of the pan to cut off the small amount of excess dough. Prick the pastry shell with a fork and refrigerate it for 30 minutes covered with plastic wrap. Then roll the leftover dough on a lightly floured work surface to a little more than $\frac{1}{16}$ inch [about 2 mm] thick. Roll it around the rolling pin and lift it over a baking sheet covered with parchment paper. Unroll it gently. This allows the dough to relax and prevents it from shrinking when it is cut. Refrigerate it for 30 minutes covered with plastic wrap. With a cookie-cutter, cut about 30 leaf shapes. Set them aside. Using a pastry brush dipped in cold water, moisten the edges of your tart. Press on the leaves, overlapping them slightly.

Preheat the oven to 350°F [180°C]. Paint your tart's decorations with a little beaten egg. Bake your tart shell blind (*see page 14*) for 15 minutes and let it cool.

Meanwhile, prepare your almond cream. Fill the pastry shell halfway with an even layer of almond cream. It might be helpful to use a pastry bag with a plain tip. Bake the tart for about 10 minutes. The tart's edges should be golden and the almond cream lightly colored and puffed. Remove your tart from the pan and place it on a rack to cool.

In a bowl, smooth the pastry cream by stirring it gently with a whip. In another bowl previously chilled for 15 minutes in the refrigerator, whip the cream. Now, lighten the pastry cream by gently incorporating the whipped cream into it.

Quickly rinse the fruit in cold water. Dry it in a kitchen towel. Stem the strawberries and cut them in half lengthwise. Cut the rhubarb in half lengthwise, then into small cubes. Remove the orange rind and pith, sliding a knife between the membranes to lift out the sections. Cut the apple in half, remove the seeds and slice each half thinly. Fill the tart with the lightened pastry cream. It might be helpful to use a pastry bag with a plain tip for this. Now create a garden of colors with the fruits, arranging them as you like on the cream.

In a small pan, heat the apple jelly with 2 Tbsp. [30 g / 3 cl] of water and bring to a simmer. Using a pastry brush, gently coat the fruit with the jelly. Dust the raspberries with confectioners' sugar and gently place them and the cherries on top.

Tart with Lemony Apples and Little Acacia Flower Fritters

11 oz. [300 g] rich flaky pastry with praline paste and hazelnuts (*see recipe page 19*)

2 lbs. [900 g] Golden Delicious apples, *or* 1½ lbs. [700 g] net

½ cup [100 g] granulated sugar

4 Tbsp. / 2 oz. [55 g] butter

Zest of 1 lemon

For the fritters:

3½ oz. [100 g / 10 cl] milk

2 Tbsp. [25 g / 2.5 cl] beer

2 eggs

1 Tbsp. [15 g] granulated sugar

Scant ¾ cup [100 g] flour

1½ Tbsp. [20 g] acacia blossom honey

Pinch of salt

8 bunches of acacia flowers

1 quart [1 liter] cooking oil

For the egg wash:

1 egg

To decorate:

Generous ⅓ cup [50 g] confectioners' sugar

To bake:

A tart pan with plain rim, 10 inches [26 cm] in diameter and 1 inch [3 cm] deep with removable bottom

The day before, prepare your rich flaky pastry and your apples with lemon: Peel the apples, remove their stems, core them, and cut them into small cubes. In a pan, melt the butter on high heat. Add the apples and lemon zest, stirring gently, still on high heat. Add the sugar in three additions, turning your apples so that they absorb the butter and sugar thoroughly. Turn into a bowl and set aside.

The next day, roll your pastry on a lightly floured work surface into a circle a little less than ⅛ inch [2.5 mm] thick and 13 inches [34 cm] in diameter.

Butter your pan and carefully place the pastry in it. Press the dough lightly with your fingertips against the bottom and sides. Roll the rolling pin across the top edges of the pan to trim off the small amount of excess dough. Prick the pastry shell with a fork and refrigerate it for 30 minutes covered with plastic wrap.

Preheat the oven to 350°F [180°C].

Bake your tart blind 10 minutes (*see page 14*). Then, using a pastry brush, paint the pastry with a little beaten egg and continue baking for about 8 minutes. This way the shell will be more "moisture-proof." It will also have a pretty golden color and will keep its crunch. Remove your shell from the pan onto a rack and let it cool.

Prepare your acacia blossom fritters: In a bowl, combine the beer, flour, sugar, honey, salt, and eggs, stirring with a whip. Gradually pour in the milk. Your fritter batter should be very smooth without any lumps.

In a large, deep saucepan or fryer, heat the oil to 350°F [180°C].

Rinse the acacia blossom bunches and dry them gently in a kitchen towel.

Dip them in the fritter batter, then immediately put them into the oil. When they are completely golden and crunchy, remove them with a skimmer and place them on paper towel. Let them cool.

To finish, fill your tart shell with the apples and lemon zest. Place your acacia blossom bunches on top so that each serving has one. Sprinkle generously with confectioners' sugar.

~:~

Acacia blossom fritters are a dessert in themselves. Dusted with cinnamon-flavored sugar, they taste wonderful with a crème anglaise or pastry cream.

Baker's Wife's Tart

1 lb. 9 oz. [700 g] semi-puff pastry (*see recipe page 20*)

2¼ lbs. [1 kg] Roseval potatoes, *or* 1¾ lbs. [750 g] net

1 large May onion

9 oz. [250 g] unsmoked, salted pork breast*

1 small bunch of chives

1½ Tbsp. / ¾ oz. [20 g] butter

1½ Tbsp. [20 g / 2 cl] peanut oil

Salt

Freshly ground black pepper

For the egg wash:

1 egg

To bake:

A tart pan with plain rim, 10 inches [26 cm] in diameter and 1 inch [3 cm] deep

The day before, prepare your semi-puff pastry.

The next day, roll 12 ounces [350 g] of dough on a lightly floured work surface into a circle a little more than $1/16$ inch [about 2 mm] thick and 13 inches [34 cm] in diameter.

Butter your pan and carefully place the pastry in it. Press the dough lightly with your fingertips against the bottom and sides. Roll the rolling pin across the top edges of your pan to cut off the small amount of excess dough. Prick the pastry shell with a fork and refrigerate it for 30 minutes covered with plastic wrap.

* This is unsmoked salt-cured pork. Use salt pork, available from butchers, or pancetta, an Italian unsmoked bacon, available in specialty markets.

Roll the remaining dough on a lightly floured work surface to a little more than ¹⁄₁₆ inch [about 2 mm] thick. Roll it around a rolling pin and lift it above a baking sheet covered with parchment paper. Unroll it gently. This allows your dough to relax and prevents it from shrinking when it is cut. Refrigerate it for 30 minutes covered with plastic wrap.

Preheat the oven to 400°F [200°C].

Bake your pastry shell blind (*see page 14*) for 15 minutes and let it cool.

Meanwhile, prepare your filling: Cut off the May onion top halfway up and slice the remaining green part into thin rounds. Peel the onion bulb and slice it thinly. Cut the piece of pork breast into small lardons. In a skillet, heat the oil. Add the butter. Fry the lardons on high heat. Remove them with a skimmer and set aside. In the same skillet, lightly brown the sliced onion and the chopped green part on low heat for a few minutes, stirring gently. Add a pinch of salt and 3 grinds of pepper. The onion should be lightly caramelized. Remove it with a skimmer and set it aside.

Wash the potatoes in cold water, peel them and cut them into thin, round slices. Dry them in a kitchen towel, then turn them into a bowl. Finely snip the chives. Add chives, lardons, and onion. Place the filling in your tart shell. Using a pastry brush dipped in cold water, moisten the edges of the tart.

Roll the chilled pastry around a rolling pin and lift it above your filled pastry shell. Unroll it gently. Using a small knife, trim the dough that extends beyond the tart pan. Paint this pastry lid using a pastry brush dipped in a little beaten egg. Make a few designs with the point of a knife to decorate the top of your tart. Prick the center with a fork.

When the pastry goes into the oven, remember to lower the oven temperature to 350°F [180°C]. Bake for an hour or a little more.

The pastry should have a pretty golden color. Check to see if the potatoes are done by inserting a knife blade into the pie. The filling should offer no resistance to the blade. Remove your tart from the pan and serve it immediately. Serve it with a nice dandelion green salad.

Bougon Goat Cheese Tartlets

9 oz. [250 g] flaky pastry with egg (*see recipe page 15*)

2 Bougon* cheeses

1 lb. 2 oz. [500 g] Belle de Fontenay** potatoes, or ⅔ lb. [300 g] cooked net

5 oz. [150 g] crème fraîche

Salt

Freshly ground black pepper

For the egg wash:

1 egg

To bake:

8 tartlet pans, 4 inches [10 cm] in diameter

The day before, prepare your flaky pastry with egg and the potatoes: Peel the potatoes. In a pot of boiling salted water, cook them until they are tender all the way through. Drain the potatoes and refrigerate them, covered with plastic wrap.

The next day, roll your pastry on a lightly floured work surface into a circle around ¹⁄₁₆ inch [1 mm] thick. Using a fluted cookie-cutter, cut 8 small pastry rounds, 5½ inches [14 cm] in diameter.

Butter your tartlet pans and carefully place the pastry in them. Press the dough lightly with your fingertips against the bottom and sides. Roll a rolling pin across the top edges of the pans to trim off the small amount of excess pastry. Prick the bottoms of the shells with a fork and refrigerate them for 30 minutes, covered with plastic wrap.

* Bougon is a large Poitou crottin that is shaped in a flat cylinder of about 7 ounces. It is aged for 2 to 3 weeks and is mild.
** Belle de Fontenay is a classic "salad" potato that is yellow, smooth and waxy. The skin is eaten.

Preheat the oven to 350°F [180°C].

Bake your tartlet shells blind (*see page 14*) for 8 minutes. Then, using a pastry brush, paint the pastries with a little beaten egg and continue baking for about 5 more minutes. The egg wash makes the shells more "moisture-proof"; they will also have a beautiful golden color and will keep their crunch. Remove your tartlet shells from the pans and place them on a rack to cool.

Now prepare the gratin filling: In a bowl, crush the potatoes with a fork, add the crème fraîche, and mix gently. Salt and pepper the mixture. Turn the potato mixture into a pan and bake it for 25 minutes. It should be browned.

Remove the rinds from the goat cheeses. Crumble one into a bowl. Add 11 ounces [300 g] of the potato gratin and combine gently. Spoon this filling into the 8 tartlet shells. Cut the second goat cheese into slices a little less than ½ inch [1 cm] thick and flatten them so that they cover the tartlets.

Increase the oven temperature to 425°F [220°C]. Bake for 5 minutes.

~:~

These tartlets are delicious with a salad of arugula and chive cream: 3½ ounces [100 g] of crème fraîche and 3½ ounces [100 g] of beaten fromage frais, (see note, page 7) with a few chopped chives, salt, and pepper.

This tartlet comes from Poitou [Poitiers] and was suggested to me by my friend Frédérick Hermé,* my irreplaceable kitchen muse.

* Wife of superstar pastry chef Pierre Hermé. The Hermés, also from Alsace, are longtime friends of the author.

Rhubarb Tart with Spiced Meringue

---

11 oz. [300 g] flaky pastry (*see recipe page 15*)

2¼ lbs. [1 kg] rhubarb, *or* scant 2 lbs. [850 g] net

2 oz. [50 g] ladyfingers

For the flan cream:

5 oz. [150 g / 15 cl] whipping cream

3½ oz. [100 g / 10 cl] whole milk

6 eggs

½ cup [100 g] granulated sugar

For the meringue:

7 egg whites

Scant 1⅓ cups [300 g] extra-fine sugar

Scant ⅛ tsp. freshly ground black pepper

Scant ⅛ tsp. freshly grated nutmeg

To decorate:

½ cup [50 g] confectioners' sugar

To bake:

A tart pan with plain rim, 10 inches [26 cm] in diameter and 1 inch [3 cm] deep

The day before, prepare your flaky pastry.

The next day, roll your pastry onto a lightly floured work surface into a circle a little more than 1/16 inch [about 2 mm] thick and 13 inches [34 cm] in diameter. Butter your pan and carefully place the pastry in it. Press the dough lightly with your fingertips against the bottom and sides. The dough should extend beyond the edge of the pan a little less than ½ inch [about 1 cm] to make a border. Pinch this border between your thumb and index finger to flute it. Prick the shell with a fork and refrigerate it for 30 minutes covered with plastic wrap.

Preheat the oven to 350°F [180°C].

Bake your tart shell blind (*see page 14*) for 15 minutes and let it cool.

Rinse the rhubarb in cold water and trim the stem ends. Cut the stalks in half lengthwise, then into small cubes.

Prepare your flan cream: In a bowl, combine the whipping cream, milk, eggs and sugar, then stir with a whip for a few minutes. Finely crumble the ladyfingers and sprinkle them in the bottom of the tart. Place the rhubarb on top. Cover with the flan cream.

Bake for approximately 45 minutes. The edges of your tart should be golden and your flan cream will be colored and set. Remove the tart from the pan onto a rack and let it cool.

Decrease the oven temperature to 325°F [160°C].

Prepare the meringue: Combine the spices and the sugar. Beat the egg whites with a mixer while sprinkling in the spiced sugar in a stream. Continue gradually adding the spiced sugar and beating until the whites are quite firm. Decorate your tart with rosettes of meringue. It might be helpful to use a pastry bag with a fluted tip. Sprinkle the meringue generously with confectioners' sugar. Bake tart for approximately 15 minutes. The meringue should be crunchy, with a nice, lightly caramelized color.

~:~

What I like particularly in this recipe is the contrast between the sugary sweetness of the meringue and the delicious acidity of the rhubarb. Crunchy on the outside, melting on the inside, the meringue is magic!

Rhubarb Tart with Sautéed Apples and Elderberry Flowers

---

1 lb. 5 oz. [600 g] semi-puff pastry (*see recipe page 20*)

2 oz. [50 g] ladyfingers

1 lb. 2 oz. [500 g] rhubarb, *or* 14 oz. [400 g] net

1¾ lbs. [750 g] Golden Delicious apples, or 1⅓ lbs. [600 g] net

½ cup [100 g] granulated sugar *plus* ⅓ cup [80 g]

3 Tbsp. / 1½ oz. [40 g] butter

3 bunches of elderberry blossoms

For the egg wash:

1 egg

To decorate:

Generous ⅓ cup [50 g] confectioners' sugar

To bake:

A tart pan with plain rim, 10 inches [26 cm] in diameter and 1 inch [3 cm] deep

The day before, prepare your semi-puff pastry and sautéed apples with elderberry flowers: Peel the apples, stem and core them and cut them into small dice. Take 2 bunches of elderberry flowers, remove the blossoms and mix them gently with ⅓ cup [80 g] of sugar. In a skillet, melt your butter on high heat. Add the apples and turn them gently, still on high heat. Then add the elderberry blossom and sugar mixture in 3 batches, continuing to turn the apples so that they absorb the butter and sugar thoroughly. Turn into a bowl and set aside.

The next day, roll 12 ounces [350 g] of pastry on a lightly floured work surface into a circle a little more than ⅟₁₆ inch [about 2 mm] thick and 13 inches [34 cm] in diameter.

Butter your pan and carefully place the pastry in it, pressing it lightly with the fingertips against the bottom and sides. Roll a rolling pin across the top edge of the pan to trim off the small amount of excess dough. Prick the tart with a fork and refrigerate it for 30 minutes covered with plastic wrap.

Preheat the oven to 350°F [180°C].

Now roll the remaining dough on a lightly floured work surface until it is a little more than ⅟₁₆ inch [about 2 mm] thick. Roll it around a rolling pin and lift it above a baking sheet covered with parchment paper. Unroll it gently. This allows the dough to relax and prevents it from shrinking when it is cut. Refrigerate it for 30 minutes, covered with plastic wrap.

Bake your tart blind (*see page 14*) for 10 minutes and let it cool.

Rinse the rhubarb in cold water. Cut the stalks in half lengthwise, then into small dice. Finely crumble the ladyfingers and sprinkle them in your tart shell. Combine the sautéed apple cubes with the rhubarb and add ½ cup [100 g] of sugar. Place this mixture in the tart shell. Using a cookie-cutter, cut about 60 leaf shapes from the refrigerated dough. Set them aside. Using a pastry brush dipped in cold water, paint the edges of your tart. Press on about 25 pastry leaves, overlapping them slightly. Cover the top of your tart with the remaining leaves. Arrange them like a canopy of foliage that lets the fruit show through. Using a pastry brush, paint the leaves with a little beaten egg.

Bake the tart for about 45 minutes. The edges of the tart and the leafy covering should be a pretty golden color. Remove your tart from the pan onto a rack and let it cool. At the last minute, sprinkle confectioners' sugar on the remaining bunch of elderberry blossoms and place it in the center of your tart.

Spring Carrot and
Little May Onion Tart
(page 45)

*Custard Tart with
Spring Fruits (page 77)*

Grandfather's Tart
(page 53)

Strawberry Tart with
Red Currant Jelly
(page 73)

Tart with Lemony
Apples and Little
Acacia Flower Fritters
(page 79)

Rhubarb Tart with Sautéed Apples and Elderberry Flowers
(page 87)

Morello Cherry Tart
with Crunchy Almonds
(page 57)

*Kugelhopf Pain Perdu
Tart with Black
Cherry Jam (page 51)*

Honeycomb Tart with Rhubarb, Orange and Apple Jam

1 lb. 9 oz. [700 g] brioche dough (*see recipe page 23*)

1¾ cups [400 g] crème fraîche

For the honeycomb topping:

Generous ¾ cup [100 g] slivered almonds

¼ cup [50 g] granulated sugar

3½ Tbsp. [50 g] floral honey

1½ Tbsp. / ¾ oz. [20 g] butter

½ cup *less* 1 Tbsp. [100 g / 10 cl] whipping cream

2 Tbsp. [25 g] candied orange peel, diced

For the jam:

1 orange

13 oz. [350 g] rhubarb, or 9 oz. [250 g] net

1 lb. [450 g] apples, *or* 11 oz. [300 g] net

½ cup [100 g] granulated sugar, *plus* 1½ cups [300 g]

3½ Tbsp. [50 g] water

Juice of ½ lemon

For the egg wash:

1 egg

To bake:

A tart pan with plain rim, 10 inches [26 cm] in diameter and 1 inch [3 cm] deep

The day before, prepare your rhubarb, orange, and apple jam: Rinse the orange in cold water and cut it into very thin rounds. In a preserving pan, poach the orange slices with ½ cup [100 g] of sugar and 3 tablespoons [50 g] of water. Cook at a boil until they become translucent. Add the washed, unpeeled rhubarb, cut into small dice; the apples, peeled, cored, and cut into thin slices; and the lemon juice and the 1½ cups of sugar. Bring the mixture to a boil and cook for about 5 minutes, stirring gently. Skim carefully. Pour into a bowl, cover, and set aside.

The next day, prepare your brioche dough. Roll the dough on a lightly floured work surface into a circle a little more than 1½ inches [4 cm] thick and 10 inches [26 cm] in diameter.

Butter and flour your pan and carefully place your dough in it, pressing it lightly with the fingertips against the bottom and sides. Cover it with a kitchen towel and let it rest at room temperature for 50 minutes to rise well.

Preheat the oven to 400°F [200°C].

When you put the brioche shell in the oven, be sure to lower the temperature to 350°F [180°C.] Bake the brioche shell for about 25 minutes.

Meanwhile, prepare your honeycomb topping: In a saucepan, bring the cream, honey, sugar, and butter to a boil. Put a candy thermometer into the mixture and continue boiling until it reaches 232°F [114°C]. Remove the pan from the heat, add the slivered almonds and candied orange peel, and stir gently. Pour into a bowl and set aside. When the brioche tart is lightly golden, use a spoon to cover it with a layer of this filling. Continue baking for 10 minutes. The tart will be puffed and prettily colored, and the honeycomb crunchy and slightly caramelized. Remove your tart from the pan onto a rack and let it cool.

You can serve this dessert a couple of ways: Slice the brioche tart horizontally into two layers and fill it with crème fraîche and a thin layer of jam. Or cut it into wedges and serve it on a plate with a spoonful of crème fraîche and a little jam.

Summer

Puff Pastry Tart with Apricots

11 oz. [300 g] semi-puff pastry (*see recipe page 20*)

2 oz. [50 g] ladyfingers

10 attractive Bergeron apricots, ripe but still firm

For the flan cream:

5 oz. [150 g / 15 cl] whipping cream

½ cup *less* 1 Tbsp. [100 g / 10 cl] whole milk

6 eggs

½ cup [100 g] granulated sugar

Generous ½ cup [50 g] slivered almonds

To decorate:

Generous ⅓ cup [50 g] confectioners' sugar

To bake:

A tart pan with plain rim, 10 inches [26 cm] in diameter and 1 inch [3 cm] deep

The day before, prepare your semi-puff pastry.

The next day, roll the pastry on a lightly floured work surface into a circle a little more than ¹⁄₁₆ inch [about 2 mm] thick and 14 inches [36 cm] in diameter.

Butter your pan and carefully place the pastry in it, pressing the dough lightly with the fingertips against the bottom and sides. The dough should extend beyond the edge of the pan a little less than ½ inch [1 cm] to make a border. Pinch this border between the thumb and index finger to flute it. Prick the pastry shell with a fork and refrigerate it for 30 minutes covered with plastic wrap.

Preheat the oven to 350°F [180°C].

Bake your pastry shell blind (*see page 14*) for 15 minutes and let it cool.

Prepare your flan cream: In a bowl, combine the whipping cream, milk, eggs, and sugar, then beat briefly with a whip. Rinse the apricots in cold water. Dry them in a kitchen towel and cut them in half to remove the pits. Finely crumble the ladyfingers and sprinkle them in the pastry shell. Place the apricot halves in a circle, cut surface turned up. Cover the fruit with flan cream and sprinkle slivered almonds over it.

Bake the flan for about 45 minutes. The edges of your tart should be nicely golden and your flan cream should be colored and set. Remove the tart from the pan onto a rack and let it cool. Before serving, sprinkle it generously with confectioners' sugar.

Apricot Tart with Almonds

---

11 oz. [300 g] rich flaky pastry No. 1 (*see recipe page 17*)

2 cups 1 oz. [500 g] almond cream (*see recipe page 27*)

8 attractive Bergeron apricots, ripe but still firm

25 blanched almonds

To decorate:

3 Tbsp. [25 g] confectioners' sugar

1½ Tbsp. [25 g / 2.5 cl] water

To bake:

A tart pan with plain rim, 10 inches [26 cm] in diameter and 1 inch [3 cm] deep with removable bottom

The day before, prepare your rich flaky pastry.

The next day, roll your pastry on a lightly floured work surface into a circle a little less than ⅛ inch [2.5 mm] thick and 13 inches [34 cm] in diameter.

Butter your pan and carefully place the pastry in it, pressing the dough lightly with the fingertips against the bottom and sides. Roll a rolling pin across the top edge of the pan trim off the small amount of excess dough. Prick the pastry shell with a fork and refrigerate it for 30 minutes, covered with plastic wrap.

Preheat the oven to 350°F [180°C].

Prepare your almond cream. Rinse the apricots in cold water and dry them in a kitchen towel. Cut them in half to remove the pits. Fill the pastry shell with an even layer of almond cream. It might be helpful to use a pastry bag with a plain tip. Arrange the apricots in a circle on the almond cream, cut surface turned up. Fill each little apricot "ear" with blanched almonds.

Bake the tart for about 45 minutes. The edges of the tart should be nicely golden and the almond cream colored and puffed. When the tart has finished baking, mix the confectioners' sugar and hot water in a bowl. When you take your tart out of the oven, use a pastry brush to coat each apricot with this sugar glaze. Remove the tart from the pan onto a rack and let it cool.

~:~

This tart is lovely with a crème anglaise.

Apricot Tart with Streusel and Citrus Zest

---

11 oz. [300 g] sweet pastry (*see recipe page 16*)

2 cups *plus* 2 Tbsp. [500 g] almond cream (see recipe page 27)

6 attractive Bergeron apricots, ripe but still firm

For the streusel:

4 Tbsp. / 2 oz. [60 g] cold butter

¼ cup *plus* 2 Tbsp. [60 g] granulated sugar

¼ cup [30 g] ground blanched almonds

Scant ½ cup [60 g] flour

⅜ tsp. finely grated orange zest

⅜ tsp. finely grated lemon zest

To decorate:

3 Tbsp. [25 g] confectioners' sugar

To bake:

A tart pan with plain rim, 10 inches [26 cm] in diameter and 1 inch [3 cm] deep
with removable bottom

The day before, prepare your sweet flaky pastry.

The next day, roll the pastry on a lightly floured work surface into a circle a little less than ⅛ inch [about 2.5 mm] thick and 13 inches [34 cm] in diameter.

Butter your pan and carefully place the pastry in it. Press the dough lightly with the fingertips against the bottom and sides. Roll a rolling pin across the top edge of the pan to trim off the small amount of excess dough. Prick the tart shell with a fork and refrigerate it for 30 minutes, covered with plastic wrap.

Preheat the oven to 350°F [180°C].

Prepare your almond cream. Rinse the apricots in cold water. Dry them in a kitchen towel, then cut them into quarters. Fill the pastry shell with an even layer of almond cream. It might be helpful to use a pastry bag with a plain tip. Arrange the apricots in a circle, placing them close together on the almond cream, cut surface turned up.

Bake them for about 40 minutes.

Meanwhile, prepare the streusel: Cut the butter into very small cubes. In a bowl, combine the butter, sugar, ground almonds, flour, and citrus zest. Work the mixture gently with the fingertips until it resembles coarse meal. Rub it together for a few seconds more to obtain a slightly lumpier consistency. When the almond cream is lightly colored and puffed, sprinkle the streusel in little clumps over the tart. Then continue baking for about 10 minutes. The edges of the tart should be golden and the streusel crusty and prettily colored. Remove your tart from the pan onto a rack and let it cool. Then dust it with confectioners' sugar.

∼:∼

This tart goes beautifully with a cinnamon- or cardamom-flavored crème anglaise.

Tart with Apricots Simmered in Honey and Blooming Thyme

---

11 oz. [300 g] rich flaky pastry with praline paste and hazelnuts (*see recipe page 19*)

2 cups 1 oz. [500 g / 50 cl] crème fraîche

½ cup [100 g] granulated sugar *plus* ¼ cup [50 g]

12 attractive Bergeron apricots, ripe but still firm

3½ Tbsp. / 1¾ oz. [50 g] butter

7 oz. [200 g] acacia blossom honey

3½ Tbsp. [50 g / 5 cl] water

4 small sprigs of thyme in flower

For the egg wash:

1 egg

To decorate:

6 small sprigs of thyme in flower

To bake:

A tart pan with plain rim, 10 inches [26 cm] in diameter and 1 inch [3 cm] deep with removable bottom

The day before, prepare your rich flaky pastry.

The next day, roll the pastry on a lightly floured work surface into a circle a little less than ⅛ inch [about 2.5 mm] thick and 13 inches [34 cm] in diameter.

Butter your pan and carefully place the pastry in it, pressing the dough lightly with your fingertips against the bottom and sides. Roll the rolling pin across the top edge of the pan to trim off the small amount of excess pastry. Prick the pastry shell with a fork and refrigerate it for 30 minutes, covered with plastic wrap.

Preheat the oven to 350°F [180°C].

Bake your pastry shell blind 10 minutes (*see page 14*). Then, using a pastry brush, paint the pastry with a little beaten egg and continue baking for about 5 to 8 minutes. This will make the shell more "moisture-proof"; it will also be beautifully golden and keep its crunch. Remove the shell from the pan onto a rack and let it cool.

Quickly rinse the apricots in cold water and dry them in a kitchen towel. Cut them in half to remove the pits. In a skillet, melt the butter and honey. Add the water, ¼ cup [50 g] of sugar, and the 4 thyme sprigs. Bring the mixture to a simmer. Arrange the apricot halves in the skillet, cut surface turned down. Let them simmer for a few minutes. Then, using two wooden spoons, turn them over. Let them simmer again until the fruit becomes almost jam-like. Then let them cool in the cooking liquid.

Cover your pastry shell with 1½ cups [350 g] of crème fraîche, sprinkle it with ½ cup [100 g] of sugar, and fill it with the half-candied apricots. Using a small spoon, place a little mound of crème fraîche in the center of each apricot. To finish, decorate your tart with the six small sprigs of thyme in flower.

∽∶∾

I advise you to fill this tart at the last minute so that the rich flaky pastry stays perfectly crunchy. It will be delicious with a little red currant jelly.

You can use a cookie-cutter to cut some little cookies from the leftover dough. Using a pastry brush, paint them with a little beaten egg. Bake them at 350°F [180°C] for about 8 minutes. These crisp, delicate little cookies contrast harmoniously with the velvety cream and the melt-in-your mouth apricots.

Nougapricot Tart

11 oz. [300 g] rich flaky pastry No. 1 (*see recipe page 17*)

2 cups [450 g] almond cream (*see recipe page 27*)

3½ Tbsp. [50 g] crème fraîche

8 attractive Bergeron apricots, ripe but still firm

16 blanched almonds

½ cup [50 g] pistachios, hulled and chopped

3½ Tbsp. [50 g] mountain honey

To decorate:

3½ Tbsp. [50 g] mountain honey

16 pistachio halves

3 Tbsp. [50 g] confectioners' sugar

To bake:

A tart pan with a plain rim, 10 inches [26 cm] in diameter and 1 inch [3 cm] deep with removable bottom

The day before, prepare your rich flaky pastry.

The next day, roll your pastry on a lightly floured work surface into a circle a little less than ⅛ inch [about 2.5 mm] thick and 13 inches [34 cm] in diameter.

Butter your pan and carefully place the pastry in it, pressing the dough lightly with your fingertips against the bottom and sides. Roll a rolling pin across the top edge of the pan to trim off the small amount of excess pastry. Prick the tart shell with a fork and refrigerate it for 30 minutes, covered with plastic wrap.

Preheat the oven to 350°F [180°C].

Prepare your almond cream. Add the chopped pistachios, slivered almonds, and crème fraîche, and combine them gently using a wooden spoon. Rinse the apricots in cold water and dry them in a kitchen towel. Cut them in half to remove the pits. Using a spoon, fill the tart shell with an even layer of almond cream. Arrange the apricots in a circle on the almond cream, cut surface turned up. Fill each apricot half with a blanched almond and a little "knob" of mountain honey.

Bake for about 45 minutes. The edges of the tart should be golden brown and the almond cream lightly colored and puffed.

In a small pan, melt the remaining honey on low heat. When you take your tart from the oven, coat each apricot with this glaze, using a pastry brush. Remove the tart from the pan onto a rack and let it cool. To finish, fill the hollow of each apricot with one half of a hulled pistachio. Sprinkle confectioners' sugar over your tart with your fingertips.

This tart is delicious with a crème anglaise flavored with citrus zest.

Lattice-Topped Tart with Apricots

---

1 lb. 9 oz. [700 g] semi-puff pastry (*see recipe page* 20)

Scant 1 cup [100 g] finely ground blanched almonds, *or* 7 oz. [200 g] almond
   cream (*see recipe page* 27)

10 attractive Bergeron apricots, ripe but still firm

½ cup [100 g] granulated sugar

1 generous cup [100 g] slivered almonds

For the egg wash:

1 egg

To decorate:

3 Tbsp. [20 g] confectioners' sugar

To bake:

A baking sheet covered with parchment paper

The day before, prepare your semi-puff flaky pastry.

The next day, roll the pastry on a lightly floured work surface into a circle a little more than ¹⁄₁₆ inch [about 2 mm] thick. Roll it around a rolling pin and lift it above the baking sheet. Unroll it gently. This allows your dough to relax and prevents it from shrinking when it is cut. Cut a rectangle about 5 inches [12 cm] wide and 12 inches [30 cm] long.

To form borders for your tart, cut two strips a little less than ½ inch [1 cm] wide and 12 inches [30 cm] long. Then cut two strips a little less than ½ inch [1 cm] wide and 4 inches [10 cm] long. Using a pastry brush dipped in cold water, moisten the edges of the pastry rectangle. Press the strips on, carefully lining up the borders. Carefully save the remaining pastry on a baking sheet covered with parchment paper. Prick the tart shell with a fork and sprinkle it with ground blanched almonds or fill it with almond cream. It might be helpful to use a pastry bag with a plain tip.

Rinse the apricots in cold water, dry them in a kitchen towel, and cut them in half to remove their pits. Place two rows of apricots, cut side turned down on the tart base, and sprinkle them with slivered almonds.

From the leftover dough, cut strips a little less than ½ inch [1 cm] wide and 5 inches [12 cm] long and crisscross them over the entire surface of the tart (*see photo on page 103*). Then refrigerate it for 30 minutes, covered with plastic wrap.

Preheat the oven to 400°F [200°C].

Using a pastry brush, paint your pastry lattice with a little beaten egg. When you put it into the oven, be sure to lower the temperature to 350°F [180°C]. Bake the tart for about 35 minutes. The semi-puff pastry should be nicely golden. When you remove the tart from the pan, sprinkle it with granulated sugar, then let it cool on a rack. Before you serve it, sprinkle it lightly with confectioners' sugar and reheat it for a few minutes in the oven. This tart is delicious with a spoonful of vanilla or cinnamon ice cream.

Brioche Tart with Apricots and Diced Mango

14 oz. [400 g] brioche dough (*see recipe page 23*)

6 Bergeron apricots, ripe but still firm

1 very ripe mango

Scant 1 cup [100 g] ground blanched almonds

For the flan cream:

1 cup *plus* 1 Tbsp. [250 g] crème fraîche

¼ cup [50 g] granulated sugar

6 egg yolks

Zest of 1 orange, finely grated

For the crunchy almonds:

1 generous cup [100 g] slivered almonds

Scant 1 cup [100 g] confectioners' sugar

1 egg white

For the egg wash:

1 egg

To decorate:

¼ cup [50 g] granulated sugar

To bake:

A tart pan with plain rim, 10 inches [26 cm] in diameter and 1 inch [3 cm] deep

The day before, prepare your dough. Roll it on a lightly floured work surface into a circle a little more than ⅛ inch [3 mm] thick and 15 inches [38 cm] in diameter.

The next day, butter and flour your pan and carefully place the dough in it, pressing it lightly with your fingertips against the bottom and sides. The dough should extend beyond the edge of the pan about ¾ inch [2 cm] to make a border. Cover with plastic wrap and let it rest 10 minutes at room temperature.

Preheat the oven to 400°F [200°C].

Meanwhile, rinse the apricots in cold water and dry them in a kitchen towel. Cut them in half to remove the pits. Peel the mango, remove the pit, and cut the flesh into very small cubes. Sprinkle the tart shell with ground blanched almonds. Place the apricots in a circle, cut side turned up. Distribute the mango cubes among the apricot halves. Fold the edge of the dough toward the inside, partly covering the fruit. Cover with a kitchen towel and let the pastry rest again for 10 minutes at room temperature.

Now, using a pastry brush, paint the edges of your tart with a little beaten egg. When you place the tart into the oven, be sure to lower the temperature to 350°F [180°C]. Bake the tart for about 20 minutes.

Meanwhile, prepare the flan cream: In a bowl, combine the crème fraîche, sugar, orange zest, and egg yolks. Then, using a spoon, cover your apricots with this flan cream. Continue baking for about 10 minutes.

Quickly prepare your crunchy almonds: In a bowl, mix the slivered almonds, confectioners' sugar, and egg white gently. When the flan cream is lightly colored and set, sprinkle the tart with the coated almonds. Continue baking for about 10 minutes. The edges of your tart will be puffed and prettily colored and the almonds crunchy and meringue-like. Remove your tart from the pan onto a rack and let it cool. Before serving, shower it generously with granulated sugar. The tart is also delicious served just slightly warm.

Apricot Tatin Topped with Dried Fruit and Gewurztraminer Sabayon

14 oz. [400 g] semi-puff pastry (*see recipe page 20*)

12 attractive Bergeron apricots, ripe but still firm

4 Tbsp. / 2 oz. [60 g] butter

¼ cup [60 g / 6 cl] water

½ cup [100 g] granulated sugar

3½ oz. [100 g] floral honey

¼ cup [25 g] blanched almonds, chopped

¼ cup [25 g] walnuts, broken into pieces

¼ cup [25 g] pistachios, hulled

Generous ¼ cup [50 g] dried figs

Generous ¼ cup [50 g] dried apricots

Zest of 1 lemon, finely grated

Zest of 1 orange, finely grated

⅛ tsp. ground cardamom

⅛ tsp. of ground star anise

For the egg wash:

1 egg

To bake:

A tart pan with plain rim, 10 inches [26 cm] in diameter and 1 inch [3 cm] deep

The day before, prepare your semi-puff pastry.

The next day, roll 12 ounces [350 g] of dough on a lightly floured work surface into a circle a little more than ¹⁄₁₆ inch [about 2 mm] thick and 13 inches [34 cm] in diameter.

Butter your pan and carefully place the pastry in it, pressing it lightly with your fingertips against the bottom and sides. Now roll a rolling pin across the top edge of the pan to trim off the small amount of excess dough. Prick the pastry shell with a fork and refrigerate it for 30 minutes covered with plastic wrap.

Roll the remaining dough on a lightly floured work surface to a little more than ¹⁄₁₆ inch [about 2 mm] thick. Roll it around a rolling pin and lift it over a baking sheet covered with parchment paper. Unroll it gently. This allows your dough to relax and prevents it from shrinking when it is cut. Refrigerate it for 30 minutes covered with plastic wrap. Then, using a cookie-cutter, cut about 30 crescent-moon shapes from the refrigerated dough. Set these cutouts aside. Using a pastry brush and cold water, paint the edges of your tart and press on the moons, overlapping them slightly.

Preheat the oven to 350°F [180°C].

Using a pastry brush, paint the tart decorations with a little beaten egg. Bake your pastry shell blind (*see page 14*) for 15 minutes. Then, using a pastry brush, paint the pastry with a little beaten egg and continue baking for about 10 more minutes. This will make the shell more "moisture-proof"; it will also have a beautiful golden color and will maintain its crunchiness. Now remove the pastry shell from the pan onto a rack and let it cool.

Quickly rinse the apricots in cold water and dry them in a kitchen towel. Cut them in half to remove their pits. In a skillet, melt the butter and sugar. Add the water and bring to a simmer. Arrange the apricot halves in the skillet, cut surface turned down. Let the fruit simmer for a few minutes. Then, using two wooden spoons, turn them over. Let them simmer until they are almost jam-like. Remove them from the skillet and let them cool. Now put into the skillet the nuts, the dried fruit, finely cut into sticks a little less than ¼ inch [5 mm] thick, the citrus zest, spices, and honey. Let the mixture simmer until the juice reduces and caramelizes very lightly.

Meanwhile, arrange the apricots in the pastry shell. At the last minute, using a spoon, cover your apricots with the cooking liquid and dried fruit. Your semi-puff pastry shell will thus remain perfectly crisp.

~:~

This tart goes well with a Gewurztraminer sabayon. This spicy wine calls to mind the flavors of candied citrus, dried apricots, and gingerbread spices. For the sabayon, you will need:

1 cup *plus* 1 Tbsp. [250 g / 25 cl] **Gewurztraminer**

⅔ cup [150 g] **granulated sugar**

6 **egg yolks**

Juice of 1 lemon

Juice of 1 orange

½ cup [125 g] **crème fraîche**

Heat water in a saucepan that will serve as a double boiler. In a bowl, combine the egg yolks, wine, sugar, lemon juice, and orange juice. Place this bowl over the saucepan of simmering water and beat it vigorously with a whip. The sabayon should become foamy and almost double in volume. Remove it from the double boiler. Continue to beat it until it is lukewarm. Add the crème fraîche and mix it in gently.

Wild Blueberry Meringue Tart

11 oz. [300 g] flaky pastry (*see recipe page 15*)

1 lb. 5 oz. [600 g] wild blueberries

For the flan cream:

5 oz. [150 g / 15 cl] whipping cream

5 oz. [150 g / 15 cl] whole milk

1⅛ cups [250 g] granulated sugar

For the meringue:

7 egg whites

½ cup [100 g] extra-fine sugar

To decorate:

½ cup [50 g] confectioners' sugar

To bake:

a tart pan with plain rim, 10 inches [26 cm] in diameter and 1 inch [3 cm] deep

The day before, prepare your flaky pastry.

The next day, roll the dough on a lightly floured work surface into a circle a little more than ¹⁄₁₆ inch [about 2 mm] thick and 13 inches [34 cm] in diameter.

Butter your pan and carefully place the pastry in it, pressing the dough lightly with the fingertips against the bottom and sides. The pastry should extend beyond the edge of the pan a little less than ½ inch [1 cm] to make a border. Pinch this border between the thumb and index finger to flute it. Prick the tart shell with a fork and refrigerate it for 30 minutes, covered with plastic wrap.

Preheat the oven to 350°F [180°C].

Bake your tart shell blind (*see page 14*) for 15 minutes and let it cool.

Quickly rinse the blueberries in cold water. Drain them in a strainer.

Prepare your flan cream: In a bowl, combine the cream, milk, eggs and sugar, then beat briefly with a whip. Fill the tart shell with the berries and pour in the flan cream.

Bake for about 45 minutes. The edges of your tart should be golden and your flan cream lightly colored and set. Remove your tart from the pan onto a rack and let it cool.

Lower the oven temperature to 325°F [160°C].

Prepare the meringue: Beat the egg whites with a mixer while adding the sugar in a stream, gradually, until the whites are quite stiff. Using a pastry bag with a fluted tip, decorate your tart by piping crisscross lines across the center and rosettes around the edge. Dust the meringue generously with confectioners' sugar. Bake the tart for 15 minutes or until the meringue is crunchy and has a nice, lightly caramelized color.

~:~

You can substitute red currants for the blueberries in this recipe. If so, sprinkle the pastry shell with 2 ounces [50 g] of crumbled ladyfingers because the red currants release more juice in the baking.

Quiche Lorraine with Brilliat-Savarin Cheese and Chives

11 oz. [300 g] flaky pastry with egg (*see recipe page 15*)

½ Brillat-Savarin* cheese

9 oz. [250 g] ham on the bone

1 small bunch of chives

Salt

Ground black pepper

For the egg custard:

7 oz. [200 g / 20 cl] whipping cream

7 oz. [200 g / 20 cl] whole milk

6 eggs

For the egg wash:

1 egg

To bake:

A tart pan with plain rim, 10 inches [26 cm] in diameter and 1 inch [3 cm] deep

The day before, prepare your flaky pastry with egg.

The next day, roll your pastry on a lightly floured work surface into a circle a little more than ¹⁄₁₆ inch [about 2 mm] thick and 13 inches [34 cm] in diameter.

Butter your pan and carefully place the pastry in it, pressing the dough lightly with the fingertips

* A rich (70% butterfat), sweet, and creamy fresh cheese that weighs just over a pound.

against the bottom and sides. Roll the rolling pin across the top edge of the pan to trim off the small amount of excess dough. Prick the pastry shell with a fork and refrigerate it for 30 minutes covered with plastic wrap.

Preheat the oven to 350°F [180°C].

Bake your pastry shell blind (*see page 14*) for 15 minutes. Then, using a pastry brush, paint the pastry with a little beaten egg white and continue baking for 5 more minutes. The pastry shell will be more "moisture-proof"; it will also have a nice golden color and will keep its crunch.

Meanwhile, prepare your egg custard: In a bowl, combine the cream, milk, eggs, 3 pinches of salt, and 5 grinds of pepper and beat briefly with a whip. Cut the ham into small dice, cut the Brillat-Savarin into very thin slices, and finely chop the chives. Fill your tart shell with the ham, sprinkling it with chives. Cover these with the cheese slices and egg custard.

Bake for about 45 minutes. The edges of your quiche should be nicely golden and your custard colored and set. Remove the quiche from the pan, unmold it and serve immediately. Serve it with a salad of peeled tomatoes sprinkled with chives.

Rich Pastry Galettes with Black Currants and Raspberries

---

14 oz. [400 g] rich flaky pastry No. 2 (*see recipe page 18*)

11 oz. [300 g] raspberries

1¼ cups [300 g] fromage blanc, 40% butterfat*

1½ Tbsp. [25 g] granulated sugar

For the black currant jam:

1 lb. 5 oz. [600 g] bunches of black currants, *or* 1 lb. 2 oz. [500 g] net

1½ cups [300 g] granulated sugar

Juice of ½ lemon

To decorate:

1½ Tbsp. [20 g] extra-fine sugar

Zest of 1 lemon, very finely slivered

To bake:

2 baking sheets covered with parchment paper

The day before, prepare your rich flaky pastry and the black currant jam: Rinse the black currants in cold water. Drain them and strip them from the stems. In a preserving pan, combine the berries, sugar, and lemon juice. Bring to a simmer, then turn this mixture into a bowl. Set aside for several hours. Then put this mixture through a food mill with a fine disk to remove the skins and seeds. In the preserving pan, bring to a boil again, stirring gently. Skim carefully and check the set. Pour into a bowl and set aside.

---

* A fresh white cheese. See Techniques and Ingredients, page 7.

The next day, roll your pastry on a lightly floured work surface into a circle a little more than ⅛ inch [3 mm] thick. Using a cookie-cutter, cut 20 small pastry rounds, 4 inches [10 cm] in diameter. Cover the 2 baking sheets with parchment paper. Place 10 pastry rounds on each, spaced a little more than 1 inch [3 cm] apart so that they bake evenly and do not stick to each other. Prick them with a fork and refrigerate them for 15 minutes, covered with plastic wrap.

Preheat your oven to 350°F [180°C].

Bake the rounds for about 8 minutes or until they are nicely golden. Take them off the baking sheet and let them cool on a rack.

Fill 10 of the rounds with black currant jam, then cover them with the remaining 10 rounds. Using a small spoon, decorate the center of each galette with a small mound of fromage blanc or crème fraîche. Place 7 raspberries on each of the fromage blanc toppings. Lightly shower your little pastries with confectioners' sugar, then sprinkle the raspberries with the finely slivered lemon zest.

Serve these galettes with fromage blanc flavored with extra-fine sugar and a few raspberries.

~:~

Some very ripe raspberries have a faint aroma of violets. You can enhance this perfume by adding a drop of essence of violet to the black currant jam.

Cauliflower Tart with Mustard Seed

11 oz. [300 g] flaky pastry with egg (*see recipe page 15*)

1 small cauliflower, about 1⅓ lbs. [600 g]

11 oz. [300 g] Comté cheese*

1½ Tbsp. / ¾ oz. [20 g] butter

Salt

Ground black pepper

For the egg custard:

7 oz. [200 g / 20 cl] light whipping cream

7 oz. [200 g / 20 cl] whole milk

6 eggs

Scant 2 Tbsp. [25 g] grainy mustard (with whole seeds)

For the egg wash:

1 egg

To bake:

A tart pan with plain rim, 10 inches [26 cm] in diameter and 1 inch [3 cm] deep

The day before, prepare your flaky pastry with egg.

The next day, roll the pastry on a lightly floured work surface into a circle a little more than 1/16 inch [about 2 mm] thick and 13 inches [34 cm] in diameter.

Butter your pan and carefully place the pastry in it, pressing the dough lightly with your fingertips

*Comté cheese is another name for Gruyère.

against the bottom and sides. Roll the rolling pin across the top edge of the pan to trim off the small amount of excess dough. Prick the tart shell with a fork and refrigerate it for 30 minutes covered with plastic wrap.

Preheat the oven to 350°F [180°C].

Bake your tart shell blind (*see page 14*) for 15 minutes. Then, using a pastry brush, paint the dough with a little beaten egg and continue baking for 5 more minutes. The pastry shell will be more "moisture-proof"; it will also have a nice golden color and will keep its crunch.

Meanwhile, prepare and cook your cauliflower: Remove the leaves and divide the head into small florets. Rinse them in cold water. In a pot, bring 1 quart [1 liter] of salted water to a boil and add the cauliflower. Add the butter and 3 grinds of pepper. Let the cauliflower boil, covered, for about 10 minutes. It should be slightly crunchy. Drain it, turn it into a bowl, and set it aside.

Prepare your egg custard: In a bowl combine the light whipping cream, milk, eggs, mustard, pinch of salt, and 2 grinds of pepper and briefly beat with a whip. Cut the Comté cheese into small dice. Fill your pastry shell with cauliflower and the cheese. Cover it with the custard.

Bake the tart for about 45 minutes. The edges of your tart should be nicely golden and your custard colored and set. Remove your tart from the pan and serve immediately.

Raspberry Tart with White Munster

11 oz. [300 g] rich flaky pastry No. 2 (*see recipe page 18*)

1 lb. 5 oz. / about 5 cups [600 g] raspberries

11 oz. [300 g] young (not aged) white Munster*

1¼ cups [300 g / 30 cl] whipping cream

½ cup [100 g] extra-fine sugar

For the egg wash:

1 egg

To decorate:

½ cup [50 g] confectioners' sugar

To bake:

A tart pan with plain rim, 10 inches [26 cm] in diameter and 1 inch [3 cm] deep
with removable bottom

The day before, prepare your rich flaky pastry.

The next day, roll the pastry on a lightly floured work surface into a circle a little less than ⅛ inch [about 2.5 mm] thick and 13 inches [34 cm] in diameter.

Butter your pan and carefully place the pastry in it, pressing it lightly with the fingertips against the bottom and sides. Roll the rolling pin across the top to cut off the small amount of excess dough. Prick the tart shell with a fork and refrigerate it for 30 minutes covered with plastic wrap.

Preheat the oven to 350°F [180°C].

---

* Munster is young, firm and dry, with russet-colored rind and a chalky interior.

Bake your pastry shell blind (*see page 14*) for 10 minutes. Then, using a pastry brush, paint the pastry with a little beaten egg and continue baking for 5 to 8 minutes. The pastry shell will be more "moisture-proof"; it will also have a pretty golden color and will keep its crunch. Remove your pastry shell from the pan onto a rack and let it cool.

In a bowl, mash the Munster and sugar with a fork. Push this mixture through a fine strainer, pressing it with the back of a spoon. In another bowl that has been chilled in the refrigerator for 15 minutes, whip the light whipping cream. Now gently incorporate the whipped cream into the creamed white Munster. Fill your tart with this slightly lumpy mixture.

Sort the raspberries but do not rinse them so that that they'll keep their aroma. On your work surface, generously dust half of the berries with confectioners' sugar. Arrange a row of the sugared raspberries around the outer edge of the tart. Then place a row of unsugared raspberries, and continue, alternating, until you reach the center of the tart.

∾⫶∾

This tart is equally delicious if you substitute well-drained raw milk faisselle* for the young white Munster. If so, add the finely chopped zest of 1 lemon when you mash the faisselle.

* *A fresh white cheese. See Techniques and Ingredients, page 7.*

Tart with Raspberries and Chocolate

1 lb. 2 oz. [500 g] rich flaky pastry No. 2 (*see recipe page 18*)

3½ oz. / scant 1 cup [100 g] raspberries

For the ganache:

5 oz. [150 g / 15 cl] whipping cream

7 oz. [200 g] bittersweet chocolate

6 oz. [175 g] raspberries

2½ Tbsp. [35 g] room-temperature butter

For the egg wash:

1 egg

To decorate:

3½ oz. / scant 1 cup [100 g] raspberries

To bake:

A tart pan with plain rim, 10 inches [26 cm] in diameter and 1 inch [3 cm] deep
with removable bottom

A baking sheet covered with parchment paper

The day before, prepare your pastry.

The next day, roll the pastry on a lightly floured work surface into a circle a little less than ⅛ inch [about 2.5 mm] thick and 13 inches [34 cm] in diameter.

Butter your pan and carefully place the pastry in it, pressing lightly against the bottom and sides. Roll the rolling pin across the top edge of the pan to cut off the small amount of excess dough. Prick the pastry shell with a fork and refrigerate it for 30 minutes covered with plastic wrap. Make a ball of the dough leftovers. Then roll it out quickly. Roll the pastry around a rolling pin and lift it above a baking sheet covered with parchment paper. Unroll it gently. If your pastry tears, gently join the pieces and press with your fingertips to make the edges stick. Then cut a disk, 9½ inches [24 cm] in diameter. Prick it with a fork and refrigerate it for 30 minutes covered with plastic wrap.

Preheat the oven to 350°F [180°C].

Bake your pastry shell and the pastry disk blind (*see page 14*) for 10 minutes. Then, using a pastry brush, paint the pastry with a little beaten egg and continue baking for 5 to 8 minutes. The pastry will be a little more "moisture-proof"; it will also have a nice golden color and will keep its crunch. Remove your shell and disk from the pan and let them cool on a rack.

Meanwhile, prepare the ganache: Pick over the raspberries but do not rinse them so that they'll keep their aroma. Put them through a food mill with a fine disk to make a purée. Finely grate the chocolate into a bowl. In a saucepan, bring the cream to a boil. In another saucepan, heat the raspberry purée. Pour the cream onto the grated chocolate and mix gently with a wooden spatula. Just as gently, add the raspberry purée. Cut the butter into small cubes and incorporate it into the mixture, stirring gently until it is melted.

Pour ⅓ of the ganache mixture into your pastry shell. Place the pastry disk on top and cover it with 3½ ounces [100 g] of raspberries and the rest of the ganache. Decorate the tart with fresh raspberries.

Raspberry Clafoutis with Wild Blackberries and Star Anise Compote

---

1 cup *plus* 1 Tbsp. [250 g / 25 cl] whipping cream

1 cup *plus* 1 Tbsp. [250 g / 25 cl] whole milk

6 eggs

5 egg yolks

⅔ cup [150 g] granulated sugar

1¾ lbs. [800 g] raspberries

1 star anise

For the compote:

1 lb. 2 oz. [500 g] wild blackberries

½ cup [100 g] granulated sugar

1 star anise

To decorate:

A few fresh raspberries

To bake:

A ceramic tart pan with a fluted rim 10 inches [26 cm] in diameter and 1½ inches [4 cm] deep

Preheat the oven to 325°F [160°C].

In a heavy-bottomed saucepan, bring the milk to a boil. Remove from the heat. Add the star anise, cover the pan, and let the mixture infuse for 10 minutes.

Pick over the raspberries but do not rinse them so that they'll keep their aroma.

Remove the star anise from the pan of milk. *Prepare the flan cream:* In a bowl, combine the cream, milk, eggs, egg yolks, and sugar and beat briefly with a whip. Then arrange the raspberries in the ceramic tart pan. Cover them with the milk mixture.

Bake for 40 minutes.

Meanwhile, prepare the blackberry compote: Pick over the blackberries and quickly rinse them in cold water without soaking them. In a saucepan, combine the blackberries, sugar, and star anise. Bring to a simmer, then pour into a bowl and set aside.

The clafoutis is done when the flan cream is set and has a pretty golden yellow color. Decorate it with a few fresh raspberries and serve it with the blackberry compote. Accompany with thin slices of brioche, toasted and buttered.

Raspberry and Blueberry Tart with Wild Blackberry Compote

---

11 oz. [300 g] semi-puff pastry (*see recipe page 20*)

11 oz. [300 g] wild blueberries

11 oz. [300 g] raspberries

1 cup *plus* 1 Tbsp. [250 g] crème fraîche

For the compote:

11 oz. [300 g] wild blackberries

½ cup *plus* 1 Tbsp. [120 g] granulated sugar

For the egg wash:

1 egg

To decorate:

3 Tbsp. [20 g] confectioners' sugar

To bake:

A baking sheet covered with parchment paper

The day before, prepare your semi-puff pastry and the blackberry compote: Pick over the blackberries and quickly rinse in cold water without soaking them. In a saucepan, combine the blackberries and sugar. Bring to a simmer, then turn into a bowl and refrigerate.

The next day, roll the pastry on a lightly floured work surface into a circle a little more than ¹⁄₁₆ inch [2 mm] thick. Then roll it around a rolling pin and lift it above the baking sheet covered with parchment paper. Unroll it gently. This allows your pastry to relax and prevents it from shrinking when it is cut. Cut a circle, 10 inches [26 cm] in diameter. Using a trefoil-shaped cookie-cutter, cut some shapes to use for decorating the edges of your tart from the pastry scraps. With a pastry brush dipped in cold water, moisten the edges of the tart and press the trefoils on, overlapping them slightly. Prick the bottom of the tart with a fork and refrigerate it for 30 minutes covered with plastic wrap.

Preheat the oven to 400°F [200°C].

Paint the decorations on your tart with beaten egg. Bake your pastry shell blind (*see page 14*) for 10 minutes. Then using a pastry brush, paint it with a little beaten egg and continue baking for about 10 more minutes. The shell will be more "moisture-proof"; it will also have a nice golden color and will keep its crunch. Place it on a rack and let it cool.

Set your oven to broil.

Quickly rinse the raspberries and blueberries in cold water without soaking them. Dry them gently in a kitchen towel. At the last minute, fill your tart with a layer of mixed raspberries and blueberries. Coat the fruit with the blackberry mixture and cover it with a nice layer of crème fraîche. It might be helpful to use a pastry bag with a plain tip. Bake in the oven for a few minutes. The cream will cling to the fruit and form a fine, golden crust. Dust lightly with confectioners' sugar.

∾:∾

This recipe offers a delicious contrast between the cooked and the fresh fruit, and between the puff pastry and the velvety cream. Eat it right away!

Red Currant Meringue Tart

---

1 lb. 2 oz. [500 g] semi-puff pastry (*see recipe page 20*)

1 lb. 9 oz. [700 g] bunches of red currants, *or* 1 lb. 5 oz. [600 g] net

1 cup [100 g] ground blanched almonds

½ cup [100 g] granulated sugar

6 egg yolks

For the egg wash:

1 egg

For the meringue:

5 egg whites

1 cup [225 g] extra-fine sugar

To decorate:

3 bunches of red currants

2½ Tbsp. [30 g] granulated sugar

1 egg white

½ cup [50 g] confectioners' sugar

To bake:

A tart pan with plain rim, 10 inches [26 cm] in diameter and 1 inch [3 cm] deep

The day before, prepare your semi-puff pastry.

The next day, roll 11 ounces [300 g] of pastry on a lightly floured work surface into a circle a little more than ¹⁄₁₆ inch [about 2 mm] thick and 13 inches [34 cm] in diameter.

Butter your pan and carefully place the pastry in it, pressing the dough lightly with your fingertips against the bottom and sides. The pastry should extend beyond the edge of the pan a little less than ½ inch [1 cm] to make a border. Pinch this border between your thumb and index finger to flute it. Prick the bottom of the tart with a fork and refrigerate it for 30 minutes covered in plastic wrap.

Now roll the remainder of the dough on a lightly floured work surface to a little more than ¹⁄₁₆ inch [about 2 mm] thick. Roll it around a rolling pin and lift it above a baking sheet covered with parchment paper. Unroll it gently. This allows your dough to relax and prevents it from shrinking when it is cut. Refrigerate it for 30 minutes covered with plastic wrap.

Preheat the oven to 400°F [200°C].

Bake your pastry shell blind (*see page 14*) for 10 minutes and let it cool.

Rinse the red currants in cold water. Drain them in a colander and strip them from the stems.

Meanwhile, prepare the meringue: Beat the egg whites with an electric beater while adding the sugar in a slow stream. Continue beating, incorporating the sugar little by little until the whites are very stiff. In a bowl, combine the red currants, ground almonds, sugar, and egg yolks. Be careful not to mash the red currants. Add the beaten egg whites and fold them in gently with a wooden spatula. Fill the tart with this mixture.

From the refrigerated pastry, cut strips a little less than ½ inch [1 cm] wide and 11 inches [28 cm] long. Using a pastry brush dipped in cold water, moisten the edges of your tart. Make an evenly spaced lattice across the entire surface of the tart with pastry strips. With a pastry brush, paint the lattice with a little beaten egg. When you are ready to put the tart into the oven, remember to lower the temperature to 350°F [180°C]. Bake the tart for about 45 minutes. The edges of your tart and the lattice should be golden brown and your meringue will have a pretty, lightly caramelized color. Remove your tart from the pan onto a rack and let it cool. Dust it with confectioners' sugar. Dip the red currant bunches into the egg white and cover them with granulated sugar. Let them dry on a plate. At the last minute, decorate your tart with the frosted red currants.

Mirabelle Plum Tart with Cardamom Sugar

---

11 oz. [300 g] **flaky pastry** (*see recipe page 15*)

2 oz. [50 g] **ladyfingers**

2¾ lbs. [1.2 kg] **Nancy mirabelle plums**, *or* about 2¼ lbs. [1 kg] net

¼ cup [50 g] **granulated sugar**

To decorate:

¼ cup [50 g] **granulated sugar** *combined with* ½ tsp. **ground cardamom**

To bake:

A **tart pan** with plain rim, 10 inches [26 cm] in diameter and 1 inch [3 cm] deep

The day before, prepare your flaky pastry.

The next day, roll your pastry on a lightly floured work surface into a circle a little more than ¹⁄₁₆ inch [about 2 mm] thick and 13 inches [34 cm] in diameter.

Butter your pan and carefully place the pastry in it, pressing it with your fingertips against the bottom and sides. The dough should extend beyond the edge of the pan a little less than ½ inch [1 cm] to make a border. Pinch this border between your thumb and index finger to flute it. Prick the bottom of the tart shell with a fork and refrigerate it for 30 minutes, covered with plastic wrap.

Preheat the oven to 350°F [180°C].

Bake your tart shell blind (*see page 14*) for 15 minutes and let it cool.

Rinse the mirabelles in cold water, dry them in a kitchen towel, and cut them in half to remove the pits. Finely crumble your ladyfingers and sprinkle them in the bottom of the tart. Stand the mirabelles on top in a circle, cut surface turned toward the center of the tart. Continue arranging them this way, making concentric circles, to the center of the tart. See that they are touching. Sprinkle the fruit with granulated sugar.

Bake the tart for about 35 minutes. The edges of the tart should be nicely golden brown and the mirabelles almost jam-like. Remove your tart from the pan onto a rack and let it cool. Sprinkle it with cardamom-flavored sugar. This tart is delicious served barely warm.

~:~

I always choose mirabelles from Nancy. This yellow, rosy-cheeked variety has a bit of a honey taste that is totally exquisite.

Puff Pastry Squares with Mirabelle Plums and Linden Blossom Honey

14 oz. [400 g] semi-puff pastry (*see recipe page 20*)

2 oz. [50 g] ladyfingers

4 lbs. [1.8 kg] Nancy mirabelle plums, *or* about 3⅓ lbs. [1.5 kg] net*

¼ cup [50 g] granulated sugar

For the egg wash:

1 egg

To decorate:

3½ oz. [100 g] linden blossom honey

Juice of 1 lemon

To bake:

A baking sheet covered with parchment paper

The day before, prepare your semi-puff pastry.

The next day, roll the pastry on a lightly floured work surface to a little more than ¹⁄₁₆ inch [about 2 mm] thick. Roll it around a rolling pin and lift it over the baking sheet covered with parchment paper. Unroll it gently. This allows your dough to relax and prevents it from shrinking when it is cut. Now cut a square about 12 inches [30 cm] on a side. Using a pastry brush dipped in cold water, moisten the edges of the square. Now fold the edges toward the inside, making a double border. Pinch and mark this border

---

* *I always choose mirabelles from Nancy. This yellow, rosy-cheeked variety has a bit of a honey taste that is totally exquisite.*

with the fingertips so it won't come apart during baking. Prick the bottom of the tart with a fork and refrigerate it for 30 minutes, covered with plastic wrap.

Preheat the oven to 400°F [200°C].

Rinse the mirabelles in cold water, dry them in a kitchen towel and cut them in half to remove the pits. Finely crumble your ladyfingers and sprinkle them in the bottom of the tart. Arrange the mirabelles on the pastry square, being careful to preserve their original round shape. Sprinkle them with granulated sugar. Paint the edges of your tart with a pastry brush dipped in a little beaten egg.

When you are ready to put the tart into the oven, remember to decrease the oven temperature to 350°F [180°C]. Bake the tart for about 40 minutes. The pastry will have a pretty golden color. The mirabelles will be half-candied.

In a small pan, melt the honey and lemon juice on low heat. When you remove your tart from the oven, coat the plums with the lemon honey, using a pastry brush. Slide your tart onto a rack and let it cool.

~:~

You can also decorate this tart with thin slices of orange and lemon dried in the oven. To prepare: Cut the citrus fruit into round slices and place them on an oven rack covered with parchment paper. Let them dry for 3 hours at 150°F [60°C]. Then cut them in half and distribute them among the mirabelles.

This tart is delicious with crème brûlée.

Puff Pastry Tart with Wild Blueberries

---

    1 lb. 5 oz. [600 g] semi-puff pastry (*see recipe page 20*)

    2 oz. [50 g] ladyfingers

    1 lb. 9 oz. [700 g] wild blueberries

    ⅔ cup [150 g] granulated sugar

For the egg wash:

    1 egg

To bake:

    A tart pan with plain rim, 10 inches [26 cm] in diameter and 1 inch [3 cm] deep

The day before, prepare your semi-puff pastry.

The next day, roll 12 ounces [350 g] of pastry on a lightly floured work surface into a circle a little more than 1/16 inch [about 2 mm] thick and 13 inches [34 cm] in diameter.

Butter the pan and carefully place the pastry in it, pressing lightly with the fingertips against the bottom and sides. The pastry should extend a little less than ½ inch [1 cm] beyond the pan to make a border. Pinch this border between the thumb and index finger to flute it. Prick the bottom of the tart with a fork and refrigerate it for 30 minutes covered with plastic wrap.

Now roll the remaining pastry on a lightly floured work surface to a little more than 1/16 inch [about 2 mm] thick. Roll it around a rolling pin and lift it above a baking sheet covered with parchment paper. Unroll it gently. This allows the pastry to relax and prevents it from shrinking when it is cut. Refrigerate it for 30 minutes, covered with plastic wrap.

Preheat the oven to 350°F [180°C].

Bake the tart shell blind (*see page 14*) for 15 minutes and let it cool.

Meanwhile, quickly rinse the blueberries in cold water without soaking them. Dry them gently in a kitchen towel. Finely crumble the ladyfingers and sprinkle the bottom of the tart with them. Arrange the blueberries on top, then sprinkle them with granulated sugar. Using a cookie-cutter, cut a few flower shapes out of the refrigerated dough. Set these aside on a sheet of parchment paper. With a pastry brush dipped in cold water, moisten the edges of the tart. Now roll the dough with the flower shapes cut out of it around the rolling pin and lift it above your filled pastry shell. Unroll it gently, without stretching or distorting the holes made by cutting out the flowers. Using a small knife, trim off the pastry that extends beyond the tart pan. Then, using a pastry brush, paint the pastry cover with a little beaten egg. Cut the reserved flower cutouts in half, press them here and there on the pastry cover, and paint them with the beaten egg.

Bake the tart for about 35 minutes. The pastry should be a pretty golden color. Unmold the tart from the pan onto a rack and let it cool. Serve this tart with thick crème fraîche.

Chantilly Tart with Wild Blueberries

11 oz. [300 g] rich flaky pastry with praline paste and hazelnuts (*see recipe page 19*)

1 lb. 2 oz. [500 g] wild blueberries

2 cups 1 oz. [500 g / 50 cl] whipping cream

Scant 1 cup [100 g] confectioners' sugar

Zest of 1 lemon, finely grated

For the egg wash:

1 egg

To decorate:

3 Tbsp. [25 g] confectioners' sugar

To bake:

A tart pan with plain rim, 10 inches [26 cm] in diameter and 1 inch [3 cm] deep with removable bottom

The day before, prepare your rich flaky pastry.

The next day, roll the pastry on a lightly floured work surface into a circle a little less than ⅛ inch [about 2.5 mm] thick and 13 inches [34 cm] in diameter.

Butter your pan and carefully place the pastry in it, pressing it lightly with the fingertips against the bottom and sides. Roll the rolling pin across the top edge of the pan to trim off the small amount of excess pastry. Prick the tart with a fork and refrigerate it for 30 minutes, covered with plastic wrap.

Preheat the oven to 350°F [180°C].

Bake your tart shell blind (*see page 14*) for 10 minutes. Then, using a pastry brush, paint the pastry with a little beaten egg and continue baking for 5 to 8 minutes. The pastry shell will be more "moisture-proof"; it will also have a nice golden color and it keep its crunch. Remove your tart onto a rack and let it cool.

Quickly rinse the blueberries in cold water without soaking them. Dry them gently in a kitchen towel. Prepare the Chantilly cream: In a bowl that has been chilled in the refrigerator for 15 minutes, combine the cream, confectioners' sugar, and finely grated lemon zest. Beat the mixture with a whip until it is quite stiff. You could also use an electric mixer. Now fill the bottom of the tart with this Chantilly cream. It might be helpful to use a pastry bag with a plain tip. Arrange the blueberries in a heap on the cream. Dust them generously with confectioners' sugar.

~:~

I suggest you fill this tart at the last minute so that the pastry stays perfectly crunchy. The little bit of lemon zest in the whipped cream gives a pleasant lift to the blueberries' flavor and lightens the richness of the cloud of crème fraîche.

Peak of Freshness Tart with Red and Black Fruit

---

14 oz. [400 g] flaky pastry (*see recipe page 15*)

1 cup *plus* 1 Tbsp. [250 g] pastry cream (*see recipe page 25*)

1 cup *plus* 1 Tbsp. [250 g / 25 cl] whipping cream

4 oz. [120 g] strawberries, *or* about 3½ oz. [100 g] net

3½ oz. [100 g] raspberries

3½ oz. [100 g] wild blueberries

4 oz. [120 g] red currants, *or* about 3½ oz. [100 g] net

3½ oz. [100 g] wild blackberries

For the egg wash:

1 egg

To decorate:

a few bunches of red currants

3½ oz. [100 g] raspberry or red currant jelly (*see recipes pages 30 and 31*)

A few additional raspberries

3 Tbsp. [20 g] confectioners' sugar

To bake:

A tart pan with plain rim, 10 inches [26 cm] in diameter and 1 inch [3 cm] deep

The day before, prepare your flaky pastry.

The next day, roll 12 ounces [350 g] of pastry on a lightly floured work surface into a circle a little more than ¹⁄₁₆ inch [about 2 mm] thick and 13 inches [34 cm] in diameter.

Butter your pan and carefully place the pastry in it, pressing the dough lightly with the fingertips against the bottom and sides. Roll the rolling pin across the top edge of the pan to cut off the small amount of excess dough. Prick the pastry shell with a fork and refrigerate it for 30 minutes covered with plastic wrap.

Roll the rest of the dough on a lightly floured work surface to a little more than ⅛ inch [about 2 mm] thick.

Roll it around a rolling pin and lift it above a baking sheet covered with parchment paper. Unroll it gently. This allows your dough to relax and prevents it from shrinking when it is cut. Refrigerate it for 30 minutes, covered with plastic wrap. Using a cookie-cutter, cut about 30 leaf shapes from the refrigerated dough. Using a pastry brush dipped in cold water, moisten the edges of your tart and press on about 25 leaves, overlapping them slightly.

Preheat the oven to 350°F [180°C].

Using a pastry brush, paint the decorations on your tart dipped in a little beaten egg. Bake your tart shell blind (*see page 14*) for 15 minutes. Using a pastry brush, paint the tart shell with a little beaten egg and continue baking for about 10 minutes. The shell will be more "moisture-proof"; it will also have a pretty golden color and keep its crunch. Remove the tart onto a rack and let it cool.

In a bowl, smooth the pastry cream by stirring it gently with a whip. In another bowl that you have chilled in the refrigerator for 15 minutes, whip the cream. Now, lighten the pastry cream by gently incorporating the whipped cream into it.

Quickly rinse the fruits in cold water. Dry them gently in a kitchen towel. Stem the strawberries and cut them in half lengthwise. Strip the red currants from their bunches. Now fill the tart with the lightened pastry cream. It might be helpful to use a pastry bag with a plain tip. Make a garden of colors, arranging the fruit on the cream as you feel inspired to.

In a small pan, gently heat the raspberry or red currant jam with 2 tablespoons [30 g / 30 cl] of water. Bring it to a simmer and, using a pastry brush, carefully coat your fruit. Dust the red currant bunches with confectioners' sugar. Gently place the red currants and raspberries on your tart.

∾:∾

I suggest you fill this tart at the last minute so that the pastry stays crisp.

Old Bachelor's Tart

---

14 oz. [400 g] rich flaky pastry with praline paste and hazelnuts (*see recipe page 19*)

7 oz. [200 g] almond cream (*see recipe page 27*)

3⅓ cups [800 g] Old Bachelor's Jam

7 oz. [200 g] crème fraîche

3½ Tbsp. [50 g / 5 cl] whipping cream

For the egg wash:

1 egg

To bake:

A baking sheet covered with parchment paper

The day before, prepare your rich flaky pastry.

The next day, roll the pastry on a lightly floured work surface to a little more than 1⁄16 inch [about 2 mm] thick. Roll it around a rolling pin and lift it above the baking sheet. Unroll it gently. If your pastry tears, carefully put the edges together and press lightly with the fingertips to make them stick. Cut a circle, 10 inches [26 cm] in diameter. Using a heart-shaped cookie-cutter, cut some shapes from the pastry scraps for decorating the edges of your circle. Using a pastry brush dipped in cold water, moisten the edges of the circle and press the hearts onto it, overlapping them slightly. Prick the pastry shell with a fork and refrigerate it for 30 minutes covered with plastic wrap.

Preheat the oven to 350°F [180°C].

Paint the decorations with beaten egg. Bake your shell blind for 10 minutes (*see page 14*). Let it cool. Meanwhile, prepare your almond cream. Now fill the tart with an even layer of almond cream. It might be helpful to use a pastry bag with a plain tip. Bake the pastry for about 8 minutes. The edges of the tart should be golden and the almond cream slightly colored and puffed. Slide your tart onto a rack and let it cool.

In a bowl, combine the crème fraîche and the cream. Using a small ladle, fill the bottom of your tart with Old Bachelor's Jam* and serve it immediately with the cream. You can also enjoy this tart with faisselle**, crème anglaise, or an oval-shaped scoop of vanilla ice cream.

~:~

In earlier times, every household made Old Bachelor's Jam using fruit and alcohol. In an earthenware pot, they would put a few handfuls of red or black fruit, gathered as it ripened in the garden or growing wild in the woods, then covering each addition with sugar and Kirsch. By fall, this jam would be enjoyed with crunchy little cakes, a semolina pudding, or fromage blanc.

Lacking Old Bachelor's Jam, you can make a little salad of fresh red and black fruit: for 1 pound 9 ounces [700 g] of fruit, allow ½ cup [100 g] of granulated sugar and 2 tablespoons [30 g / 30 cl] of Kirsch.

* *The author's recipe for Old Bachelor's Jam appears in* Mes Confitures: The Jams and Jellies of Christine Ferber.
** *A fresh white cheese. See Techniques and Ingredients, page 7.*

Peach and Raspberry Tart with Lemongrass

1 lb. 2 oz. [500 g] semi-puff pastry (*see recipe page 20*)

2 cups 1 oz. [500 g] pastry cream (*see recipe page 25*)

5 oz. [150 g] raspberries

8 small white peaches

Juice of 1 lemon

1 cup [200 g] granulated sugar

8 small, fresh lemongrass leaves

For the egg wash:

1 egg

To decorate:

8 small, fresh lemongrass leaves

3 Tbsp. [40 g] granulated sugar

1 egg white

To bake:

A baking sheet covered with parchment paper

The day before, prepare your semi-puff pastry and your pastry cream. In a pot of boiling water, blanch your peaches for 1 minute. Refresh them in ice water. Peel the peaches, cut them in half, remove the pits, and cut each half into quarters. In a preserving pan, combine the peach sections, lemon juice, sugar, and finely chopped lemongrass. Bring to a simmer, then turn into a bowl, cover, and refrigerate.

The next day, roll your pastry on a lightly floured work surface to a little more than 1⁄16 inch [about 2 mm] thick. Roll it around a rolling pin and lift it above the baking sheet covered with parchment paper. Unroll it gently. This allows your pastry to relax and prevents it from shrinking when it is cut. Cut a rectangle about 5 inches [12 cm] wide and 12 inches [30 cm] long. To make borders for your tart, cut 2 pastry strips a little less than ½ inch [1 cm] wide and 12 inches [30 cm] long. Then cut 2 strips a little less than ½ inch [1 cm] wide and a little more than 4 inches [10 cm] long. Using a pastry brush dipped in water, moisten the edges of the pastry rectangle. Press these strips along the edges, carefully aligning the ends. Prick the pastry with a fork and refrigerate it for 30 minutes covered with plastic wrap.

Preheat the oven to 400°F [200°C].

Using a pastry brush, paint the edges of your tart with a little beaten egg. When you put it into the oven, remember to lower the temperature to 350°F [180°C]. Bake your tart shell blind (*see page 14*) for 15 minutes. The edges of the pastry will be lightly browned. Using a pastry brush, paint the inside of the tart with a little egg. Continue baking for about 10 more minutes. The shell will be more "moisture-proof"; it will also have a nice golden color and keep its crunch. Slide your tart onto a rack and let it cool.

In a bowl, smooth the pastry cream by stirring it gently with a whip. Now fill the tart. It might be helpful to use a pastry bag with a plain tip. Remove the peach slices from their juice. Drain them for a few minutes and arrange them on the pastry cream. Arrange the raspberries among the peach sections. Dip the lemongrass leaves in beaten egg white and cover them with granulated sugar. Let them dry on a plate. At the last minute, decorate your tart with the frosted lemongrass leaves.

White and Yellow Peach Clafoutis with Lavender

5 small white peaches

5 small yellow peaches

For the flan cream:

1 cup *plus* 1 Tbsp. [250 g / 25 cl] whipping cream

1 cup *plus* 1 Tbsp. [250 g / 25 cl] whole milk

6 eggs

5 egg yolks

⅔ cup [150 g] granulated sugar

5 sprigs of fresh, fragrant lavender

To decorate:

6 sprigs of fresh, fragrant lavender

To bake:

A ceramic pan with fluted rim, 10 inches [26 cm] in diameter and 1 inch [3 cm] deep

Preheat the oven to 325°F [160°C].

In a heavy-bottomed saucepan, bring the milk to a boil. Remove from the heat. Add the lavender tied in a piece of cheesecloth, cover the pan, and let the mixture infuse for 10 minutes.

Blanch the white and yellow peaches for 1 minute in a pot of boiling water. Refresh them in ice water. Peel them, cut them in half, remove the pits and cut each half into quarters.

Remove the lavender from the pan of milk.

Prepare the flan cream: In a bowl, combine the cream, milk, eggs, egg yolks, and sugar and beat briefly with a whip. Arrange the peach sections in the ceramic tart pan. Cover them with the flan cream mixture.

Bake for about 45 minutes. The clafoutis is done when the flan cream is set and has a pretty golden yellow color. Decorate it with a few sprigs of fresh lavender and serve it with vanilla ice cream. Pass thin slices of toasted and buttered brioche.

Caramelized Peach Tart with Rosemary

---

14 oz. [400 g] rich flaky pastry No. 2 (*see recipe page 18*)

7 oz. [200 g] almond cream (*see recipe page 27*)

10 small yellow peaches

3½ Tbsp. / 1¾ oz. [50 g] butter)

3½ Tbsp. [50 g / 5 cl] water

½ cup [100 g] granulated sugar

3½ Tbsp. [50 g] acacia blossom honey

1 small sprig of rosemary

For the egg wash:

1 egg

To bake:

A baking sheet covered with parchment paper

The day before, prepare your rich flaky pastry.

The next day, roll the pastry on a lightly floured work surface to a little more than ¹⁄₁₆ inch [about 2 mm] thick. Then roll it around a rolling pin and lift it above the baking sheet. Unroll it gently. If your pastry tears, carefully put the edges together and press lightly with the fingertips to make them stick. Cut a circle, 10 inches [26 cm] in diameter. Use a round cookie-cutter to cut some shapes from the pastry scraps to use for decorating the rim of your circle. With a pastry brush dipped in cold water, moisten the outside of the pastry circle and press the little rounds on, overlapping them slightly. Prick the bottom of the shell with a fork and refrigerate it for 30 minutes, covered with plastic wrap.

Preheat the oven to 350°F [180°C].

Paint the tart decorations with beaten egg. Bake your tart shell blind (*see page 14*) for 10 minutes, and let it cool.

Meanwhile, prepare your almond cream. Fill your tart with an even layer. It might be helpful to use a pastry bag with a plain tip. Bake it for about 8 minutes. The edges of the tart should be golden and the almond cream lightly colored and puffed. Slide your tart onto a rack and let it cool.

Now prepare your caramelized peaches: Blanch them for 1 minute in a pan of boiling water. Refresh them in a bowl of ice water. Peel them, cut them in half, and remove the pits. In a skillet, melt the butter and the sugar. Add the water, honey, and the small sprig of rosemary. Bring to a simmer. Put the peach halves into the skillet, cut surface turned down. Let them simmer for a few minutes. Then, using two wooden spoons, turn them over. Let them simmer again until they are half-candied. Remove the peaches and the rosemary from the skillet. Reduce the liquid until it has caramelized very slightly.

Arrange the peaches in the bottom of the tart and at the last minute, using a spoon, coat them with the caramelized juices. Serve this tart with thick crème fraîche. You will also enjoy it with faisselle*, crème anglaise, or a scoop of vanilla ice cream.

* A fresh white cheese. See Techniques and Ingredients, page 7.

Leek Tart

11 oz. [300 g] flaky pastry with egg (*see recipe page 15*)

2 lbs. [900 g] leeks, *or* 1⅓ lbs. [600 g] net

3½ Tbsp. / 1¾ oz. [50 g] butter

Salt

Freshly ground black pepper

For the custard filling:

¼ cup *plus* 2 Tbsp. [150 g] crème fraîche

5 oz. [150 g] ricotta cheese

7 oz. [200 g] faisselle*, drained

6 eggs

For the egg wash:

1 egg

To bake:

A tart pan with plain rim, 10 inches [26 cm] in diameter and 1 inch [3 cm] deep

The day before, prepare your flaky pastry with egg.

The next day, roll the pastry on a lightly floured work surface into a circle a little more than 1/16 inch [about 2 mm] thick and 13 inches [34 cm] in diameter.

Butter your pan and carefully place the pastry in it, pressing the dough lightly with the fingertips against the bottom and sides.

* A fresh white cheese. See Techniques and Ingredients, page 7.

Preheat the oven to 350°F [180°C].

Bake your tart shell blind (*see page 14*) for 15 minutes. Then, using a pastry brush, paint the pastry with beaten egg and continue baking for about 5 minutes. The bottom will be more "moisture-proof"; it will also have a pretty golden color and will keep its crunch.

Meanwhile, prepare your leeks: Rinse them in cold water. Peel them and keep only the white and a small part of the green. Cut them into round slices about ¼ inch [5 mm] thick, then wash them carefully. Drain them. In a pan, melt the butter, add 3 pinches of salt, 2 grinds of black pepper, and 3½ ounces [100 g / 10 cl] of cold water. Add the sliced leeks and mix with a wooden spatula. Cook for about 10 minutes, covered and on low heat, stirring occasionally. The leeks should be somewhat soft and the water almost entirely evaporated. Turn into a bowl and set aside.

Prepare your custard filling: In a bowl combine the crème fraîche, faisselle, ricotta, eggs, 2 pinches of salt, and 2 grinds of black pepper and beat briefly with a whip. Arrange the braised leeks in the bottom of your tart, being careful not to include any of the cooking liquid. Pour in the custard. It should cover the leeks.

Bake for about 45 minutes. The edges of your tart should be nicely browned and the custard colored and set. Remove the tart from the pan and serve immediately.

Alsatian Quetsch Plum Tart with Cinnamon Sugar

11 oz. [300 g] semi-puff pastry (*see recipe page 20*)

2 oz. [50 g] ladyfingers

2¾ lbs. [1.2 kg] Alsatian quetsch plums, *or about* 2¼ lbs. [1 kg] net

¼ cup [50 g] granulated sugar

To decorate:

¼ cup [50 g] granulated sugar

⅝ tsp. ground cinnamon

To bake:

A tart pan with plain rim, 10 inches [26 cm] in diameter and 1 inch [3 cm] deep

The day before, prepare your semi-puff pastry.

The next day, roll the pastry on a lightly floured work surface into a circle a little more than ¹⁄₁₆ inch [about 2 mm] thick and 13 inches [34 cm] in diameter.

Butter your pan and carefully place the pastry in it, pressing lightly with your fingertips against the bottom and sides. The pastry should extend beyond the edge of the pan a little less than ½ inch [1 cm] to make a border. Pinch this border between the thumb and index finger to flute it. Prick the tart with a fork and refrigerate it for 30 minutes covered with plastic wrap.

Preheat the oven to 350°F [180°C].

Bake your tart shell blind (*see page 14*) for about 15 minutes and let it cool.

Rinse the plums in cold water, dry them in a kitchen towel, and cut them in half to remove the pits. Finely crumble your ladyfingers and sprinkle them in the bottom of the tart. Arrange your plums in a circle, cut surface turned toward the center of the tart. Continue arranging them this way, making concentric circles to the center of the tart. See that they are touching. Sprinkle the fruit with granulated sugar.

Bake for about 35 minutes. The edges of the tart should be nicely brown and the plums soft and half-candied. Remove your tart onto a rack and let it cool. Sprinkle it with cinnamon sugar. This tart is delicious served just barely warm.

~:~

Quetsch plums are best when they are fully ripe. Their skins should be velvety blue and their flesh a pretty gold color with a slight taste of jam. If you choose them even riper, they will have a delicious aroma of spice and caramel.

Old-Fashioned Rich Flaky Pastry Tart with Quetsch Plum Jam

11 oz. [300 g] rich flaky pastry No. 1 (*see recipe page 17*)

2 cups *plus* 2 Tbsp. [500 g] almond cream (*see recipe page 27*)

3 Tbsp. [50 g] crème fraîche

For the jam:

2½ lbs. [1.1 kg] Alsatian quetsch plums, *or* 2¼ lbs. [1 kg] net

Scant 2 cups [200 g] walnuts, broken into pieces

1 cup [200 g] granulated sugar

Juice of 1 lemon

1 cinnamon stick

2 star anise

For the egg wash:

1 egg

To bake:

A tart pan with plain rim, 10 inches [26 cm] in diameter and 1 inch [3 cm] deep with removable bottom

The day before, prepare your rich flaky pastry.

The next day, roll the pastry on a lightly floured work surface into a circle a little less than ⅛ inch [2.5 mm] thick and 13 inches [34 cm] in diameter.

Butter your pan and carefully place the pastry in it, pressing it lightly with the fingertips against the bottom and sides. Roll the rolling pin across the edge of the pan to cut off the small amount of excess pastry. Prick the tart with a fork and refrigerate it for 30 minutes covered with plastic wrap.

Preheat the oven to 350°F [180°C].

Bake your tart shell blind (*see page 14*) for 10 minutes and let it cool.

Meanwhile, prepare your almond cream. Add the crème fraîche and stir gently with a wooden spatula. Fill the tart with an even layer of the cream. It might be helpful to use a pastry bag with a plain tip.

Bake for about 15 minutes. The edges of the tart should be nicely brown and the almond cream lightly colored and puffed. Remove your tart onto a rack and let it cool.

Prepare the quetsch jam: Quickly rinse the plums in cold water. Dry them in a kitchen towel and cut them in half to remove the pits. Combine them with the sugar, lemon juice, star anise, and cinnamon. Let them macerate for 10 minutes, then turn this mixture into a preserving pan and bring it to a simmer. Pour into a bowl and set aside. When the jam is cool, remove the spices and add the broken walnuts.

At the last minute, using a small ladle, coat the bottom of the tart with the quetsch jam.

~:~

This tart is delicious with crème fraîche or a crème anglaise, given a little boost with the finely chopped zest of 1 orange.

Alsatian Tart with Quetsch Plums and Streusel

---

11 oz. [300 g] rich flaky pastry No. 1 (*see recipe page 17*)

2 cups 1 oz. [500 g] almond cream (*see recipe page 27*)

1⅓ lbs. [600 g] quetsch plums, *or* 1 lb. 2 oz. [500 g] net

For the streusel:

2 Tbsp. / 1 oz. [30 g] cold butter

2½ Tbsp. [30 g] sugar

1 generous Tbsp. [15 g] ground blanched almonds

3 Tbsp. [30 g] flour

⅜ tsp. ground cinnamon

To decorate:

3 Tbsp. [25 g] confectioners' sugar

To bake:

A tart pan with plain rim, 10 inches [26 cm] in diameter and 1 inch [3 cm] deep with removable bottom

The day before, prepare your rich flaky pastry.

The next day, roll your pastry on a lightly floured work surface into a circle a little less than ⅛ inch [about 2.5 mm] thick and 13 inches [34 cm] in diameter.

Butter your pan and carefully place the dough in it, pressing it lightly with the fingertips against the bottom and the sides. Roll the rolling pin across the top to trim off the small amount of excess dough. Prick the tart with a fork and refrigerate it for 30 minutes covered with plastic wrap.

Preheat the oven to 350°F [180°C].

Prepare your almond cream.

Rinse the plums in cold water, dry them in a kitchen towel, and cut them in half to remove the pits. Fill the bottom of the tart with an even layer of almond cream. It might be helpful to use a pastry bag with a plain tip. Arrange your plums in a circle, cut surface turned up. Continue arranging them this way, making concentric circles to the center of the tart. See that they are touching.

Bake for 40 minutes.

Meanwhile, prepare the streusel: Cut the butter into very small cubes. In a bowl, combine the butter, sugar, ground almonds, flour, and ground cinnamon. Work this mixture gently with the fingertips until it has a texture like coarse meal. Rub it together for a few seconds more to obtain a slightly lumpier consistency.

When the almond cream is lightly colored and puffed, sprinkle the streusel in little mounds on the tart. Then continue baking for 10 more minutes. The edges of the tart should be nicely golden and the streusel crunchy and well colored. Remove your tart onto a rack and let it cool before dusting it with confectioners' sugar.

∾:∾

This tart is lovely with a cinnamon-flavored crème anglaise.

My Grandmother's Quetsch Tart

For the rich flaky pastry with cinnamon:

> 1½ cups [200 g] Wondra flour
>
> 7 Tbsp. / 3½ oz. [100 g] softened butter
>
> ½ cup [100 g] granulated sugar
>
> ⅔ cup [50 g] blanched almonds, finely chopped
>
> Finely grated zest of ½ lemon
>
> Pinch of salt
>
> ¼ tsp. ground cinnamon
>
> 1 Tbsp. [5 g] cocoa
>
> 2 small eggs
>
> ½ tsp. [2 g] baking powder
>
> 1 tsp. [5 g] vanilla sugar

For the jam:

> 1 lb. 5 oz. [600 g] quetsch plums, *or* about 1 lb. 2 oz. [500 g] net
>
> ½ cup [100 g] granulated sugar
>
> 1 cinnamon stick

For the egg wash:

> 1 egg

To decorate:

> A few plums
>
> 2 tsp. [10 g] granulated sugar

To bake:

A tart pan with plain rim, 10 inches [26 cm] in diameter and 1 inch [3 cm] deep with removable bottom

The day before, prepare your rich flaky pastry with cinnamon: Sift the flour. Make a hollow. Sprinkle the almonds, lemon zest, salt, cinnamon, and cocoa around the edge of the hollow. Place the butter, sugar, and vanilla sugar in the center. Work the butter and the two sugars with the fingertips until it is velvety. Gather up the flour little by little and rub it with the butter and sugar mixture gently between your hands until you have a texture that resembles coarse meal. Now make another hollow. Beat two eggs in a bowl and pour them into the center. Gather the flour, butter, and sugar mixture toward the center, lightly kneading the pastry. Be careful not to work it too much. Now roll the pastry into a ball. Protect it by wrapping it in plastic wrap. Let it rest in the refrigerator for three hours or overnight.

Prepare the quetsch jam: Quickly rinse the plums in cold water, dry them in a kitchen towel and cut them in half to remove the pits. Mix them with the sugar, lemon juice, star anise, and cinnamon. Let them macerate for 10 minutes. Then pour this preparation into a preserving pan and bring to a simmer. Pour into a bowl and set aside. When the jam is cool, remove the spices.

The next day, roll your pastry on a lightly floured work surface into a circle a little more than ⅛ inch [4 mm] thick and 13 inches [34 cm] in diameter.

Butter your pan and carefully place the pastry in it, pressing it lightly with the fingertips against the bottom and sides. Roll the rolling pin across the top edges of the pan to trim off the small amount of excess dough. From the pastry scraps, using a cookie-cutter, cut about 30 heart shapes to decorate the top and the edges of your tart. Place the hearts on a lightly floured sheet of parchment paper. Prick the tart with a fork. Fill it with 1¾ cups [400 g] of quetsch jam. Using a pastry brush dipped in cold water, moisten the edges of your tart and press the hearts on, overlapping them slightly. Refrigerate your tart for 30 minutes, covered with plastic wrap.

Preheat the oven to 400°F [200°C].

Paint the decorations with a little beaten egg. Cut the reserved plums in quarters. Arrange them in a circle, cut surface turned up in the center of your tart. They should be touching.

When you are ready to put the tart into the oven, be sure to lower the temperature to 350°F [180°C]. Bake for about 40 minutes. The edges and the heart decorations on your tart should be nicely golden and the plums almost jam-like. Remove the tart onto a rack and let it cool.

~:~

You have some latitude about serving this tart. Make it the day before and it will only be better!

Lattice-Topped Tart with Greengage Plums and Almonds

---

1 lb. 5 oz. [600 g] semi-puff pastry (*see recipe page 20*)

1 cup *plus* 1 Tbsp. [250 g] almond cream (*see recipe page 27*)

1 lb. 14 oz. [850 g] greengage plums, *or* about 1 lb. 9 oz. [700 g] net

¼ cup [50 g] granulated sugar

For the egg wash:

1 egg

To bake:

A tart pan with plain rim, 10 inches [26 cm] in diameter and 1 inch [3 cm] deep

The day before, prepare your semi-puff pastry.

The next day, roll 12 ounces [350 g] of pastry on a lightly floured work surface into a circle a little more than ¹⁄₁₆ inch [2 mm] thick and 13 inches [34 cm] in diameter.

Butter your pan and carefully place the pastry in it, pressing it lightly with the fingertips against the bottom and sides. The dough should extend beyond the edge of the pan a little less than ½ inch [1 cm] to make a border. Pinch this border between the thumb and index finger to flute it. Prick the bottom of the tart with a fork and refrigerate it for 30 minutes covered with plastic wrap.

Roll the remainder of the dough on a lightly floured work surface to a little more than ¹⁄₁₆ inch [2 mm] thick. Roll it around a rolling pin and lift it above a baking sheet covered with parchment paper. Unroll it gently. This allows your pastry to relax and prevents it from shrinking when it is cut. Refrigerate it for 30 minutes, covered with plastic wrap.

Preheat the oven to 400°F [200°C].

Bake your tart shell blind (*see page 14*) for about 10 minutes and let it cool.

Meanwhile, prepare your almond cream.

Rinse the greengages in cold water, dry them in a kitchen towel and cut them in half to remove the pits. Fill the bottom of the tart with an even layer of almond cream. It might be helpful to use a pastry bag with a plain tip. Arrange the greengages in a circle on the cream filling. See that they keep their original round shape. Sprinkle them with granulated sugar.

From the refrigerated pastry, cut strips a little less than 1 inch [2 cm] wide and 11 inches [28 cm] long. Using a pastry brush dipped in cold water, moisten the edges of your tart. Then make an evenly spaced lattice across the top surface with the pastry strips. Using a pastry brush, paint this lattice with a little beaten egg.

When you are ready to put the tart into the oven, remember to lower the temperature to 350°F [180°C]. Bake for about 45 minutes. The edges of the tart and the lattice should be nicely colored. Remove your tart onto a rack and let it cool.

Tomato Zucchini Puffs with Brin d'Amour Cheese

1 lb. 5 oz. [600 g] true puff pastry (*see recipe page 21*)

½ Brin d'Amour* cheese

5 attractive stem tomatoes

3 small zucchini

1½ Tbsp. / ¾ oz. [20 g] butter

2 sprigs of fresh thyme

1 small sprig fresh rosemary

Salt

Freshly ground black pepper

For the egg wash:

1 egg

To bake:

A baking sheet covered with parchment paper

The day before, prepare your puff pastry.

The next day, prepare your vegetables: Rinse the zucchini in cold water. Cut them into small cubes. In a pan melt the butter, then add 3 pinches of salt, 2 grinds of black pepper, a sprig of thyme, and the diced zucchini and mix with a wooden spatula. Cook for about 10 minutes, covered and on low heat, stirring occasionally. The zucchini should be slightly softened. Turn them into a bowl and set aside.

Plunge the tomatoes into boiling water for 1 minute. Refresh them in a bowl of ice water, then remove

* Brin D'Amour is a Corsican ewe's cheese with aromatic herbs.

their skins. Cut them in quarters, then core, seed, and juice them. Let the tomato flesh drain in a colander.

Cut the Brin d'Amour into 20 very thin slices and set aside.

Roll your pastry on a lightly floured work surface to about ⅟₁₆ inch [1.5 mm] thick. Then roll it around a rolling pin and lift it above a baking sheet covered with parchment paper. Unroll it gently. This allows your pastry to relax and prevents it from shrinking when it is cut. Cut 10 approximately 4-inch [10-cm] squares. Space the squares 2 inches [5 cm] apart so that they bake evenly and don't stick to each other. Cut 10 additional approximately 4½ inches [12 cm] pastry squares and put them on a lightly floured sheet of parchment paper. Cut a few leaf shapes from the pastry scraps as well, using a cookie-cutter.

Using a fork, prick the first 10 squares. Put a slice of Brin d'Amour on each square and cover it with diced zucchini. Be careful not to include any of the cooking liquid. Then lay on another slice of cheese. Cover the cheese with two quarters of peeled tomato and flavor with a bit of rosemary. Salt and pepper them lightly. Using a pastry brush dipped in cold water, moisten the edges of the squares. Align the remaining 10 pastry squares edge to edge over the filled bottoms. Press gently on the edges to seal the two layers of pastry perfectly together. Prick the puff pastry puffs with the point of a sharp knife. Using a pastry brush dipped in cold water, moisten the leaf cutouts and press them lightly on the center of each puff. Refrigerate the puffs for 30 minutes, covered with plastic wrap.

Preheat the oven to 400°F [200°C].

Using a pastry brush, paint your puffs with a little beaten egg. When you are ready to put them in the oven, remember to decrease the temperature to 350°F [180°C].

Bake them for about 15 minutes. The puff pastry should be nicely golden. Serve the puffs immediately. Accompany them with a good green salad with fresh herbs.

Square Tart of Tomato Confit with Eggplant

For 1 pound 3 ounces [550 g] of bread dough:

> 2 cups *plus* 1 Tbsp. [300 g] wheat flour
>
> ⅔ cup [100 g] rye flour
>
> Slightly more than ½ a 0.6-oz. [17 g] package compressed fresh yeast
>
> 4 Tbsp. [60 g / 6 cl] olive oil
>
> Scant 1 tsp. [4 g] salt
>
> 7 oz. [200 g / 20 cl] warm water
>
> 10 small stem tomatoes
>
> 5 small eggplants
>
> 8 cloves of garlic
>
> 4 sprigs fresh thyme
>
> 7 oz. [200 g / 20 cl] olive oil, divided
>
> Salt
>
> Freshly ground black pepper

To decorate:

> A few sprigs thyme

To bake:

> A baking sheet covered with parchment paper

The day before, prepare the eggplant: Rinse them in cold water and remove the stems. Cut them into quarters. In a pan, bring 1 quart [1 liter] of salted water to a boil, add the eggplants and cook, covered, on low heat for about 10 minutes. They should still be a little firm. Drain them and put them in a bowl and set aside.

Peel 4 garlic cloves and cut them into round slices. In a bowl, combine the garlic, thyme, and 3½ ounces [100 g / 10 cl] of olive oil. Pour this mixture into a bowl and, with the fingertips, coat the eggplants. Salt and pepper them lightly. Cover the bowl with plastic wrap and let the eggplant macerate.

The next day, prepare your bread dough: Sift the flours, make a well, and sprinkle the salt and sugar around the edge. Pour 2 ounces [60 g] of oil and the water into your well. Little by little, gather the flour toward the center and knead the dough for a few minutes. It should become a little lighter in color, be very smooth and no longer stick to the fingers. Cover with a kitchen towel and let rest in the refrigerator for about 3 hours, or until you are finished drying the tomatoes.

Preheat the oven to 200°F [90°C].

Peel the last four garlic cloves and slice them thinly. Rinse the tomatoes in cold water and remove the green part of their stems. Cut them in half widthwise. Place them on a plate, cut surface face up. Salt and pepper them, then sprinkle with garlic. Coat each tomato with olive oil. Let the tomatoes gently dry in the oven for about 3 hours. They will shrink and wrinkle and the garlic will turn a nice golden color.

When the tomatoes are ready, roll your pastry on a lightly floured work surface. Roll it approximately square a little more than ¹⁄₁₆ inch [about 2 mm] thick. Then roll it around a rolling pin and lift it above a baking sheet covered with parchment paper. Unroll it gently. This allows your pastry to relax and prevents it from tearing. Now cut a 12-inch [30-cm] square. Using a pastry brush dipped in cold water, moisten the edges of your square a little less than 1 inch [2 cm]. Then fold the edges toward the inside, as if making a hem. Pinch and mark the hem with the fingertips so it doesn't come apart in baking. Prick the bottom of the tart with a fork and refrigerate it for 10 minutes, covered with a kitchen towel.

Increase the oven temperature to 395°F [200°C].

Distribute the eggplant quarters on your pastry base. Bake it for about 25 minutes. The edges of your tart will be puffed, the bread dough deliciously crunchy, and your eggplants tender. Now arrange the tomatoes on the eggplant. Decrease the oven temperature to 350°F [180°C]. Continue baking for about 10 minutes more. Garnish with fresh thyme leaves and serve immediately.

This tart can be made more quickly if you omit the step of oven-drying the tomatoes. You could garnish the eggplant instead with peeled tomato quarters, with the seeds and juice removed. The flavor will be fresher. Personally, I prefer the taste of the cooked tomatoes.

Tomato Galette with Olives and Grilled Peppers

---

11 oz. [300 g] flaky pastry with egg (*see recipe page 15*)

10 small stem tomatoes

6 black olives

2 onions

2 red bell peppers

5 cloves of garlic

3½ oz. [100 g / 10 cl] olive oil *plus* 3½ oz. [100 g / 10 cl]

1 sprig of fresh lemon thyme

1 tsp. granulated sugar

Salt

Freshly ground black pepper

To bake:

A baking sheet covered with parchment paper

The day before, prepare your flaky pastry with egg and marinate your peppers: Wash them, cut them in quarters, and remove the seeds. Set the oven to broil and grill them, cut surface turned down, for a few minutes. As soon as they look wrinkled you can easily remove the skins. Put them in a bowl. Peel the garlic cloves and cut them into round slices. In a bowl, mix the garlic and 3½ ounces [100 g / 10 cl] of olive oil. Pour the oil mixture into the bowl with the peppers and, with the fingertips, coat the peppers. Salt and pepper them lightly. Cover them with plastic wrap and let them macerate.

The next day, roll the pastry on a lightly floured work surface into a circle a little more than ¹⁄₁₆ inch [about 2 mm] thick. Then roll it around a rolling pin and lift it above the baking sheet covered with parchment paper. Unroll it gently. This allows it to relax and prevents it from shrinking when it is cut. Cut a circle, 11 inches [28 cm] in diameter. Refrigerate it for 30 minutes covered with plastic wrap.

Peel the onions and slice them thinly. Cut the macerated peppers into thin slices and brown them in a skillet. Add the onion, sugar, 3 pinches of salt, and 5 grinds of pepper and simmer covered on low heat for a few minutes, stirring occasionally. The peppers should be soft and the onions lightly caramelized. Scrape this mixture into a bowl and set aside.

Preheat your oven to 350°F [180°C].

Blanch the tomatoes in boiling water for 1 minute. Refresh them in a bowl of ice water, remove their skins, slice them horizontally about ⅛ inch [3 mm] thick, and remove their seeds and juice. Set aside in a bowl.

Prick your tart base with a fork and bake it for about 15 minutes. The flaky pastry should be nicely golden brown. Slide the pastry base onto a rack and let it cool.

Arrange the pepper and onion filling on the pastry base. Be careful to leave a border a little less than 1 inch [about 2 cm] wide. Arrange the round tomato slices on top in concentric circles, overlapping slightly.

In a bowl, combine the pitted and finely chopped black olives, chopped lemon thyme, and 3½ ounces [100 g] of olive oil. Using a small spoon, coat your tart with this aromatic oil. Bake for about 15 minutes. Serve immediately.

Old Bachelor's Tart
(page 138)

Puff Pastry Tart
with Wild Blueberries
(page 132)

*Red Currant Meringue
Tart (page 126)*

Alsatian Quetsch Plum Tart with Cinnamon Sugar (page 148)

Lattice-Topped Tart with Greengage Plums and Almonds (page 157)

Puff Pastry Squares with Mirabelle Plums and Linden Blossom Honey (page 130)

Lattice-Topped
Tart with Apricots
(page 103)

Apricot Tart Topped with Dried Fruit and Gewurztraminer Sabayon (page 107)

*Raspberry Tart
with White Munster
(page 118)*

*Square Tart of
Tomato Confit with
Eggplant (page 161)*

Fall

Almond Tart with Vineyard Peach Jam Flavored with Pinot Noir and Cinnamon

---

1 lb. [450 g] rich flaky pastry No. 1 (*see recipe page 17*)

1 cup *plus* 1 Tbsp. [250 g] almond cream (*see recipe page 27*)

3½ Tbsp. [50 g] crème fraîche

Finely grated zest of ½ orange

For the jam:

2¾ lbs. [1.25 kg] vineyard peaches, or 2¼ lbs. [1 kg] net*

1 cup [200 g] granulated sugar

Juice of 1 orange

1 cinnamon stick

1 cup [250 g] Alsatian Pinot Noir

For the egg wash:

1 egg

To decorate:

1¾ cups [400 g] crème fraîche

To bake:

A baking sheet covered with parchment paper

The day before, prepare your rich flaky pastry and your vineyard peach jam: Poach the peaches for 1 minute in a pan of boiling water, refresh them in a bowl of ice water, peel them, remove the pits, and cut

* Substitute small, flavorful homegrown yellow peaches.

them in quarters. In a preserving pan, combine the peach quarters, sugar, lemon juice, Pinot Noir, and cinnamon stick. Bring to a simmer, then pour this mixture into a bowl and refrigerate.

The next day, roll the pastry on a lightly floured work surface into a circle a little more than 1/16 inch [about 2 mm] thick. Roll it around a rolling pin and lift it above the baking sheet. Unroll it gently. If your pastry should tear, gently put the edges together and press with the fingertips to rejoin them. Cut a circle, 10 inches [26 cm] in diameter. Using a heart-shaped cookie-cutter, cut some shapes from the pastry scraps for decorating the edges of your pastry. Now, using a pastry brush, paint the edges of the circle with a little beaten egg and press on the hearts, overlapping them slightly. Prick the bottom of the tart with a fork and refrigerate the pastry for 30 minutes covered with plastic wrap.

Preheat the oven to 350°F [180°C].

Now paint the tart's decorations with a little beaten egg. Bake your tart shell blind (*see page 14*) for 10 minutes and let it cool.

Meanwhile, prepare your almond cream. Add the crème fraîche and finely grated orange zest and mix them in gently with a wooden spatula. Fill the tart base with an even layer of this cream. It might be helpful to use a pastry bag with a plain tip for this.

Bake the tart for about 8 minutes. The edges of the pastry should be golden and the almond cream slightly colored and puffed. Slide your tart onto a rack and let it cool. At the last minute, decorate the pastry shell with rosettes of thick crème fraîche, possibly using a pastry bag with a plain tip. Serve this tart with vineyard peach jam.

~:~

You can find vineyard peaches with white or red flesh. Choose the red—their pulp, with its slight flavor of bitter almond, is firmer.

Lattice-Topped Tart with Cèpes, Chanterelles and Shallots

1 lb. 5 oz. [600 g] semi-puff pastry (*see recipe page 20*)

1 lb. 9 oz. [700 g] chanterelles

1 lb. 9 oz. [700 g] young cèpes*

8 shallots

2 Tbsp. [60 g] peanut oil

2½ oz. [80 g / 8 cl] aged wine vinegar

2 Tbsp. / 1 oz. [30 g] butter

1 small bunch of parsley

4 cloves of garlic, finely chopped

For the egg wash:

1 egg

To bake:

A tart pan with plain rim, 10 inches [26 cm] in diameter and 1 inch [3 cm] deep

The day before, prepare your semi-puff pastry.

The next day, roll 12 ounces [350 g] of the pastry on a lightly floured work surface into a circle about ¹⁄₁₆ inch [1.5 mm] thick and 13 inches [34 cm] in diameter.

Butter your pan and carefully place the pastry in it, pressing it lightly with the fingertips against the

---

* Cèpes, also known as Porcini or boletes, are hard to find fresh in the United States. Specialty markets might order them for you in late spring or fall. Otherwise you might substitute cremini, adding some reconstituted dried cèpes (usually sold as Porcini).

bottom and sides. Roll the rolling pin across the top edge of the pan to cut off the small amount of excess pastry. Prick the bottom of the tart with a fork and refrigerate it for 30 minutes covered with plastic wrap.

Roll the remaining pastry on a lightly floured work surface. Your pastry should be about ¹⁄₁₆ inch [1.5 mm] thick. Roll it around a rolling pin and lift it above a baking sheet covered with parchment paper. Unroll it gently. This allows your pastry to relax and prevents it from shrinking when it is cut. Refrigerate it for 30 minutes covered with plastic wrap.

Preheat the oven to 400°F [200°C].

Bake your pastry shell blind (*see page 14*) for 15 minutes and let it cool.

Meanwhile, prepare your mushroom filling: With the edge of a knife, scrape the mushroom stems and trim off the ends. Clean the caps, rinsing them carefully in cold water and drying them gently in a kitchen towel. Then cut the chanterelles in half and slice the cèpes thinly.

Peel and slice the shallots. In a pan, heat the oil and brown the shallots on high heat for 2 minutes. Add the sugar and caramelize them for 2 more minutes, stirring constantly. Pour in the vinegar, stirring, and let it evaporate. Now add the mushrooms. Salt and pepper them and let them brown for 5 minutes. When this is finished, add 3 tablespoons / 1½ oz. [42 g] of butter, garlic, and the finely chopped parsley. Then remove this filling with a skimmer and put it onto your tart shell.

From the refrigerated pastry, cut strips a little more than 1 inch [3 cm] wide and 11 inches [28 cm] long. Using a pastry brush dipped in cold water, paint the edges of your tart. Now make an even, closely spaced lattice across the entire surface of the tart. Using a pastry brush, paint the top of the tart with a little beaten egg.

When you are ready to put the tart into the oven, remember to lower the temperature to 350°F [180°C].

Bake the tart for about 30 minutes. The edges of the tart and the lattice should be nicely golden. Serve immediately.

Sauerkraut and Munster Tart

---

11 oz. [300 g] flaky pastry with egg (*see recipe page 15*)

11 oz. [300 g] aged Munster, made with unpasteurized milk

11 oz. [300 g] sauerkraut

1½ Tbsp. [20 g / 20 cl] peanut oil

2 Tbsp. [30 g] butter

1 shallot

5 oz. [150 g] Alsatian white wine (Edelzwicker)

5 oz. [150 g] water

3 pinches of cumin

For the egg custard:

5 oz. [150 g] crème fraîche

7 oz. [200 g / 20 cl] whole milk

3 eggs

Salt

Freshly ground black pepper

For the egg wash:

1 egg

To bake:

A tart pan with plain rim, 10 inches [26 cm] in diameter and 1 inch [3 cm] deep

The day before, prepare your flaky pastry with egg.

The next day, roll the pastry on a lightly floured work surface into a circle about ¹⁄₁₆ inch [2 mm] thick and 13 inches [34 cm] in diameter.

Butter your pan and carefully place the pastry in it, pressing it lightly with the fingertips against the bottom and sides. Roll a rolling pin across the top edge of your pan to cut off the small amount of excess pastry. Prick the bottom of the tart with a fork and refrigerate it for 30 minutes covered with plastic wrap.

Preheat the oven to 350°F [180°C].

Bake your tart shell blind (*see page 14*) for 15 minutes. Then, using a pastry brush, paint the pastry with a little beaten egg and continue baking for about 5 minutes. The bottom of the tart will be more "moisture-proof"; it will also have a pretty golden color and keep its crunch.

Prepare your sauerkraut: Rinse it in tap water. Peel the garlic and shallot and slice them thinly. In an enameled cast-iron casserole, heat the oil, then add 1½ tablespoons [20 g] of butter. Brown the sliced garlic and the shallot for a few minutes on high heat, stirring gently. Deglaze with the white wine and bring to a simmer. Add the sauerkraut, water, 2 pinches of salt, 3 grinds of pepper, and 3 pinches of cumin. Continue cooking, covered, on low heat for about 20 minutes. The sauerkraut should be slightly softened. Turn into a bowl and set aside.

Prepare the egg custard: In a bowl, combine the crème fraîche, milk, eggs, 3 pinches of salt, and 5 grinds of pepper and beat briefly with a whip.

Fill your tart with the sauerkraut, being careful not to include any of the cooking liquid. Cover the sauerkraut with the Munster, cut into thin slices. Cover the filling with custard and bake it for about 45 minutes. The edges of your tart should be nicely golden and the custard colored and set. Unmold the tart and serve immediately.

Quince Tart with Slivered Citrus Zest and Spices

11 oz. [300 g] rich flaky pastry with praline paste and hazelnuts (*see recipe page 19*)

4 attractive apple-quinces *or* pear-quinces

2 cups 1 oz. [500 g] almond cream (*see recipe page 27*)

3½ Tbsp. [50 g] crème fraîche

Zest of 1 lemon, slivered very finely

Zest of 1 orange, slivered very finely

⅛ tsp. ground cardamom

⅛ tsp. ground star anise

For the syrup:

1⅛ cups [250 g] granulated sugar

1 cup [250 g / 25 cl] water

To bake:

A tart pan with plain rim, 10 inches [26 cm] in diameter and 1 inch [3 cm] deep with removable bottom

The day before, prepare your rich flaky pastry.

The next day, prepare your quinces: Dry them in a kitchen towel to remove the fine down from their skins. Wash them in cold water, then peel them and remove the stems, the remainder of the blossoms and any hard parts. Cut them in quarters and remove the core and the seeds.

Prepare a poaching syrup for the quinces. In a saucepan, bring the water, sugar and lemon juice to a boil. Add the quince quarters and let them simmer until they are soft. Remove them with a skimmer and let them cool. In the same syrup, poach the slivered citrus zests, letting them simmer for 5 minutes.

Remove them with a skimmer and let them cool.

Roll your pastry on a lightly floured work surface into a circle a little less than ⅛ inch [about 2.5 mm] thick and 13 inches [34 cm] in diameter.

Butter your pan and carefully place the pastry in it, pressing it lightly with the fingertips against the bottom and sides. Roll the rolling pin across the top edge of the pan to trim off the small amount of excess dough. Prick the bottom of the tart with a fork and refrigerate it for 30 minutes covered with plastic wrap.

Preheat the oven to 350°F [180°C].

Prepare your almond cream. Add the crème fraîche, slivered citrus zests, and spices and stir gently with a wooden spatula. Fill the bottom of the tart with an even layer of almond cream. It might be helpful to use a pastry bag with a plain tip for this. Distribute the quince quarters in a circle on the almond cream, cut surface turned down.

Bake the tart for about 45 minutes. The edges of the tart should be nicely golden and the almond cream lightly colored and puffed. When the tart has nearly finished baking, mix the confectioners' sugar and very hot water in a bowl. When you remove your tart from the oven, coat each quince quarter with this glaze using a pastry brush. Unmold your tart onto a rack and let it cool.

~:~

This tart goes nicely with a spiced crème anglaise (use cinnamon, cardamom, or star anise).

My Father's Quince Tart with Raspberries and Kirsch

11 oz. [300 g] flaky pastry (*see recipe page 15*)

1 lb. 2 oz. [500 g] raspberries

4 attractive apple-quinces *or* pear-quinces

For the flan cream:

3½ oz. [100 g / 10 cl] whipping cream

3½ oz. [100 g / 10 cl] whole milk

6 egg yolks

¼ cup [50 g] granulated sugar

2 Tbsp. [30 g / 3 cl] Kirsch

Juice of 1 lemon

To decorate:

¼ cup [50 g] granulated sugar

A few raspberries for garnish

To bake:

A tart pan with plain rim, 10 inches [26 cm] in diameter and 1 inch [3 cm] deep

The day before, prepare your pastry.

The next day, prepare your quinces: Dry them in a kitchen towel to remove the fine down from their skins. Wash them in cold water, then peel them and remove the stems, the remainder of the blossoms and any hard parts. Cut them in half and remove the cores and seeds, then slice them a little less than a ¼ inch [5 mm] thick.

Prepare a poaching syrup for the quinces: In a pan, bring water to a boil with the sugar and lemon juice. Add the quince slices and let them simmer for a few minutes. Remove them with a skimmer and let them cool.

Roll your pastry on a lightly floured work surface into a circle a little more than ¹⁄₁₆ inch [about 2 mm] thick and 13 inches [34 cm] in diameter.

Butter your pan and carefully place the pastry in it, pressing it lightly with the fingertips against the bottom and sides. Roll the rolling pin across the top edge of the pan to cut off the small amount of excess dough. Prick the bottom of the tart with a fork and refrigerate it for 30 minutes covered with plastic wrap.

Preheat the oven to 350°F [180°C].

Bake your tart shell blind (*see page 14*) for 15 minutes and let it cool.

Prepare your flan cream: In a bowl, combine the cream, milk, eggs, sugar, and Kirsch, then stir briefly with a whip.

Pick over the raspberries but do not rinse them so that they'll keep their aroma. Fill the bottom of the tart with a layer of raspberries, placed close together. Cover them with the flan cream and on that arrange the quince slices in concentric circles, overlapping them slightly, to the center of your tart. Sprinkle with granulated sugar.

Bake for about 40 minutes. The edges of the tart should be nicely golden and the quince slices almost jam-like. Unmold your tart onto a rack and let it cool. Before serving, decorate it with a few fresh raspberries.

Dartois* with Morbier Cheese and Tarragon

1 lb. 9 oz. [700 g] puff pastry *or* semi-puff pastry (*see recipe pages 20 and 21*)

6 slices of ham on the bone, ⅛ inch [3 mm] thick

14 oz. [400 g] Morbier cheese**

For the béchamel:

6½ Tbsp. [60 g] flour

4 Tbsp. / 2 oz. [60 g] butter

2 cups 1 oz. [500 g / 50 cl] milk

3 oz. [80 g] grated Gruyère

5 egg yolks

2 sprigs of tarragon

Salt

Freshly ground black pepper

For the egg wash:

1 egg

To bake:

A baking sheet covered with parchment paper

The day before, prepare your puff pastry or semi-puff pastry.

The next day, prepare your béchamel: In a heavy-bottomed saucepan, heat the milk. In another

---

* Dartois is a savory covered tart made with puff pastry.
** Morbier is a semi-soft cow's milk cheese with a creamy brown crust. The interior is two layers of glossy, yellowish-ivory paste separated by a thin, flavorless layer of ash. Morbier has a compelling flavor of nuts and fruit and fresh hay aroma.

saucepan, melt the butter. Pour the flour into the butter in a stream, stirring gently with a whip to make a light roux. Then pour in the hot milk all at once and bring to a boil, stirring hard. Add the grated Gruyère, tarragon, 2 pinches of salt, and 3 grinds of pepper and return to a boil. Pour into a bowl and set aside.

Divide your pastry in half. Roll the first piece on a lightly floured work surface into a circle about 1/16 inch [1.5 mm] thick. Then roll it around a rolling pin and lift it above the baking sheet covered with parchment paper. Unroll it gently. This allows the dough to relax and prevents it from shrinking when it is cut. Now cut a circle, 11 inches [28 cm] in diameter. Roll the second piece of dough. Cut a second circle the same size and set it aside on a lightly floured sheet of parchment paper.

Remove the rind from the Morbier and cut the cheese into very small dice. Add the egg yolks and Morbier to the cooled béchamel and stir gently with a whip.

Prick the first pastry circle with a fork. Cover it with one-third of the béchamel mixture and smooth the surface with the back of a spoon. Be careful to leave an uncovered border a little more than 1 inch [3 cm]. Place 3 slices of ham on top. Cover with another third of the béchamel mixture, smoothing this layer with the back of a spoon. Then put on 3 more slices of ham. Finish by adding the remaining béchamel mixture and sprinkling the top with tarragon leaves. Using a pastry brush dipped in cold water, moisten the edges of your pastry base.

Now take your second pastry circle. Using a knife, make 5 slits, each 6 inches [15 cm] long, in the center of the circle. Then, matching up the edges, place the pastry circle onto the filled tart base. Spread the slits slightly so that the béchamel shows. Press gently on the edges to seal the two layers of pastry well. Refrigerate the tart for 30 minutes, covered with plastic wrap.

Preheat your oven to 400°F [200°C]. Using a pastry brush, paint the tart with a little beaten egg. Make a few designs with the point of a knife to decorate the top of the dartois. When you are ready to put it into the oven, remember to decrease the temperature to 350°F [180°C]. Bake the tart for about 35 minutes. The pastry should be a nice golden color. Serve immediately.

Rich Pastry Galettes with Rose Hip Jam

---

11 oz. [300 g] rich flaky pastry No. 2 (*see recipe page 18*)

For the jam:

1¾ cups [400 g] rose hip purée

1½ cups [300 g] granulated sugar

Juice of ½ lemon

To decorate:

3 Tbsp. [20 g] confectioners' sugar

Zest of 1 orange, finely slivered

To bake:

2 baking sheets covered with parchment paper

To prepare the rose hip purée: Collect the rose hips, quickly rinse them in cold water and remove the stems and caps. Place them in a pan with water to cover. Bring to a boil and let it simmer for 30 minutes, stirring occasionally. After the mixture cools, put it through a food mill several times, using a finer disk each time to remove the seeds and hairs. Last, work the purée through a fine sieve to catch the remaining hairs.

The day before, prepare your rich flaky pastry and your rose hip jam: In a preserving pan, combine the rose hip purée, sugar, and lemon juice. Bring to a boil for 5 minutes, stirring consistently. Pour the mixture into a bowl and set aside.

The next day, roll your pastry on a lightly floured surface to a little more than 1⁄16 inch [about 2 mm] thick. Using a round cookie-cutter, cut 20 small pastry rounds 4 inches [10 cm] in diameter. Cover the

2 baking sheets with parchment paper. Place 10 pastry rounds on each, spaced a little more than 1 inch [3 cm] apart so that they bake evenly and don't stick to each other. Prick them with a fork and refrigerate them for 15 minutes, covered with plastic wrap.

Preheat your oven to 350°F [180°C].

Bake the pastry rounds for about 10 minutes or until they are golden. Take them out of the oven, remove them from the baking sheet, and let them cool on a rack. Spread 10 of the rounds with 2 table-spoons of rose hip jam, then cover them with the remaining 10 rounds. Dust your pastries lightly with confectioners' sugar, then sprinkle them with orange zest slivers. Serve these galettes with a crème anglaise flavored with finely grated orange zest.

~:~

You will also enjoy these galettes with a good wine. A noble grape Alsatian Muscat would be perfect.

Fig Tart with Oranges and Walnuts

1 lb. 5 oz. [600 g] semi-puff pastry (*see recipe page 20*)

1 cup *plus* 1 Tbsp. [250 g] almond cream (*see recipe page 27*)

3½ Tbsp. [50 g] crème fraîche

6 attractive fresh figs

3 attractive oranges

½ cup [50 g] fresh walnuts, broken into pieces

¼ cup [50 g] granulated sugar

For the egg wash:

1 egg

To bake:

A baking sheet covered with parchment paper

The day before, prepare your semi-puff pastry.

The next day, roll the pastry on a lightly floured surface to a little more than ¹⁄₁₆ inch [1.5 mm] thick. Then roll it around a rolling pin and lift it above the baking sheet. Unroll it gently. This will allow your pastry to relax and prevent it from shrinking when it is cut. Cut a 10-inch [26-cm] square. Cut a second square the same size and set it aside on a lightly floured sheet of parchment paper. Prick the first square with a fork.

Prepare your almond cream. Add the crème fraîche. Spread the first pastry square with an even layer of cream, leaving clear a border a little more than 1 inch [3 cm] on each side. It might be helpful to use a pastry bag with plain tip.

Rinse the figs in cold water and dry them in a kitchen towel. Remove the stems and cut the fruits in quarters. Peel the oranges, removing the white pith and sliding your knife between the membranes to remove the sections. Sprinkle the broken walnut meats on the almond cream. Place your fig quarters on top, alternating them with orange sections. Using a pastry brush dipped in cold water, moisten the edges of your square. Sprinkle the fruit with granulated sugar.

Take the second square of pastry. Starting 2 inches [5 cm] inside the edges, make 6 slits at evenly spaced intervals of 6 inches [15 cm]. Then place this pastry square onto the filled pastry base, matching up the edges. Open the slits slightly to let the fruit show. Press lightly on the edges of the top pastry so that edges of the top and bottom squares are perfectly joined. Refrigerate the tart for 30 minutes, covered with plastic wrap.

Preheat the oven to 400°F [200°C].

Using a pastry brush, paint your tart with a little beaten egg. When you are ready to put it into the oven, remember to decrease the temperature to 350°F [180°C]. Bake the tart for about 45 minutes. The semi-puff pastry will have a beautiful golden color and the figs will be almost jam-like. Slide your tart onto a rack and let it cool.

Fig Tart with Caramel

11 oz. [300 g] rich flaky pastry with praline paste and hazelnuts (*see recipe page 19*)

2 cups *plus* 1 Tbsp. [500 g] almond cream (*see recipe page 27*)

18 small fresh figs

1¼ cups [300 g] crème fraîche

For the caramel:

1½ cups [300 g] extra-fine sugar

1¼ cups [300 g / 30 cl] whipping cream

3½ Tbsp. [50 g] lightly salted butter

½ vanilla bean

To poach the figs:

¼ cup [50 g] granulated sugar

2 cups 1 oz. [500 g / 50 cl] water

Juice of 1 lemon

To decorate:

3 Tbsp. [20 g] confectioners' sugar

To bake:

A tart pan with plain rim, 10 inches [26 cm] in diameter and 1 inch [3 cm] deep with removable bottom

The day before, prepare your rich flaky pastry. Then prepare the figs in syrup: Rinse them in cold water, and dry them in a kitchen towel. Remove the stems. In a pan, bring the water, sugar, and lemon juice to a boil. Add the figs and let them simmer for 10 minutes. Let them cool in this syrup and refrigerate them overnight.

The next day, roll your pastry on a lightly floured work surface into a circle a little less than ⅛ inch [about 2.5 mm] thick and 13 inches [34 cm] in diameter.

Butter your pan and carefully place the pastry in it, pressing it lightly with the fingertips against the bottom and sides.

Roll the rolling pin across the top edge of your pan to trim off the small amount of excess pastry. Prick the bottom of the tart with a fork and refrigerate it for 30 minutes, covered with plastic wrap.

Preheat the oven to 350°F [180°C].

Bake your tart shell blind (*see page 14*) for 10 minutes and let it cool.

Meanwhile, prepare your almond cream. Add the crème fraîche and stir gently with a wooden spatula. Spread an even layer of the cream in the tart. It might be helpful to use a pastry bag with a plain tip.

Bake the tart for about 15 minutes. The edges of the tart should be nicely golden and the almond cream lightly colored and puffed. Unmold your tart onto a rack and let it cool.

Meanwhile prepare your caramel: In a saucepan, heat the cream with ½ vanilla bean split lengthwise on low heat. Then, in a much larger saucepan, melt dry ¼ of the sugar, stirring gently with a wooden spatula. As soon as the sugar is a light caramel color, add another ¼ of the remaining sugar. Stir gently with the spatula and wait until the sugar is a light caramel color once more. Repeat this procedure twice more. Remove the vanilla bean from the cream. Then gradually add the cream to the caramelized sugar, stirring gently with the wooden spatula. Let the mixture mount and boil until the last sugar crystals have disappeared. Pour the caramel into a bowl, add the butter, and stir gently. Let it cool.

Remove the figs from their syrup with a skimmer. Put them on a plate. Cut them in quarters with scissors. Fill the quarters with crème fraîche. It might be helpful to use a pastry bag with a plain tip. Now spread a little caramel over your tart base and arrange the filled figs in a circle on top. Coat each fig with caramel. Sprinkle confectioners' sugar on the tart with the fingertips.

∼:∼

This tart is delicious with a scoop of vanilla or cinnamon ice cream.

Clafoutis with Marrons Glacés, Pears and Fresh Walnuts

For the flan cream:

> 1 cup *plus* 1 Tbsp. [250 g / 25 cl] whipping cream
> 1 cup *plus* 1 Tbsp. [250 g / 25 cl] whole milk
> 4 eggs
> 5 egg yolks
> ¼ cup [50 g] granulated sugar
> 5 very ripe William pears
> ½ cup [50 g] fresh walnuts, broken into pieces
> 2 vanilla beans

To decorate:

> 3 marrons glacés

To bake:

> A ceramic tart pan with a fluted rim, 10 inches [26 cm] in diameter and 1½
> inches [4 cm] deep

Preheat the oven to 325°F [160°C].

In a heavy-bottomed saucepan, bring the milk to a boil. Remove it from the heat. Add the 2 vanilla beans, split lengthwise. Cover the pan and let the mixture infuse for 10 minutes.

Peel the pears, core them, and cut them into small dice. Remove the vanilla beans from the pan of milk.

Prepare your flan cream: In a bowl, combine the cream, milk, eggs, egg yolks, and sugar and beat briefly with a whip. Put the diced pear into the ceramic tart dish. Break up the marrons glacés and nuts with the fingertips. Sprinkle them on the pears. Cover the fruit with the clafoutis cream.

Bake for 40 minutes. The clafoutis is done when the flan cream is set and has a nice golden yellow color. Decorate the flan with the 3 marrons glacés and serve it with vanilla ice cream.

~:~

Thinly sliced, buttered, and toasted kugelhopf offers a crunchy note to this velvety dessert.

Caramel Tartlets with Fresh Walnuts

11 oz. [300 g] rich flaky pastry No. 1 (*see recipe page 17*)

1½ cups [150 g] fresh walnuts*

For the caramel:

1½ cups [300 g] granulated sugar

1¼ cups [300 g / 30 cl] whipping cream

3½ Tbsp. [50 g] lightly salted butter

½ vanilla bean

For the egg wash:

1 egg

To decorate:

4 Tbsp. [30 g] confectioners' sugar

To bake:

8 tartlet pans, 4 inches [10 cm] in diameter

The day before, prepare your rich flaky pastry.

The next day, roll the pastry on a lightly floured work surface to a little more than ¹⁄₁₆ inch [2 mm] thick. Using a fluted cookie-cutter, cut 8 small pastry rounds, 5½ inches [14 cm] in diameter.

Butter the tartlet pans and carefully place the pastry in them, pressing lightly with the fingertips against the bottom and sides. Roll a rolling pin across the top edges of the pans to trim off the small

* "Fresh" means shortly after harvest, not subjected to long storage or the grocery shelf. Often called "new crop" at farmers' markets.

amount of excess pastry. Prick the bottoms of the shells with a fork and refrigerate them for 30 minutes covered with plastic wrap.

Preheat the oven to 350°F [180°C].

Bake your tartlet shells blind (*see page 14*) for 10 minutes. Then using a pastry brush, paint them with a little beaten egg and continue baking for about 5 to 8 minutes. The shells will be more "moisture-proof"; they will also have a nice golden color and will keep their crunch.

Unmold the tartlet shells on a rack and let them cool.

Meanwhile, prepare your caramel: In a small saucepan, heat the cream with ½ vanilla bean, split lengthwise on low heat. Then, in a much larger saucepan, melt dry ¼ of the sugar, stirring gently with a wooden spatula. As soon as the sugar is a light caramel color, add another ¼ of the remaining sugar. Stir gently with the spatula and wait until the sugar is a light caramel color once more. Repeat this procedure twice more. Remove the vanilla bean from the cream. Now gradually mix the cream into the caramelized sugar, stirring gently with the wooden spatula. Let the mixture mount and boil until the last sugar crystals have disappeared. Pour the caramel into a bowl, add the butter, and stir gently. Let the mixture cool.

Distribute the fresh walnuts in your tartlets and, using a spoon, coat them with caramel. Sprinkle confectioners' sugar on the edges with the fingertips.

~:~

These tartlets are nice with vanilla tea.

Puff Pastry Pillows with Pears and Figs Sautéed with Vanilla

---

1 lb. 5 oz. [600 g] true puff pastry (*see recipe page 21*)

1 cup *plus* 1 Tbsp. [250 g] almond cream (*see recipe page 27*)

3½ Tbsp. [50 g] crème fraîche

10 small, very ripe figs

1½ lbs. [650 g] William pears, ripe but still firm, *or* 1 lb. 2 oz. [500 g] net

½ cup [100 g] granulated sugar

5⅓ Tbsp. / 2¾ oz. [75 g] butter

2 Tbsp. [30 g / 3 cl] water)

2 vanilla beans

For the egg wash:

1 egg

To bake:

A baking sheet covered with parchment paper

The day before, prepare your puff pastry.

The next day, prepare the pears and the figs with vanilla: Peel the pears, remove the stems, core them, and cut them into small dice. Rinse the figs in cold water and dry them in a kitchen towel. Remove the stems and cut them into 8 pieces. In a skillet, melt the butter over high heat. Add the water. Add the pears and figs, mixing gently with a wooden spatula, still on high heat. Then pour in the sugar in thirds, continuing to turn your fruit so that it absorbs the butter and sugar thoroughly. Turn this preparation into a bowl. Split the vanilla beans in half lengthwise, scrape the inside and remove the seeds with the point of a knife. Then carefully mix the vanilla bean pods and seeds with the fruit. Set the mixture aside.

Roll the pastry on a lightly floured work surface to about ⅟₁₆ inch [1.5 mm] thick. Then roll it around a rolling pin and lift it above a baking sheet covered with parchment paper. Unroll it gently. This allows your pastry to relax and prevents it from shrinking when it is cut. Cut 10 approximately 4-inch [10-cm] squares. Arrange them spaced an 1½ inches [5 cm] apart so that they bake evenly and do not stick together. Cut 10 additional 4½-inch [11-cm] squares and set them aside on a lightly floured sheet of parchment paper. Using a cookie-cutter, cut a few leaf shapes from the pastry scraps as well. Prick the first 10 squares with a fork.

Prepare your almond cream. Add the crème fraîche and stir gently with a wooden spatula. Place about 2 tablespoons of almond cream in the center of each of the first 10 squares. It might be helpful to use a pastry bag with a plain tip. Remove the vanilla beans pods from your fruit. Mound 2 tablespoons of pear and sautéed figs on top of the almond cream on each square. Using a pastry brush dipped in cold water, moisten the edges of your squares. Now place the 10 remaining squares, aligning the edges, over the filled bottoms. Press gently on the edges to seal the two layers of pastry together perfectly. Prick the puff pastry pillows with the point of a knife. Using a pastry brush dipped in cold water, moisten the leaf shapes and press them on the center of each pillow. Refrigerate the tartlets for 30 minutes covered with plastic wrap.

Preheat the oven to 400°F [200°C].

Paint the pillows with a little beaten egg. When you are ready to put them into the oven remember to decrease the temperature to 350°F [180°C]. Bake them for about 30 minutes. The puff pastry should be nicely golden. Slide your puff pastry pillows onto a rack and let them cool.

Spiced Pears in Party Dress

---

1 lb. 5 oz. [600 g] semi-puff pastry (*see recipe page 20*)

8 small William or Bartlett pears, ripe but still firm

For the syrup:

2⅓ cups [500 g] granulated sugar

2 cups 1 oz. [500 g / 50 cl] water

Juice of 1 lemon

1 cinnamon stick

1 vanilla bean

1 clove of garlic~~X~~ — *Clove*

1 star anise

⅜ tsp. ground cardamom

To decorate:

1 egg

¼ cup [50 g] granulated sugar

To bake:

A baking sheet covered with parchment paper

The day before, cook the pears in spiced syrup: In a pan, combine the water, sugar, lemon juice, spices, and vanilla bean (split lengthwise) and bring the mixture to a simmer. Meanwhile, peel the pears, leaving the stems on. Add them to the syrup and poach them, letting them simmer for about 25 minutes so that the syrup cooks them gently. Turn them into a bowl and refrigerate them in the spiced syrup.

The next day, roll the pastry on a lightly floured work surface to about ¹⁄₁₆ inch [**1.5 mm**] thick. Then roll it around a rolling pin. Lightly flour your work surface again and unroll the pastry gently onto it. This allows the pastry to relax and prevents it from shrinking when it is cut.

Cut 6 approximately 6-inch [15-cm] squares. From the pastry scraps, cut some leaf shapes with a cookie-cutter. Set them aside on a lightly floured sheet of parchment paper. Using a pastry brush, paint the squares with a little beaten egg and in the center of each gently stand a pear.

Now wrap your pears: Lift the points of your pastry squares one by one and bring them up to the stem of the pear. With the palm of your hand, press the pastry against the fruit so that it molds itself perfectly to the shape of the pear. To finish, arrange the reserved pastry leaves around the stem of each pear, attaching them with a little beaten egg. Refrigerate the pears for 30 minutes, covered with plastic wrap.

Preheat the oven to 400°F [200°C].

Using a pastry brush and beaten egg, paint the pears in their party garb and sprinkle them with granulated sugar.

Be careful to decrease the oven temperature to 350°F [180°C], then bake the pears for about 35 minutes. The pastry should be nicely golden and crunchy. Place your pears on a rack. Serve them warm with a crème anglaise or a chocolate sauce.

Three Pirates Tart

1 lb. [450 g] semi-puff pastry (*see recipe page 20*)

8 small William or Bartlett pears, ripe but still firm

4 Tbsp. / 2 oz. [60 g] butter

½ cup [100 g] granulated sugar

1 cup [100 g] fresh walnuts, broken into pieces

3½ oz. [100 g] acacia blossom honey

Finely grated zest of ½ orange

For the syrup:

2⅓ cups [500 g] granulated sugar

2 cups 1 oz. [500 g / 50 cl] water

Juice of 1 lemon

2 cinnamon sticks

1 vanilla bean

1 clove

1 star anise

⅜ tsp. ground cardamom

For the egg wash:

1 egg

To bake:

A baking sheet covered with parchment paper

The day before, prepare your semi-puff pastry and cook the pears in spiced syrup: In a pan, combine the water, sugar, lemon juice, spices, and vanilla bean split lengthwise and bring the mixture to a simmer. Meanwhile, peel the pears, remove the stems, cut them in half, and core them. Place them in the syrup and poach them at a simmer for about 15 minutes so that they cook gently in the syrup. Turn them into a bowl and refrigerate them in their spiced syrup.

The next day, roll the pastry on a lightly floured work to a little more than ¹⁄₁₆ inch [2 mm] thick. Then roll it around a rolling pin and lift it above a baking sheet covered with parchment paper. Unroll it gently. This allows it to relax and prevents it from shrinking when it is cut. Cut a circle, 10 inches [26 cm] in diameter. From the pastry scraps, using a star-shaped cookie-cutter, cut shapes for decorating the edges of the circle. Using a pastry brush, paint the edges of the circle with a little beaten egg and press on the stars, overlapping them slightly. Prick the bottom of the tart with a fork and refrigerate it for 30 minutes, covered with plastic wrap.

Preheat the oven to 400°F [200°C].

Paint the tart decorations with beaten egg. When you are ready to put the tart into the oven decrease the temperature to 350°F [180°C].

Bake the tart shell blind (*see page 14*) for 15 minutes. Using a pastry brush, paint the bottom of the tart with a little beaten egg and continue baking for about 10 minutes. The bottom of the tart will be more "moisture-proof"; it will be also be nicely golden and will keep its crunch. Slide it onto a rack and let it cool.

Prepare your caramelized pears: In a skillet, melt the butter and sugar and add 3½ ounces [100 g / 10 cl] of the spiced pear syrup. Bring to a simmer. Place the pear halves in the skillet, cut surface turned down. Let them simmer for a few minutes. Then, using two wooden spoons, turn them over. Let them simmer again until they are almost jam-like. Remove them from the pan and let them cool. Now add the broken walnuts, honey, and orange zest. Let the fruit simmer until the liquid reduces and caramelizes lightly.

Arrange the pears on the tart base. At the last minute, using a spoon, coat the fruit with the walnuts and caramelized juice. Serve this tart with crème fraîche. It is also delicious with faisselle*, crème anglaise, or cinnamon ice cream.

~:~

And the three pirates? They know who they are.

* A fresh white cheese. See Techniques and Ingredients, page 7.

Sunburst Tart

12 oz. [350 g] rich flaky pastry with praline paste and hazelnuts (*see recipe page 19*)

6 small William or Bartlett pears, ripe but still firm

2½ cups *plus* 2 Tbsp. [600 g] pastry cream (*see recipe page 25*)

For the syrup:

2⅓ cups [500 g] granulated sugar

2 cups 1 oz. [500 g / 50 cl] water

Juice of 1 lemon

3 vanilla beans

To decorate:

½ cup [100 g] granulated sugar

To bake:

A tart pan with plain rim, 10 inches [26 cm] in diameter and 1 inch [3 cm] deep with removable bottom

The day before, prepare your rich flaky pastry and pastry cream, and cook the pears in a vanilla syrup: In a pan, combine the water, sugar, lemon juice, and the vanilla beans split lengthwise and bring the mixture to a simmer. Meanwhile, peel the pears, remove the stems, cut them in half and core them. Put them in the pan of syrup and poach them at a simmer for about 15 minutes so that the syrup cooks them gently. Turn them into a bowl and refrigerate them in their vanilla syrup.

The next day, roll your pastry on a lightly floured work surface into a circle a little less than ⅛ inch [2.5 mm] thick and 13 inches [34 cm] in diameter.

Butter your pan and carefully place the pastry in it, pressing the dough lightly with the fingertips against the bottom and sides. Roll a rolling pin across the top edge to trim off the small amount of excess pastry. Prick the bottom of the tart with a fork and refrigerate it for 30 minutes covered with plastic wrap.

Preheat the oven to 350°F [180°C].

Bake your pastry shell blind (*see page 14*) for 10 minutes. Then, using a pastry brush, paint it with a little beaten egg and continue baking for about 5 to 8 minutes. The bottom will be more "moisture-proof"; it will also have a pretty golden color and will keep its crunch. Unmold your tart onto a rack and let it cool.

In a bowl, smooth the pastry cream by stirring it gently with a whip. Cover the bottom of the tart with a layer of cream a little less than ½ inch [1 cm] deep. It might be helpful to use a pastry bag with a plain tip.

Drain the pear halves. Cut them into thin slices widthwise without spoiling their shape, and arrange the slices like sunrays on the tart. Cover them with the rest of the pastry cream. It might be helpful to use a pastry bag with a plain tip. Smooth the pastry cream well with the back of a spoon.

Set your oven to broil.

Sprinkle your tart with granulated sugar and let it brown under the boiler for a few minutes. The sugar will bubble and caramelize lightly. Serve it immediately, because this tart is best right out of the oven!

Lydia Jacob Tart

11 oz. [300 g] rich flaky pastry with praline paste and hazelnuts (*see recipe page 19*)

8 small William or Bartlett pears, ripe but still firm

1¾ cups [400 g] almond cream (*see recipe page 27*)

3½ Tbsp. [50 g] crème fraîche

Finely grated zest of ½ orange

⅜ tsp. fresh ginger, finely grated

⅜ tsp. ground cinnamon

For the syrup:

2⅓ cups 5 granulated sugar

2 cups 1 oz. [500 g / 50 cl] water

Juice of 1 lemon

2 star anise

2 cinnamon sticks

To decorate:

7 Tbsp. [100 g] apple jelly (*see recipe page 29*)

Zest of 1 orange, slivered very finely

To bake:

A tart pan with plain rim, 10 inches [26 cm] in diameter and 1 inch [3 cm] deep with removable bottom

The day before, prepare your rich flaky pastry and cook the pears: In a pan, combine the water, sugar, lemon juice, and spices and bring to a simmer. Meanwhile, peel the pears and set aside three whole pears.

Remove the stems from the remaining pears, cut them in half, and core them. Put all of the pears into the syrup and poach them, letting them simmer for about 15 minutes so that the syrup cooks them gently; the whole pears should cook for about 25 minutes. Turn the pears into a bowl and refrigerate them in their spiced syrup.

The next day, roll your pastry on a lightly floured work surface into a circle a little less than ⅛ inch [2.5 mm] thick and 13 inches [34 cm] in diameter.

Butter your pan and carefully place the dough in it, pressing the dough lightly with your fingertips against the bottom and sides. Roll the rolling pin across the top edge of the pan to trim off the small amount of excess pastry. Prick the bottom of the tart with a fork and refrigerate it for 30 minutes, covered with plastic wrap.

Preheat the oven to 350°F [180°C].

Meanwhile, prepare your almond cream. Add the crème fraîche, ground cinnamon, grated ginger, and orange zest and stir gently with a wooden spatula. Place an even layer of almond cream in the bottom of the tart. It might be helpful to use a pastry bag with a plain tip. Drain the pear halves. Cut them into thin slices widthwise, being careful not to spoil their shape, and place them like sun rays in the tart.

Bake for about 45 minutes. The edges of the tart should be golden and the almond cream lightly colored and puffed.

In a small saucepan, melt the apple jelly with 2 tablespoons [30 g / 3 cl] of water on low heat and bring it to a simmer. When you remove your tart from the oven, coat each pear with the apple jelly, using a pastry brush. Unmold your tart onto a rack and let it cool. Decorate the center of the tart with the 3 whole pears glazed with apple jelly and sprinkled with slivers of citrus zest.

~:~

Enjoy this tart with an Alsatian Gewurztraminer—a surprising harmony!
"Lydia Jacob was a fashion designer and world-traveling adventurer born in Strasbourg-Neudorf in the last century. The subtle perfumes of this tart also express impressions of her travels." (Raymond Émile Waydelich)

Warm Tart with Pears and Chocolate

11 oz. [300 g] sweet pastry (*see recipe page 16*)

1¾ cups [400 g] almond cream (*see recipe page 27*)

3½ Tbsp. [50 g] crème fraîche

1 cup [100 g] hazelnuts, lightly toasted and chopped

3½ oz. [100 g] extra-bittersweet chocolate, 70% cocoa butter

Zest of 1 orange, finely grated

5 small William pears, fully ripe but firm

For the chocolate sauce:

7 oz. [200 g / 20 cl] whipping cream

1½ Tbsp. [20 g] extra-fine sugar

3½ oz. [100 g] extra-bittersweet chocolate, 70% cocoa butter

1½ Tbsp. [15 g] unsweetened cocoa

To decorate:

Zest of 1 orange, very finely slivered

To bake:

A tart pan with plain rim, 10 inches [26 cm] in diameter and 1 inch [3 cm] deep with removable bottom

The day before, prepare your sweet pastry and chocolate sauce: In a heavy-bottomed saucepan, bring the light whipping cream and sugar to a boil. Remove from the heat and add the cocoa and grated bittersweet chocolate, mixing gently with a whip. Then bring this mixture to a simmer on low heat and cook for 2 minutes, stirring constantly, so that the bottom does not stick. Turn into a bowl and set aside.

The next day, roll your pastry on a lightly floured work surface into a circle a little less than ⅛ inch [about 2.5 mm] thick and 13 inches [34 cm] in diameter.

Butter your pan and carefully place the pastry in it, pressing the dough lightly with your fingertips against the bottom and sides. Roll the rolling pin across the top edge to trim off the small amount of excess pastry. Prick the bottom of the tart with a fork and refrigerate it for 30 minutes covered with plastic wrap.

Preheat the oven to 350°F [180°C].

Lightly toast the hazelnuts. Then rub them between your fingers to remove the last bits of skin.

Meanwhile, prepare your almond cream.

Peel the pears, remove the stems, cut them in half, and core them. Cut them into small dice. With a wooden spatula, incorporate the crème fraîche, toasted chopped hazelnuts, grated chocolate, finely grated orange zest and diced pear into the almond cream. Mix gently. Spread the bottom of the tart with an even layer of almond cream. Bake for about 45 minutes. The tart borders should be golden. The chocolate-flecked almond cream will be lightly colored and puffed. Unmold your tart onto a rack and let it cool.

At the last minute, in a heavy-bottomed saucepan, reheat your chocolate sauce on low heat and, using a small ladle, coat your tart with it. Then very finely, chop the orange slivers and sprinkle them over your tart.

∽:∼

This tart goes well with a crème anglaise.

Pear and Apple Tart with Vanilla Sugar

---

14 oz. [**400 g**] **semi-puff pastry** (*see recipe page 20*)

3 Passe-Crassane* pears, fully ripe but still firm

3 Ida Red apples

3 Tbsp. / 1½ oz. [**40 g**] **butter**

¼ cup [**50 g**] **vanilla sugar** (*see page 10*)

For the egg wash:

1 egg

To decorate:

¼ cup [**50 g**] **vanilla sugar**

To bake:

A baking sheet covered with parchment paper

The day before, prepare your semi-puff pastry.

The next day, roll the pastry to a little more than ¹⁄₁₆ inch [**about 2 mm**] thick on a lightly floured work surface. Now roll it around a rolling pin and lift it above the baking sheet covered with parchment paper. Unroll it gently. This allows it to relax and prevents it from shrinking when it is cut. Now cut a circle, 12 inches [**30 cm**] in diameter. Prick the tart with a fork and refrigerate it for 30 minutes, covered with plastic wrap.

Preheat the oven to 400°F [**200°C**].

---

*Passe-Crassane is a French pear resulting from a cross between a pear and a quince. It is an outstanding winter pear because it keeps well. This pear is large and round with thick skin. It has white, slightly granular flesh and is juicy and flavorful. Use a firm Bartlett pear.

Meanwhile, rinse the apples and pears in cold water and dry them with a kitchen towel. Remove the stems, cut them in half and core them. Cut each half in quarters.

Arrange the apple and pear pieces on the tart base 1 inch [3 cm] from the edge, cut surface turned toward the center. Overlap them slightly, alternating a piece of apple and a piece of pear, making concentric circles to the center of the tart. Distribute bits of butter on the fruit, then sprinkle it with ¼ cup of the vanilla-flavored granulated sugar. Using a pastry brush, paint the pastry edges with a little beaten egg. When you are ready to put the tart into the oven, remember to decrease the temperature to 350°F [180°C].

Bake the tart for about 40 minutes. The pastry should be a nice golden color. Slide your tart onto a rack. Sprinkle it with the remaining vanilla sugar and serve it warm with crème fraîche.

∾:∾

This rustic tart brings to mind old-fashioned baked apples with butter and sugar.

Alsatian Apple Tart

---

11 oz. [300 g] flaky pastry (*see recipe page 15*)

6 attractive Reine des Reinettes* apples

For the flan cream:

7 oz. [200 g / 20 cl] whipping cream

3½ oz. [100 g / 10 cl] whole milk

6 eggs

¼ cup [50 g] granulated sugar

For the crunchy almonds:

1½ cups [150 g] slivered almonds

⅞ cup [100 g] confectioners' sugar

2 egg whites

To decorate:

3 Tbsp. [25 g] confectioners' sugar

To bake:

A tart pan with plain rim, 10 inches [26 cm] in diameter and 1 inch [3 cm] deep

The day before, prepare your flaky pastry.

The next day, roll your pastry on a lightly floured work surface into a circle a little more than ¹⁄₁₆ inch [about 1.5 mm] thick and 14 inches [36 cm] in diameter.

Butter your pan and carefully place the pastry in it, pressing the dough lightly with your fingertips

---

* Reine des Reinettes are slightly tart, juicy apples, yellow with red color, from southwestern France.

against the bottom and sides. The pastry should extend a little less than 1 inch [2 cm] beyond the edge of the pan. Using scissors, snip this pastry edge at an angle to make "teeth" a little less than ½ inch [about 1 cm] wide. Now fold the crenellations under alternately, one toward the inside, one toward the outside. This diagonal border creates a wonderfully pretty effect. Prick the bottom of the tart with a fork and refrigerate it for 30 minutes, covered with plastic wrap.

Preheat the oven to 350°F [180°C].

Bake your tart shell blind (*see page 14*) for 15 minutes and let it cool.

Meanwhile, prepare your flan cream: In a bowl, mix the cream, milk, eggs, and sugar, stirring briefly with a whip. Then peel the apples, remove the stems, core them and cut them into quarters. Lightly score a crisscross pattern with a knife on the rounded side of the apples. Place the quarters into the tart, arranging them in circles, scored surface turned up. Then cover them with flan cream and bake for about 40 minutes.

Meanwhile, in a bowl gently mix the almonds, confectioners' sugar and egg white with your fingertips. When the edges of the tart are golden and the flan custard lightly colored and puffed, sprinkle the tart with the coated almonds. Continue baking for about 10 more minutes. The almonds will form a delicate, crunchy, and slightly meringue-like layer. Unmold your tart onto a rack and let it cool. Before serving, dust it generously with confectioners' sugar.

Grated Apple Tart with Cinnamon Streusel

11 oz. [300 g] rich flaky pastry No. 1 (*see recipe page 17*)

1¾ cups [400 g] almond cream (*see recipe page 27*)

3½ Tbsp. [50 g] crème fraîche

5 Ida Red apples

For the streusel:

4 Tbsp. / 2 oz. [60 g] cold butter

4½ Tbsp. [60 g] extra-fine sugar

⅓ cup [30 g] ground blanched almonds

3 Tbsp. [30 g] flour

⅜ tsp. ground cinnamon

To decorate:

3 Tbsp. [25 g] confectioners' sugar

To bake:

A tart pan with plain rim, 10 inches [26 cm] in diameter and 1 inch [3 cm] deep with removable bottom

The day before, prepare your flaky pastry.

The next day, roll your pastry on a lightly floured work surface into a circle a little less than ⅛ inch [about 2.5 mm] thick and 13 inches [34 cm] in diameter.

Butter your pan and carefully place the pastry in it, pressing the dough lightly with the fingertips against the bottom and sides. Roll the rolling pin across the top edge of the pan to trim off the small amount of excess dough. Prick the bottom of the tart with a fork and refrigerate it for 30 minutes, covered with plastic wrap.

Preheat the oven to 350°F [180°C].

Meanwhile, prepare your almond cream. Then peel the apples, remove their stems, cut them in half and core them. Grate the apples on the coarse holes of a grater. Add the crème fraîche and grated apples to the almond cream and mix gently with a wooden spatula.

Spread an even layer of this cream in the bottom of the tart.

Bake for about 40 minutes.

Meanwhile, prepare the streusel: Cut the butter into very small cubes. In a bowl, combine the butter, sugar, ground almonds, flour, and ground cinnamon. Work this mixture gently with the fingertips until it looks like coarse meal. Rub it together a few seconds more to obtain a slightly lumpier consistency. When the almond cream is lightly colored and puffed, sprinkle the streusel in little clumps over the tart. Continue baking for about 10 more minutes. The edges of the tart should be golden and the streusel crunchy and prettily colored. Unmold your tart onto a rack and let it cool. Then dust it with confectioners' sugar.

~:~

This tart is delicious with a cinnamon- or cardamom-flavored crème anglaise.

Flambéed Apple Square

---

14 oz. [400 g] semi-puff pastry (*see recipe page 20*)

6 attractive Ida Red apples

3½ Tbsp. / 1¾ oz. [50 g] cold butter

¼ cup [50 g] granulated sugar

1¾ oz. [50 g / 5 cl] Calvados

To decorate:

¼ cup [50 g] granulated sugar

To bake:

A baking sheet covered with parchment paper.

The day before, prepare your semi-puff pastry.

The next day, roll your pastry on a lightly floured work surface to about ¹⁄₁₆ inch [1.5 mm] thick. Then roll it around a rolling pin and lift it above a baking sheet covered in parchment paper. Unroll it gently. This allows your pastry to relax and prevents it from shrinking when it is cut. Now cut an approximately 12-inch [30-cm] square. Using a pastry brush dipped in cold water, moisten the edges of your square about 1 inch [2 cm] in. Fold the edges toward the inside, as if making a hem. Pinch and mark this hem with your fingertips so it won't come apart during baking. Prick the bottom of the tart with a fork and refrigerate it for 30 minutes covered with plastic wrap.

Preheat the oven to 400°F [200°C].

Rinse the apples in cold water and dry them in a kitchen towel. Remove the stems and core them, using an apple corer. Then slice them very thinly. Arrange the slices in rows on the pastry square, overlapping them slightly. Distribute bits of butter on the apples, then sprinkle them with granulated sugar. Using a pastry brush, paint the edges of the tart with a little beaten egg.

Bake the tart for about 30 minutes. The pastry should be a pretty golden color. When you remove the tart from the oven, sprinkle the apples with the Calvados and flame them. Serve immediately.

~:~

This tart is wonderful with thick crème fraîche.

Apple Tatin

---

11 oz. [300 g] semi-puff pastry (*see recipe page 20*)

10 Reine des Reinettes apples*

3½ Tbsp. / 1¾ oz. [50 g] butter

½ cup [100 g] extra-fine sugar

½ cup [100 g] granulated sugar

To decorate:

½ cup [100 g] granulated sugar

The egg wash:

1 egg

To bake:

A baking sheet covered with parchment paper and a heavy, nonstick cake pan 10 inches [26 cm] in diameter and 2 inches [5 cm] deep

The day before, prepare your semi-puff pastry.

The next day, roll the pastry on a lightly floured work surface to a little more than ¹⁄₁₆ inch [about 2 mm] thick. Roll it around the rolling pin and lift it above the baking sheet covered with parchment paper. Unroll the pastry gently. This allows it to relax and prevents it from shrinking when it is cut. Cut a circle, 12 inches [30 cm] in diameter. Refrigerate it for 1½ hours, covered with plastic wrap.

Preheat the oven to 425°F [220°C].

In a saucepan, melt half of the extra-fine sugar over low heat, stirring gently with a wooden spatula. As

* *Reine des Reinettes are slightly tart, juicy apples, yellow with red color, from southwestern France.*

soon as the sugar is a light caramel color, add the remaining half of the sugar. Stir gently with the wooden spatula until all of the sugar is a light caramel color. Now pour the caramel in a spiral pattern into your cake pan. Rinse the apples in cold water, and dry them in a kitchen towel. Remove their stems, cut them in half, and core them. Stand the apples vertically in two concentric circles. See that they are very close to each other. Sprinkle them with ½ cup [100 g] of granulated sugar, then dot them with bits of butter.

When you are ready to put the tart into the oven, remember to decrease the temperature to 400°F [200°C].

Bake the tart for about 50 minutes. The apples should be jam-like. Place the cake pan on a rack and let it cool.

Now bake the pastry base. Using a pastry brush, paint a border a little less than 1 inch [about 2 cm] wide with a little beaten egg. Prick the center with a fork.

Remember to decrease the oven temperature to 350°F [180°C] and bake the tart for about 15 minutes. The pastry should have a nice golden color. Slide it onto a rack and let it cool. Then place it upside down over the cake pan. Now put a serving plate on top of the pastry base. Turn both over. Remove the cake pan—the caramelized apples will fill the tart base.

Now set the oven to broil.

Sprinkle the tart with granulated sugar and let it brown under the broiler for a few minutes. The sugar will bubble and caramelize lightly. Serve it immediately because this tatin is best as soon as it comes out of the oven. Serve it with crème fraîche or an assertively vanilla-accented crème anglaise.

Apple Strudel

For the strudel pastry:

3⅓ cups [500 g] King Arthur unbleached all-purpose flour

2¾ oz. [80 g / 8 cl] peanut oil

7 oz. [200 g / 92 cl] water

1 tsp. [5 g] salt

2 tsp. [10 g] granulated sugar

For the filling:

5 Reine des Reinettes apples*

1 cup [100 g] fresh walnuts, broken into pieces

1 scant tsp. [5 g] ground cinnamon

2 Tbsp. [30 g / 3 cl] rum

4 Tbsp. [50 g] raisins

3½ Tbsp. / 1¾ oz. [50 g] melted butter

½ cup [50 g] unblanched almonds, ground

To decorate:

3½ Tbsp. / 1¾ oz. [50 g] melted butter

3 Tbsp. [25 g] confectioners' sugar

To bake:

A baking sheet covered with parchment paper

The day before, prepare your strudel pastry and filling. Prepare your pastry using an electric mixer or food processor: Sift the flour. Dissolve the salt and sugar in the water. In the mixer bowl, place the flour, oil, and

---

* *Reine des Reinettes are slightly tart, juicy apples, yellow with red color, from southwestern France.*

water. Using the hook, mix at low speed just until the pastry is very smooth. Shape the pastry into a ball and coat it with oil so that it doesn't form a crust. Wrap it carefully in plastic wrap and refrigerate overnight.

Prepare your filling: Peel the apples, remove their stems, cut them in half and core them. Cut them into thin slices. In a bowl, combine the granulated sugar and cinnamon. Add the apple slices, broken walnut meats, raisins, and rum. Mix gently. Cover with plastic wrap and press well to make a firm seal. Refrigerate overnight.

The next day, roll the strudel pastry on a lightly floured work surface into a rectangle about 16 inches [40 cm] by 12 inches [30 cm]. The pastry should be extremely thin and somewhat translucent, like tracing paper. Roll it around the rolling pin and lift it above a lightly floured kitchen towel. Unroll it gently with the short edges top and bottom. This allows your pastry to relax and prevents it from tearing.

Preheat the oven to 400°F [200°C].

Using a pastry brush, paint the pastry with melted butter, then sprinkle it with ground almonds. Now spoon the filling along top short edge of the pastry, leaving a generous 1-inch [3-cm] strip uncovered at the top and along both sides. The filling should make a strip 3½ inches [10 cm] wide, 9½ inches [24 cm] long, and about 3½ inches [10 cm] deep. Take hold of the towel, fold the little bare edge of the pastry over onto the filling, and roll it tightly until you get to the other edge. You will have a sort of giant rolled package that you can close on the ends by folding the pastry under the roll. Prick your roll with a fork. Lift it onto a baking sheet covered with parchment paper and paint it again with melted butter.

Bake it for about 40 minutes. The dough should be a pretty golden color. Slide the strudel onto a rack, paint it generously with melted butter, dust it with confectioners' sugar, and let it cool. Serve it warm with whipped cream, thick crème fraîche, or a crème anglaise.

~:~

When you taste this strudel, which is Austrian in origin, you'll discover a pastry texture similar to puff pastry, although lighter.

Crunchy Tart with Dried Fruit and Sautéed Apple Quarters

***

14 oz. [400 g] semi-puff pastry (*see recipe page 20*)

6 Golden Delicious apples

4 Tbsp. / 2 oz. [60 g] butter

½ cup [120 g / 12 cl] water

½ cup [100 g] granulated sugar

3½ oz. [100 g] floral honey

¼ cup [25 g] blanched almonds, chopped

¼ cup [25 g] walnuts, broken into pieces

¼ cup [25 g] hazelnuts, toasted and chopped

4 dried figs

6 dried apricot halves

6 pitted prunes

Zest of 1 lemon, finely grated

Zest of 1 orange, finely grated

⅛ tsp. ground cinnamon

⅛ tsp. ground star anise

For the egg wash:

1 egg

To bake:

A tart pan with plain rim, 10 inches [26 cm] in diameter and **1 inch** [3 cm] deep

The day before, prepare your semi-puff pastry.

The next day, roll 12 ounces [350 g] of pastry on a lightly floured work surface into a circle a little more than 1/16 inch [about 1.5 mm] thick and 13 inches [34 cm] in diameter.

Butter your pan and carefully place the pastry in it, pressing the dough lightly with your fingertips against the bottom and sides. Roll the rolling pin across the top edge of the pan to trim off the small amount of excess pastry. Prick the bottom of the tart with a fork and refrigerate it for 30 minutes, covered with plastic wrap. Then roll the remaining pastry on a lightly floured work surface to a little more than 1/16 inch [about 1.5 mm] thick. Roll it around the rolling pin and lift it above a baking sheet covered with parchment paper. Unroll it gently. This allows your pastry to relax and prevents it from shrinking when it is cut. Refrigerate it for 30 minutes, covered with plastic wrap. Then with a small cookie-cutter cut about 30 hearts from the refrigerated pastry. Set the hearts aside. Using a pastry brush dipped in cold water, moisten the edges of the tart and press on the hearts, overlapping them slightly.

Preheat the oven to 350°F [180°C].

Using a pastry brush, paint your tart's decorations with a little beaten egg and bake it blind (*see page 14*) for 15 minutes. Then, using a pastry brush, paint the bottom of the tart with a little beaten egg and continue baking for about 10 minutes. The tart base will be more "moisture-proof"; it will also have a good golden color and will keep its crunch. Unmold your tart shell onto a rack and let it cool.

Prepare your caramelized apples: Peel the apples, remove the stems, core them and cut them into quarters. In a skillet, melt the butter and sugar, then add the water. Bring to a simmer. Put the apples into the skillet and let them simmer for a few minutes. Then, using two wooden spoons, turn them over. Let them simmer again until they are almost jam-like. Remove them from the skillet and let them cool. Add the dried fruit, finely cut into little sticks a little less than 1/4 inch [5 mm] wide, and the citrus zest, spices, and honey. Let this mixture simmer until the liquid reduces and caramelizes very lightly.

Place the apple quarters onto the bottom of the tart. At the last minute, using a spoon, coat your apples with the cooking liquid and dried fruit. Your semi-puff pastry will stay perfectly crunchy that way.

~:~

This tart may be served with a vanilla-flavored crème anglaise.

Aligoté Tartlets with Three Cheeses

1 lb. 2 oz. [500 g] flaky pastry with egg (*see recipe page 15*)

1 lb. 2 oz. [500 g] Belle de Fontenay potatoes*, *or* 11 oz. [300 g] net

2¼ oz. [60 g] Cantal cheese**

2¼ oz. [60 g] Beaufort cheese***

2¼ oz. [60 g] Tomme de Savoie cheese****

2 Tbsp. / 1 oz. [25 g] butter

3 Tbsp. [40 g / 4 cl] whipping cream

5 Tbsp. [75 g / 7.5 cl] milk

4 egg yolks

1 clove of garlic, mashed

Salt

Freshly ground black pepper

To bake:

12 tartlet pans, 4 inches [10 cm] in diameter

The day before, prepare your flaky pastry with egg.

The next day, on a lightly floured work surface, roll your pastry a little less than ¹⁄₁₆ inch [1.5 mm] thick. Using a fluted cookie-cutter, cut 12 small pastry rounds, 5½ inches [14 cm] in diameter.

---

* Belle de Fontenay is a firm-textured potato, like the Roseval, that won't disintegrate during cooking.

** Cantal, from Auvergne, is made from cow's milk. It is semi-firm and pressed, with an almost crumbly texture and a mild, buttery flavor.

*** Beaufort, from Savoie, comes in a wheel, 8 inches thick. It has a creamy texture and a mild, fruity, sweet flavor. Beaufort has an extraordinary melting capacity and is not readily available here.

**** Tomme de Savoie is made from cow's milk. It is a semi-firm, pressed curd, with tiny holes. The flavor is slightly saline and mild but savory.

Butter the tartlet pans and carefully place the pastry in them, pressing it lightly with your fingertips against the bottom and sides. Roll the rolling pin across the top edges of the pans to trim off the small amount of excess dough. Prick the bottoms of the shells with a fork and refrigerate them for 30 minutes, covered with plastic wrap.

Preheat the oven to 350°F [180°C].

Bake your tartlet shells blind (*see page 14*) for 10 minutes. Then, using a pastry brush, paint the pastry with a little beaten egg and continue baking for about 5 minutes. The shells will be more "moisture-proof"; they will also have a nice golden color and will keep their crunch. Unmold your tarts onto a rack and let them cool.

Prepare your potatoes: Rinse them in cold water. Put them in a pan with cold water to cover. Add salt, then bring them to a boil and cook on low heat, covered, until they are soft all the way through.

Meanwhile, remove the rinds from your cheeses, grate them in thin shavings, and set aside. Drain the potatoes, peel them while they are still warm, and put them through a food mill with a very fine disk. Add the butter and mix gently with a wooden spatula. Add the cream, milk, egg yolks, 3 pinches of salt, 5 grinds of pepper, mashed garlic clove, and grated cheese. Mound this filling in the 12 tartlet shells.

Increase the oven temperature to 400°F [200°C]. Bake the tartlets for about 10 minutes. Serve immediately. Accompany them with a fresh green salad and chives and chervil.

Tartiflette*

11 oz. [300 g] flaky pastry with egg (*see recipe page 15*)

12 oz. [350 g] Reblochon** cheese, made with unpasteurized milk

1 onion

1 lb. 5 oz. [600 g] Belle de Fontenay potatoes, *or* 14 oz. [400 g] net

5 oz. [150 g] salted, smoked pork breast***

1½ Tbsp. [20 g / 20 cl] peanut oil

1½ Tbsp. / ¾ oz. [20 g] butter

1 clove of garlic, mashed into a paste

For the egg custard:

⅔ cup [150 g / 15 cl] crème fraîche

5 oz. [150 g / 15 cl] whole milk

3 eggs

Salt

Freshly ground black pepper

For the egg wash:

1 egg

To bake:

A tart pan with plain rim, 10 inches [26 cm] in diameter and 1 inch [3 cm] deep

---

* Tartiflette refers to a dish made with potatoes, Alsatian cheese, salt pork, onions, and crème fraîche.

** Reblochon is a sweet, nutty, aromatic Savoyard cheese made from cow's milk. The texture is Brie-like.

*** Use a good double-thick cut bacon.

The day before, prepare your flaky pastry with egg.

The next day, roll the pastry on a lightly floured work surface into a circle a little more than ⅟₁₆ inch [about 2 mm] thick and 13 inches [34 cm] in diameter.

Butter your pan and carefully place the pastry in it, pressing the dough lightly with the fingertips against the bottom and sides. Roll the rolling pin across the top edge of the pan to trim off the small amount of excess dough. Prick the bottom of the tart with a fork and refrigerate it for 30 minutes, covered with plastic wrap.

Preheat the oven to 350°F [180°C].

Bake the pastry shell blind (*see page 14*) for 15 minutes. Then, using a pastry brush, paint the pastry with a little beaten egg and continue baking for about 5 minutes. The bottom will be more "moisture-proof"; it will also have a nice golden color and will keep its crunch.

Prepare your potatoes: Rinse them in cold water and put them in a pan with cold water to cover. Salt them and bring them to a boil, then cook on low heat, covered, until they are soft all the way through. When they are cool, peel them and cut them into thick round slices.

Peel the onion and slice it thinly. Cut the piece of salt pork into small lardons. In a skillet, heat the oil. Add 2 tablespoons of butter. Fry the lardons, on high heat, then remove them with a skimmer and set aside. In the same skillet, brown the sliced onion on low heat for a few minutes, turning them gently. They should be lightly caramelized. Now add the potatoes and mashed garlic. Continue cooking for 5 more minutes. Turn them into a bowl and set aside.

Prepare the custard: In a bowl, combine the crème fraîche, milk, eggs, 3 pinches of salt, and 5 grinds of pepper and beat briefly with a whip. Place the potatoes, lardons, and onions in the tart and cover them with the Reblochon, sliced thinly. Nap the filling with the custard and bake for about 45 minutes. The edges of the tart should be well browned and your custard colored and set. Unmold your tart and serve immediately.

Alsatian Quiche

---

11 oz. [300 g] flaky pastry with egg (*see recipe page 15*)

3 onions

3½ oz. [100 g] ham on the bone

5 oz. [150 g] salted, smoked pork breast*

3½ oz. [100 g] grated Gruyère

1½ Tbsp. [20 g / 20 cl] peanut oil

1½ Tbsp. / ¾ oz. [20 g] butter

For the egg custard:

1 cup *plus* 1 Tbsp. [250 g / 25 cl] whipping cream

1 cup *plus* 1 Tbsp. [250 g / 25 cl] whole milk

6 eggs

¼ tsp. ground nutmeg

Salt

Freshly ground black pepper

For the egg wash:

1 egg

To bake:

A tart pan with plain rim, 10 inches [26 cm] in diameter and 1 inch [3 cm] deep

The day before, prepare your flaky pastry with egg.

* *Use a good double-thick cut bacon.*

The next day, roll the pastry on a lightly floured work surface into a circle a little more than ¹⁄₁₆ inch [about 2 mm] thick and 13 inches [34 cm] in diameter.

Butter your pan and carefully place the pastry in it, pressing it lightly with the fingertips against the bottom and sides. Roll the rolling pin across the top edge of the pan to trim off the small amount of excess pastry. Prick the bottom of the tart with a fork and refrigerate it for 30 minutes, covered with plastic wrap.

Preheat the oven to 350°F [180°C].

Bake your tart shell blind (*see page 14*) for 15 minutes. Then, using a pastry brush, paint the pastry with a little beaten egg and continue baking for about 5 minutes. The pastry base will be more "moisture-proof"; it will also have a nice golden color and will keep its crunch.

Meanwhile, prepare your egg custard: In a bowl, combine the cream, milk, eggs, 3 pinches of salt, 5 grinds of pepper, and ¼ teaspoon of ground nutmeg and beat briefly with a whip.

Now prepare your filling: Peel the onions and slice them thinly. Cut the smoked pork into small lardons. In a skillet, heat the oil. Add 1½ tablespoons [20 g] of butter. Fry the lardons on high heat. Remove them with a skimmer and set aside. In the same skillet, brown the sliced onions for a few minutes over low heat, turning them gently. They should be lightly caramelized. Remove them with a skimmer and set aside. Cut the ham into small cubes. Fill the tart shell with the cubed ham, lardons, and onions. Sprinkle with grated Gruyère. Cover the filling with the custard.

Bake for about 45 minutes. The edges of your quiche should be nicely browned and the custard colored and set. Unmold the quiche and serve immediately.

Grape Harvester's Tart

---

11 oz. [300 g] rich flaky pastry No. 1 (*see recipe page 17*)

1¾ cups [400 g] hazelnut cream (*see recipe page 28*)

1¾ lb. [800 g] Alsace Muscat grapes, *or* about 1 lb. 2 oz. [500 g] stemmed grapes

For the streusel:

4 Tbsp. / 2 oz. [60 g] cold butter

4½ Tbsp. [60 g] sugar

¼ cup [30 g] ground hazelnuts

3 Tbsp. [30 g] flour

Finely grated zest of 1 orange

To decorate:

3 Tbsp. [25 g] confectioners' sugar

To bake:

A tart pan with plain rim, 10 inches [26 cm] in diameter and 1 inch [3 cm] deep with removable bottom

The day before, prepare your rich flaky pastry.

The next day, roll the pastry on a lightly floured work surface into a circle a little less than ⅛ inch [about 2.5 mm] thick and 13 inches [34 cm] in diameter.

Butter your pan and carefully place the dough in it, pressing the dough lightly with your fingertips against the bottom and sides. Prick the bottom of the tart with a fork and refrigerate it for 30 minutes, covered with plastic wrap.

Preheat the oven to 350°F [180°C].

Meanwhile, prepare your hazelnut cream.

Rinse the grapes in cold water, stem them, and dry them in a kitchen towel. Fill the bottom of your tart with an even layer of hazelnut cream. It might be helpful to use a pastry bag with a plain tip. Arrange the grapes on top. Bake the tart for 35 minutes.

Meanwhile, prepare the streusel: Cut the butter into very small cubes. In a bowl, combine the butter, sugar, ground hazelnuts, flour, and orange zest. Work this mixture gently with your fingertips until it resembles coarse meal. Then rub it together a little longer until it has a slightly lumpier consistency.

When the hazelnut cream is lightly colored and puffed, sprinkle the streusel in little clumps over the tart. Continue baking for about 10 minutes. The edges of the tart should be browned and the streusel crunchy and prettily colored. Unmold your tart onto a rack and let it cool. Dust it lightly with confectioners' sugar.

~:~

This tart goes beautifully with a Muscat d'Alsace sabayon. Wine and grapes, elegantly aromatic and appetizing, create a delicate harmony with the flavor of hazelnuts. For the sabayon:

1 cup [250 g / 25 cl] Muscat wine
⅔ cup [150 g] extra-fine sugar
6 egg yolks
Juice of 1 orange
½ cup plus 2 Tbsp. [125 g] crème fraîche

Heat water in a pan that will serve as a double boiler. In a bowl, combine the egg yolks, wine, sugar, and orange juice. Put this bowl over the boiling water and beat vigorously with a whip. The sabayon should foam up and nearly double in volume. Remove it from the double boiler. Beat it until the mixture cools to lukewarm. Add the crème fraîche and gently incorporate.

Lydia Jacob Tart
(page 200)

Sauerkraut Munster
Tart (page 173)

*Fig Tart with
Oranges and Walnuts
(page 183)*

Three Pirates' Tart
(page 195)

Spiced Pears in Party Dress (page 193)

Fig Tart with Caramel
(page 185)

Flambéed Apple
Square (page 210)

Pear and Apple Tart
with Vanilla Sugar
(page 204)

Winter

Florentine Almond Tart

---

11 oz. [300 g] sweet pastry (*see recipe page 16*)

3 cups [700 g] almond cream (*see recipe page 27*)

½ cup *less* 1 Tbsp. [100 g] crème fraîche

Zest of ½ orange, finely grated

For the Florentine:

1 cup [100 g] slivered almonds

3½ Tbsp. [50 g] extra-fine sugar

3½ Tbsp. [50 g] honey

1½ Tbsp. / ¾ oz. [20 g] butter

2 Tbsp. [25 g] candied lemon peel, diced small

3½ oz. [100 g / 10 cl] whipping cream

Zest of 1 lemon, slivered very finely

To bake:

A tart pan with plain rim, 10 inches [26 cm] in diameter and 1 inch [3 cm] deep
with removable bottom

The day before, prepare your sweet pastry.

The next day, roll the pastry on a lightly floured work surface into a circle a little less than ⅛ inch [about 2.5 mm] thick and 13 inches [34 cm] in diameter.

Butter your pan and carefully place the pastry in it, pressing the dough lightly with the fingertips against the bottom and sides. Roll the rolling pin across the top edge of the pan to trim off the small amount of excess pastry. Prick the bottom of the tart with a fork and refrigerate it for 30 minutes, covered with plastic wrap.

Preheat the oven to 350°F [180°C].

Meanwhile, prepare your almond cream. Add the cream fraîche and finely grated orange zest and mix gently with a wooden spatula. Fill the bottom of the tart with an even layer of the cream mixture. It might be helpful to use a pastry bag with a plain tip. Bake the tart for about 35 minutes.

Meanwhile, prepare the Florentine: In a pan bring the cream, honey, sugar, butter, and slivers of lemon peel to a boil. Place a sugar thermometer in the pan and continue boiling until it reaches 237°F [114°C]. Remove the pan from the heat, add the slivered almonds and candied lemon peel and stir gently. Turn the mixture into a bowl and set aside. When the almond cream is lightly colored and puffed, use a wooden spoon to coat the tart with the Florentine topping. Continue baking for about 10 minutes. The edges of your tart should be nicely browned and the Florentine topping crunchy and lightly caramelized. Unmold the tart onto a rack and let it cool.

∾:∾

This tart is wonderful with a cardamom-flavored crème anglaise or a fresh fruit salad.

Rich Pastry Hearts with Sautéed Tropical Fruits

---

15 oz. [400 g] rich flaky pastry No. 2 (*see recipe page 18*)

10½ oz. [300 g] lime jelly

1 Victoria pineapple

1 well-ripened mango

2 passion fruit

⅛ tsp. grated ginger

Juice of 1 lemon

3½ Tbsp. / 1¾ oz. [50 g] butter

½ cup [100 g] granulated sugar

Juice of 1 lime

To decorate:

3 Tbsp. [20 g] confectioners' sugar

To bake:

2 baking sheets covered with parchment paper

The day before, prepare your rich flaky pastry.

The next day, roll your dough on a lightly floured work surface to a little more than ¹⁄₁₆ inch [about 2 mm] thick. With a cookie-cutter, cut 20 small pastry hearts about 4 inches [10 cm] long. Cover the 2 baking sheets with parchment paper. Arrange 10 pastry hearts on each of the sheets, spacing them 1 inch [3 cm] apart so that they bake evenly and do not stick together. Prick them with a fork and refrigerate them for 15 minutes, covered with plastic wrap.

Preheat the oven to 350°F [180°C].

Bake the hearts for about 10 minutes, until they are golden. Remove them and let them cool on a rack.

Meanwhile, peel and cut the pineapple into small sticks. Peel and cut the mango into ½ inch dice. Place them into a bowl. Cut the passion fruit in half, scoop out the pulp and the seeds, and add to the bowl. In a skillet, melt the butter and sugar and add the lemon juice and ginger. Bring to a simmer. Place the fruit in the skillet and let it simmer for 3 minutes. Turn it gently with a wooden spatula and continue simmering for 2 more minutes. Turn the fruit onto a serving plate. Season it with a few drops of lime juice and let it cool. Spread 10 of the pastry hearts with a small spoonful of jelly, then cover them with the remaining 10 hearts. Dust them lightly with confectioners' sugar. The pastry hearts and sautéed fruit are delicious with crème fraîche.

⁓:⁓

If you don't have lime jelly, you can flavor apple jelly (see recipe page 29) with a few thin lime sections and some zest.

Pierre Hermé's Pineapple Macaroon Tart

9 oz. [250 g] almond paste, available in the pastry shop*

1 egg white

For the macaroon layer:

5 Tbsp. [65 g] extra-fine sugar

⅛ cup [25 g] grated coconut

Scant ¼ cup [20 g] blanched, ground almonds

1½ Tbsp. [15 g] flour

2½ egg whites

For the coconut cream:

1 stick *plus* 1 Tbsp. / 4½ oz. [125 g] butter

Scant 2 Tbsp. [25 g / 2.5 cl] unsweetened coconut milk

¼ cup *plus* 1 Tbsp. [65 g] grated coconut

1¼ cups [300 g] pastry cream (*see recipe page 25*)

2 Tbsp. [30 g / 3 cl] white rum

For the filling:

1 Victoria pineapple, 1⅓ lbs. [600 g]

Zest of 1 lime, finely grated

2 tsp. [10 g] apple jelly (*see recipe page 29*)

3 bunches of red currants

To bake:

A baking sheet covered with parchment paper

* *Specialty markets carry almond paste.*

Peel the pineapple. Cut into slices about ⅛ inch thick, then into sticks. Let it drain for an hour on paper towels.

Preheat the oven to 350°F [180°C].

Put the almond paste in the bowl of an electric mixer equipped with a paddle and incorporate the egg white gradually on low speed. The mixture will be a dough but not a soft one, which is the reason it works better not to add the egg whites all at once.

Put the almond paste into a pastry bag with the largest fluted tip, the one usually used for Chantilly cream. Draw a circle, 9 inches [22 cm] in diameter, on the parchment paper covering the baking sheet. Make a rosette in the center of the circle, and beginning there, squeeze the bag to make a delicate, thin spiral. This will be the foundation for the tart.

Now prepare the macaroon layer: Combine 4½ tablespoons [60 g] of the sugar, the ground almonds, and the flour. Sift these ingredients, then add the coconut. In a bowl, beat the egg whites to soft peaks with the remaining sugar, and add the sifted mixture in a stream, folding it in gently with a wooden spatula. Put this batter into a pastry bag with a plain tip. Hold the bag vertically with the tip a little less than ½ inch [1 cm] from the almond paste. Make a spiral overlapping the almond spiral.

Bake for about 25 minutes with the oven door a little ajar to prevent steam condensing, which would cause the pastry to puff and fall, distorting its shape.

Prepare the coconut cream: Put the butter in the bowl of an electric mixer equipped with a whip. Beat it to make it as light as possible. Add the grated coconut, coconut milk, rum, and pastry cream. Using a pastry bag with a fluted tip, spread this custard in a spiral on the cookie crust.

Distribute the pineapple pieces and finely grated lime zest on top. Using a pastry brush, coat the top with the warmed apple jelly. Sprinkle with the stemmed red currants.

∾∶∾

This tart is a gift from my friend Pierre Hermé. "I really love this dessert," he says. "It is a subtle and delicious compromise between a tart and a cake. You can make a berry macaronade using the same base, replacing the coconut cream with pistachio mousseline cream, and the pineapple with raspberries. Sprinkle it with chopped pistachios."

Chocolate Tart

11 oz. [300 g] rich flaky pastry with praline paste and hazelnuts (*see recipe page 19*)

2⅔ oz. [75 g] extra-bittersweet chocolate, 66% cocoa butter

1 stick / 4 oz. [110 g] butter

2 eggs

½ cup [100 g] extra-fine sugar

½ cup *plus* 1 Tbsp. [65 g] flour

1 scant cup [100 g] hazelnuts, finely chopped

For the ganache:

5½ oz. [150 g] extra-bittersweet chocolate, 66% cocoa butter

1 egg

2 egg yolks

2 Tbsp. [30 g] extra-fine sugar

6 Tbsp. / 3 oz. [80 g] softened butter

To bake:

A tart pan with plain rim, 10 inches [26 cm] in diameter and 1 inch [3 cm] deep with removable bottom

The day before, prepare your rich flaky pastry.

The next day, roll your pastry on a lightly floured work surface into a circle a little less than ⅛ inch [about 2.5 mm] thick and 13 inches [34 cm] in diameter.

Butter your pan and carefully place the pastry in it, pressing it lightly with the fingertips against the bottom and sides. Roll the rolling pin across the top edge of the pan to cut off the small amount of excess pastry. Prick the bottom of the tart with a fork and refrigerate it for 30 minutes covered with plastic wrap.

Preheat the oven to 350°F [**180°C**].

Bake your tart shell blind (*see page 14*) for 10 minutes and let it cool.

Meanwhile, prepare your hazelnut cookie layer: Finely chop the hazelnuts. Heat water in a pan that will serve as a double boiler. Grate the chocolate into a bowl, then melt it in the double boiler. In a bowl, beat the eggs with the sugar until the mixture becomes a little lighter and is smooth. Add the melted chocolate, stirring gently with a wooden spatula. Add the melted butter, continuing to stir. Add the flour and hazelnuts. Fill the bottom of the tart with an even layer of the hazelnut cookie batter, pouring carefully.

When you are ready to put the tart into the oven, remember to decrease the temperature to midway between 325°and 350°F [**170°C**].

Bake the tart for about 12 minutes. The edges of the tart should be lightly golden and the hazelnut layer a little puffed. Unmold your tart onto a rack and let it cool.

Now prepare your ganache: Heat water in the double boiler. Grate the chocolate into a bowl, then melt it in the double boiler. In another pan, melt the butter. Add the whole egg to the melted chocolate first and then the egg yolks, incorporating them gently with a whip. Last, add the sugar and then the melted butter, continuing to stir.

Preheat the oven to 350°F [**180°C**].

Fill the bottom of the tart with an even layer of ganache, pouring it in carefully. Smooth the ganache with the back of a spoon. Before serving, reheat the tart for about 10 minutes.

~:~

This tart is nice with sliced oranges, flavored with finely chopped orange zest, or a crème anglaise.

Lemon Tart

11 oz. [300 g] rich flaky pastry with praline paste and hazelnuts (*see recipe page 19*)

For the lemon cream:

3 oz. [90 g / 9 cl] lemon juice, *or* about 3 lemons

3 small eggs

Zest of 1 lemon, finely grated

⅞ cup [180 g] granulated sugar

2 sticks / 8 oz. [225 g] butter

For the egg wash:

1 egg

To decorate:

3½ oz. [100 g] apple jelly (*see recipe page 29*)

Zest of 1 lemon, slivered

To bake:

A tart pan with plain rim, 10 inches [26 cm] in diameter and 1 inch [3 cm] deep with removable bottom

The day before, prepare your rich flaky pastry and the lemon cream: Finely grate the zest of 1 lemon. Squeeze the other 3 lemons and reserve the juice. In a pan, melt the butter, then add the juice and grated zest, and bring the mixture to a simmer, stirring occasionally with a whip. In a bowl, combine the eggs and sugar. Beat until the mixture becomes light in color and slightly foamy. Pour this mixture into a pan and cook, stirring constantly with a whip, bringing it gradually to a simmer. Then pour it into a bowl and refrigerate.

The next day, roll your pastry on a lightly floured work surface into a circle a little less than ⅛ inch [about 2.5 mm] thick and 13 inches [34 cm] in diameter.

Butter your pan and carefully place the pastry in it, pressing it lightly with the fingertips against the bottom and the sides. Roll the rolling pin across the top edge of the pan to trim off the small amount of excess pastry. Prick the bottom of the tart with a fork and refrigerate it for 30 minutes, covered with plastic wrap.

Preheat the oven to 350°F [180°C].

Bake your tart shell blind (*see page 14*) for 10 minutes. Then, using a pastry brush, paint the pastry with a little beaten egg and continue baking for about 5 to 8 more minutes. The pastry base will be more "moisture-proof"; it will also have a nice golden color and will keep its crunch. Unmold your pastry shell onto a rack and let it cool.

At the last minute, fill the shell with the lemon cream and sprinkle it with finely slivered citrus zest. In a small pan, heat the apple jelly with 2 tablespoons [30 g / 3 cl] of water, and bring it to a simmer. Then, carefully glaze your tart.

Brioche Tart with Thick Crème Fraîche

---

1 lb. 9 oz. [700 g] **brioche dough** (*see recipe page 23*)

1 cup *plus* **1 Tbsp.** [250 g] **crème fraîche**

½ cup [100 g] **granulated sugar or cassonade***

For the egg wash:

1 egg

To decorate:

4 Tbsp. [30 g] **confectioners' sugar**

To bake:

A tart pan with plain rim, 10 inches [26 cm] **in diameter and 1 inch** [3 cm] **deep**

Prepare your brioche dough: Roll it on a lightly floured work surface into a circle a little more than ⅛ inch [4 mm] thick and 10 inches [26 cm] in diameter.

Butter and flour your pan, and carefully place the dough in it, pressing it lightly with the fingertips against the bottom and sides. Then cover it with a kitchen towel and let it rest at room temperature for 15 minutes to enable it to rise well.

Preheat the oven to 400°F [200°C].

Mark the surface of the dough with twelve little indentations, using your finger and pressing on the dough until you touch the bottom of the pan. Fill each of these little hollows with a spoonful of crème fraîche. Sprinkle the hollows with sugar. Let your tart rest for 10 minutes. Using a pastry brush, paint the dough with beaten egg without touching the filled hollows.

*Cassonade is an orange-red cane sugar from the French Antilles.

When you are ready to put the tart into the oven, remember to decrease the temperature to 350°F [**180°C**].

Bake the tart for about 35 minutes. The edges of the tart should be puffed and nicely golden. The crème fraîche in the hollows should be crusty and lightly caramelized. Unmold the tart onto a rack and let it cool. Sprinkle it generously with confectioners' sugar before serving. You can also serve it warm.

~:~

This tart has an exquisite sweetness. I love the way it tastes with my Christmas jam.

Tartlets Tatin with Christmas Flavors

---

11 oz. [300 g] rich flaky pastry with praline paste and hazelnuts (*see recipe page 19*)

10 small apple-quinces

3½ Tbsp. / 1¾ oz. [50 g] softened butter

1 cup [200 g] granulated sugar

Zest of 1 lemon, finely slivered

Zest of 1 orange, finely slivered

⅛ tsp. ground cinnamon

⅛ tsp. ground cardamom

⅛ tsp. ground star anise

For the egg wash:

1 egg

To decorate:

½ cup [100 g] granulated sugar

⅛ tsp. ground cardamom

To bake:

8 tartlet pans, 4 inches [10 cm] in diameter and a nonstick cake pan, 10 inches [26 cm] in diameter and 2 inches [5 cm] deep

The day before, prepare your rich flaky pastry.

The next day, roll your pastry on a lightly floured work surface to a little more than 1/16 inch [about 2 mm] thick. Using a fluted cookie-cutter, cut 8 small pastry rounds, 5½ inches [14 cm] in diameter.

Butter the tartlet pans and carefully place the pastry in them, pressing it lightly with the fingertips against the bottom and sides. Roll the rolling pin across the top edges of the pans to trim off the small amount of excess pastry. Prick the bottoms of the shells with a fork and refrigerate them for 30 minutes, covered with plastic wrap.

Preheat the oven to 350°F [180°C].

Bake your tartlet shells for 10 minutes. Then, using a pastry brush, paint them with a little beaten egg and continue baking for about 5 more minutes. The bottoms of the shells will be more "moisture-proof"; they will also have a nice golden color and will keep their crunch.

Unmold your tartlet shells onto a rack and let them cool.

Preheat the oven to 425°F [220°C].

In a bowl, combine the sugar, spices, and slivered citrus zest. Now prepare your quinces: Rub them with a kitchen towel to remove their fine down. Wash them in cold water, then peel them and remove the stems, the remains of the blossoms, and any hard parts. Cut them in half and remove their cores and seeds.

Sprinkle your cake pan with half of the spiced sugar. Then stand the quince halves vertically in two concentric circles. Place them very close together. Sprinkle the remaining spiced sugar over the quinces and then distribute the bits of butter.

When you are ready to put them into the oven, remember to decrease the temperature to 400°F [200°C].

Bake the quinces for about 50 minutes. They should be almost jam-like. Put your cake pan onto a rack and let it cool.

Set your oven to broil. Using a small ladle, mound some spiced quince in each tartlet shell. Sprinkle them with the cardamom-flavored granulated sugar. Brown your tartlets under the broiler for a few minutes. The sugar will bubble and lightly caramelize. Serve them immediately because this tatin is best right out of the oven. Accompany them with thick crème fraîche or a crème anglaise flavored with citrus zest.

Flan Tart

---

11 oz. [300 g] brioche dough (*see recipe page 23*)

For the flan cream:

2 cups *plus* 1 oz. [500 g / 50 cl] milk

4 egg whites

5 egg yolks

3½ Tbsp. [50 g] crème fraîche

½ cup [100 g] vanilla sugar (*see page 10*)

¼ cup [50 g] extra-fine sugar

¼ cup *plus* 2 Tbsp. [70 g] flour

Zest of ½ orange, finely grated

For the egg wash:

1 egg

To bake:

A tart pan with plain rim, 10 inches [26 cm] in diameter and 1 inch [3 cm] deep

Prepare your dough. Roll the dough on a lightly floured work surface into a circle a little more than ¹⁄₁₆ inch [about 2 mm] thick and 13 inches [34 cm] in diameter.

Butter and flour your pan and carefully place the dough in it, pressing it lightly with the fingertips against the bottom and sides. Cover with a kitchen towel and let the dough rest at room temperature for 10 minutes. Then roll the rolling pin across the top edge of the pan to trim off the small amount of excess dough.

Preheat the oven to 350°F [180°C].

Meanwhile, prepare the flan cream: In a bowl, combine the vanilla sugar, flour, crème fraîche, ¼ of the milk, and the egg yolks. Gradually pour in the rest of the milk, stirring gently with a whip. Then beat the egg whites into soft peaks with an electric mixer while sprinkling in ¼ cup [50 g] of extra-fine sugar. When the whites are firm, gently incorporate them into the flan cream with a whip.

Lightly prick the bottom of the tart with a fork. Using a pastry brush, paint the edges of the tart with a little beaten egg. Pour in the flan cream.

When you are ready to put the tart into the oven, remember to decrease the temperature to midway between 325°and 350°F [170°C].

Bake the tart for about 30 minutes. The edges of your tart will be nicely golden and the flan cream lightly colored and puffed. Put a rack over the tart and turn it over. Remove the pan and let the tart cool. Place the tart right side up on a serving plate. The rack will have imprinted a decoration on the flan!

Fromage Blanc Tart

11 oz. [300 g] flaky pastry (*see recipe page 15*)

For the cream:

15 oz. [400 g] faisselle*, 0% butterfat, well-drained

4 egg whites

8 egg yolks

½ cup *less* 1 Tbsp. [100 g] crème fraîche

½ cup [100 g] granulated sugar

¼ cup [50 g] extra-fine sugar

1½ Tbsp. [20 g / 2 cl] Kirsch

¼ tsp. finely chopped lemon zest

To decorate:

4 Tbsp. [30 g] confectioners' sugar

To bake:

A tart pan with plain rim, 10 inches [26 cm] in diameter and 1 inch [3 cm] deep

The day before, prepare your flaky pastry and set your faisselle to drain.

The next day, roll your pastry on a lightly floured work surface into a circle a little more than 1/16 inch [about 2 mm] thick and 13 inches [34 cm] in diameter.

Butter your pan and carefully place the pastry in it, pressing lightly with your fingertips against the bottom and sides. The pastry should extend beyond the edge of the pan a little less than ½ inch [about 1

* *A fresh white cheese. See Techniques and Ingredients, page 7.*

cm] to make a border. Pinch this border between your thumb and index finger to flute it. Prick the bottom of the tart with a fork and refrigerate it for 30 minutes covered with plastic wrap.

Preheat the oven to 395°F [200°C].

Bake your tart shell blind (*see page 14*) for 15 minutes.

Meanwhile, in a bowl, combine ½ cup [100 g] of the granulated sugar and the egg yolks, crème fraîche, faisselle, Kirsch, and finely chopped lemon zest, mixing gently with a whip. Beat the egg whites with an electric mixer while adding ¼ cup [50 g] of extra-fine sugar in a gradual stream. When the whites are firm, gently incorporate them into the cheese mixture with a whip. Pour the cream into your tart shell.

When you are ready to put the tart into the oven, remember to decrease the temperature to 350°F [180°C].

Bake the tart for about 45 minutes. The edges of your tart will be nicely golden and the cheese filling lightly colored and puffed. Place a rack over your tart and turn it over. Remove the pan and let it cool. Now reverse the tart onto a service plate. The rack will have imprinted a design on the cheese filling. Dust the tart lightly with confectioners' sugar.

Puréed Chestnut Tart

---

12 oz. [350 g] rich flaky pastry No. 2 (*see recipe page 18*)

For the chestnut purée:

    1 lb. 2 oz. [500 g] blanched and peeled chestnuts

    7 oz. [200 g / 20 cl] light whipping cream

    ½ cup [100 g / 10 cl] milk

    ½ cup [100 g] extra-fine sugar

    1 vanilla bean

    2 Tbsp. [30 g / 3 cl] cognac

For the egg wash:

    1 egg

For the almond cream:

    7 oz. [200 g] almond cream (*see recipe page 27*)

    3 Tbsp. [50 g] crème fraîche

For the Chantilly cream:

    1¼ cups [300 g / 30 cl] light whipping cream

    4 Tbsp. [30 g] confectioners' sugar

To decorate:

    1 marron glacé

To bake:

    A baking sheet covered with parchment paper

The day before, prepare your rich flaky pastry and chestnut purée: In a heavy-bottomed saucepan, bring the light whipping cream, milk, and sugar to a simmer. Add the vanilla bean, split lengthwise, then the chestnuts. Stir gently with a wooden spatula and simmer for about 15 minutes, or until the chestnuts are tender all the way through. Mash them with a fork. Turn this mixture into a bowl and let it cool. Remove the vanilla bean and add the cognac. Put this preparation through a food mill with a fine disk. Refrigerate, covered with plastic wrap.

The next day, roll the pastry on a lightly floured work surface into a circle a little more than 1/16 inch [about 2 mm] thick. Then roll it around the rolling pin and lift it above the baking sheet. Unroll it gently. If the pastry tears, carefully put the edges together and press with the fingertips to join them. Cut a circle, 10 inches [26 cm] in diameter. With the pastry scraps, using a cookie-cutter, cut small shapes of your choice for decorating the edges of the pastry. Using a pastry brush dipped in cold water, moisten the edges of the circle and press on the cutouts, overlapping them slightly. Prick the bottom of the tart with a fork and refrigerate it for 30 minutes, covered with plastic wrap.

Preheat the oven to 350°F [180°C].

Paint the tart decorations with beaten egg. Bake your pastry shell blind (*see page 14*) for 10 minutes and let it cool.

Meanwhile, prepare your almond cream. Add the crème fraîche and incorporate it gently with a wooden spatula. Spread an even layer of the cream in the pastry shell. It might be helpful to use a pastry bag with a plain tip.

Bake the tart for about 10 minutes. The edges of the tart should be golden and the almond cream lightly colored and puffed. Slide your tart onto a rack and let it cool.

In a bowl that you have chilled in the refrigerator for 15 minutes, whip the cream and confectioners' sugar. The cream should be quite stiff. At the last minute, mound this Chantilly cream in the center of your tart. Put the chestnut purée into a food mill with a very fine disk and cover the whipped cream dome with these "vermicelli." Place a marron glacé carefully on the top.

‿:∾

My childhood friend Pierre Hermé often pairs rose hip purée with a chestnut tart. For him, the rose hips are a bright, fresh note in this rustic, wintry harmony.

Hazlenut Tart with Orange and Caramel

---

11 oz. [300 g] rich flaky pastry with praline paste and hazelnuts (*see recipe page 19*)

1 cup [100 g] ground blanched almonds

2 Tbsp. [25 g] crème fraîche

1 stick *plus* 3½ Tbsp. [160 g] butter

3 eggs

½ cup [100 g] extra-fine sugar

Scant ½ cup [65 g] flour

1 cup [100 g] hazelnuts, toasted and chopped

Zest 1 orange, finely grated

For the caramel:

1½ cups [300 g] extra-fine sugar

1¼ cups [300 g] whipping cream

3½ Tbsp. [50 g] butter

1 vanilla bean

To bake:

A tart pan with plain rim, 10 inches [26 cm] in diameter and 1 inch [3 cm] deep with removable bottom.

The day before, prepare your rich flaky pastry.

The next day, roll your pastry on a lightly floured work surface into a circle a little less than ⅛ inch [about 2.5 mm] thick and 13 inches [34 cm] in diameter.

Butter your pan and carefully place the pastry in it, pressing the dough lightly with the fingertips against the bottom and sides. Roll the rolling pin across the top edge of the pan to trim off the small amount of excess dough. Prick the bottom of the tart with a fork and refrigerate it for 30 minutes, covered with plastic wrap.

Preheat the oven to 350°F [180°C].

Bake your tart shell blind (*see page 14*) for 10 minutes and let it cool.

Meanwhile, prepare your hazelnut cookie layer: Lightly toast the hazelnuts and rub them with your fingertips to remove the skins. Finely chop them. In a pan, melt the butter. In a bowl, beat the eggs and sugar until the mixture is a little lighter in color and smooth. Add the thick crème fraîche and mix gently with a wooden spatula. Add the melted butter, continuing to stir. Add the flour, hazelnuts, ground almonds, and grated orange zest, stirring constantly with the wooden spatula. Fill the bottom of the tart with an even layer of the hazelnut cookie batter, pouring it carefully. When you are ready to put the tart into the oven, remember to decrease the temperature to midway between 325°and 350°F [170°C].

Bake the tart for about 20 minutes. The edges of the tart should be lightly browned and the hazelnut cookie layer slightly puffed. Unmold the tart onto a rack and let it cool.

Prepare your caramel: In a small saucepan, heat the whipping cream and ½ vanilla bean split lengthwise on low heat. Then, in a much larger pan, melt dry ¼ of the sugar, stirring gently with a wooden spatula. As soon as the sugar is a light caramel color, pour in another ¼ of the remaining sugar. Stir gently with the spatula and wait until all of the sugar is a light caramel color. Repeat this procedure twice more. Remove the vanilla bean from the crème fraîche. Gradually add the light whipping cream to the caramelized sugar, stirring gently with the wooden spatula. Let the mixture mount and boil until all of the sugar crystals have disappeared. Pour the caramel into a bowl, add the butter and stir gently. Let it cool. Cover the tart with an even layer of caramel, pouring it carefully.

~:~

You can serve this tart with a salad of oranges enlivened with finely slivered lemon zest.

Galette from My Childhood

---

1 lb. 5 oz. [600 g] puff pastry *or* semi-puff pastry (*see recipe page 20 and 21*)

2 cups 1 oz. [500 g] almond cream (*see recipe page 27*)

Scant 1½ cups [150 g] fresh walnuts, broken into pieces

⅜ tsp. finely grated lemon zest

2 Tbsp. [30 g] crème fraîche

For the egg wash:

1 egg

To bake:

A baking sheet covered with parchment paper

The day before, prepare your puff pastry or semi-puff pastry.

The next day, divide your pastry in half. On a lightly floured work surface, roll the first piece into a circle about ¹⁄₁₆ inch [1.5 mm] thick. Then roll it around the rolling pin and lift it above the baking sheet covered with parchment paper. Unroll the pastry gently. This allows it to relax and prevents it from shrinking when it is cut. Cut a circle 11 inches [28 cm] in diameter. Roll the second piece of dough. Cut another circle the same size and set it aside on a sheet of parchment paper.

Prepare your almond cream. Add the crème fraîche, walnut pieces, and finely grated lemon zest, mixing gently with a wooden spatula.

Prick the first pastry circle with a fork. Cover it with an even layer of walnut cream, leaving a clear 1-inch [3-cm] border around the edges. You can use a pastry bag with a plain tip to make this easier. Using a pastry brush dipped in cold water, moisten the edges of the tart. On the other pastry circle, use a knife to make 5 slits, each 6 inches [15 cm] long, radiating from the center. Set it onto the filled bottom pastry circle, lining up the edges. Press gently on the edges to join the two pastry layers securely together. Refrigerate the tart for 30 minutes, covered with plastic wrap.

Preheat your oven to 400°F [200°C].

Using a pastry brush, paint your tart with a little beaten egg. Make a few designs with the point of a knife to decorate the top of the tart.

When you are ready to put the tart into the oven, remember to decrease the temperature to 350°F [180°C]. Bake it for about 40 minutes. The pastry will be a pretty golden color. Slide your tart onto a rack and let it cool.

~:~

When I was a child, every fall we'd go around in the vicinity of the village gathering nuts, knocking them out of the trees with a stick. We'd put them in the attic to dry until Christmas. Then my grandparents would spend the evenings telling stories while they cracked nuts. And we loved my grandmother's wonderful galettes with nuts and lemon.

Walnut Tart with Orange and Chocolate

---

11 oz. [300 g] rich flaky pastry with praline paste and hazelnuts (*see recipe page 19*)

3½ oz. [100 g] extra-bittersweet chocolate, 66% cocoa butter

1 stick *plus* 3½ Tbsp. / 5¾ oz. [160 g] butter

3 eggs

⅔ cup [150 g] extra-fine sugar

Scant ¾ cup [100 g] flour

Scant 1½ cups [150 g] fresh walnuts, broken into small pieces

Zest of 1 orange, finely grated

To decorate:

3 Tbsp. [25 g] confectioners' sugar

To bake:

A tart pan with plain rim, 10 inches [26 cm] in diameter and 1 inch [3 cm] deep, with removable bottom

The day before, prepare your flaky pastry

The next day, roll your pastry on a lightly floured work surface into a circle a little less than ⅛ inch [about 2.5 mm] thick and 13 inches [34 cm] in diameter.

Butter your pan and carefully place the pastry in it, pressing it lightly with your fingertips against the bottom and sides. Roll the rolling pin across the top edge of the pan to trim off the small amount of excess pastry. Prick the bottom of the tart with a fork and refrigerate it for 30 minutes, covered with plastic wrap.

Preheat the oven to 350°F [180°C].

Bake your tart shell blind (*see page 14*) for 10 minutes and let it cool.

Meanwhile, prepare your walnut cookie layer: Break the walnuts into small pieces. Heat water in a saucepan that will serve as a double boiler. Grate the chocolate into a bowl, then melt it in the double boiler. In another pan, melt the butter. In a bowl, beat the eggs with the sugar until the mixture turns a little lighter in color and is very smooth. Add the melted chocolate and mix gently with a wooden spatula. Add the melted butter, continuing to stir. Add the flour, walnuts, and finely grated orange zest. Fill the tart shell with an even layer of the walnut cookie batter, pouring it in carefully.

When you are ready to put the tart into the oven, remember to decrease the temperature to midway between 325°and 350°F [170°C].

Bake the tart for about 20 to 25 minutes. The edges of your tart should be lightly browned and the walnut cookie layer gently puffed. Unmold the tart onto a rack and let it cool. Dust it with confectioners' sugar.

~:~

You can serve this tart with an orange salad flavored with ⅛ teaspoon of ground cardamom.

Rich Pastry Galettes with Walnut Meringue Filling

11 oz. [300 g] rich flaky pastry No. 2 (*see recipe page 18*)

1¼ cups [300 g] lemon jelly

Zest of 1 lemon, finely slivered

For the walnut meringue filling:

Generous ½ cup [60 g] ground, blanched almonds

Generous ½ cup [60 g] ground walnuts

Scant 1 cup [100 g] fresh walnuts, finely chopped

¾ cup [100 g] confectioners' sugar

2 egg whites

4 egg whites

¼ cup [50 g] extra-fine sugar

To decorate:

3 Tbsp. [20 g] confectioners' sugar

To bake:

2 baking sheets covered with parchment paper

The day before, make your rich flaky pastry.

The next day, roll your pastry on a lightly floured work surface to a little more than 1⁄16 inch [about 2 mm] thick. Using a fluted cookie-cutter, cut 20 small pastry rounds, 4 inches [10 cm] in diameter. Cover the 2 baking sheets with parchment paper. Place 10 pastry rounds on each, spaced 1 inch [3 cm] apart so that they don't stick together. Prick them with a fork.

Preheat your oven to 350°F [180°C].

Bake the first 10 rounds for about 10 minutes, or until they are golden. Let them cool on a rack.

Prepare the walnut meringue filling: In a bowl, combine the ground almonds, ground walnuts, finely chopped walnuts, confectioners' sugar, and 2 egg whites [60 g]. Beat the remaining 4 whites with an electric mixer, while sprinkling in ¼ cup [50 g] of extra-fine sugar in a stream. When the whites are stiff, gently incorporate them into the walnut mixture with a wooden spatula. Mound some walnut meringue filling on each of the remaining 10 pastry rounds. A small ladle is helpful for this.

When you are ready to put them into the oven, remember to decrease the temperature to 325°F [160°C].

Bake them for about 20 to 25 minutes. The walnut meringue filling will be crunchy. Remove the pastry rounds and let them cool on a rack.

Place a small spoonful of lemon jelly on each of the first 10 pastry rounds. Sprinkle with the slivered lemon zest, then cover them with the 10 walnut meringue-topped rounds. Dust the galettes lightly with confectioners' sugar. Serve them with crème fraîche.

∽:∼

If you don't have lemon jelly, you can use apple jelly (see recipe page 29) given a little more zing with a few thin lemon sections and lemon zest.

Onion Tart

---

11 oz. [300 g] flaky pastry with egg (*see recipe page 15*)

8 attractive onions

7 oz. [200 g] salted, smoked pork breast*

1½ Tbsp. [20 g / 2 cl] peanut oil

3½ Tbsp. / 1¾ oz. [50 g] butter

2 Tbsp. [20 g] flour

1¼ cups [300 g / 30 cl] whole milk

⅛ tsp. ground nutmeg

Salt

Freshly ground black pepper

For the egg custard:

3½ oz. [100 g] crème fraîche

3 eggs

To bake:

A tart pan with plain rim, 10 inches [26 cm] in diameter and 1 inch [3 cm] deep

The day before, prepare your flaky pastry with egg.

The next day, roll the pastry on a lightly floured work surface into a circle a little more than ¹⁄₁₆ inch [about 2 mm] thick and 13 inches [34 cm] in diameter.

Butter your pan and carefully place the pastry in it, pressing it lightly with the fingertips against the

---

* Use a good double-thick cut bacon.

bottom and sides. The dough should extend slightly beyond the edge of the pan to make a border. Pinch this border between your thumb and index finger to flute it. Prick the bottom of the tart with a fork and refrigerate it for 30 minutes, covered with plastic wrap.

Preheat the oven to 350°F [180°C].

Bake your tart shell blind (*see page 14*) for 10 minutes.

Meanwhile, make your onion and lardon filling: Peel the onions, slice them thinly, and set aside. Cut the piece of salt pork into small lardons. In a skillet, heat the oil. Brown the lardons on high heat. Remove them with a skimmer and set aside. In the same skillet melt the butter on low heat. Scrape the sliced onions into the pan and mix with a wooden spatula. Add 3 pinches of salt, 3 grinds of pepper, and ⅛ teaspoon of ground nutmeg. Let the onions sweat for a few minutes, covered, then moisten them with 7 ounces [200 g / 20 cl] of water. Continue cooking, covered, on low heat for about 10 more minutes, stirring occasionally. The onions should be tender and the water entirely evaporated. To bind the filling, add the flour and stir with the wooden spatula. Then pour in the milk and bring to a boil. The onions will be coated with a little béchamel sauce. Turn them into a bowl, let them cool, and set aside.

Prepare your egg custard: In a bowl, mix the crème fraîche, eggs, a pinch of salt, a grind of pepper, and ¼ teaspoon of ground nutmeg and beat briefly with a whip. Add the onions and lardons. Then pour the preparation into the tart shell.

Bake for about 40 minutes. The edges of your tart should be nicely golden and the filling lightly colored and set. Unmold your tart and serve it immediately.

Orange Tart with Cardamom Streusel

---

11 oz. [300 g] sweet pastry (*see recipe page 16*)

4 attractive oranges

2 cups *plus* 2 Tbsp. [500 g] almond cream (*see recipe page 27*)

2½ Tbsp. [40 g] crème fraîche

Finely grated zest of ½ orange

For the streusel:

4 Tbsp. / 2 oz. [60 g] cold butter

4½ Tbsp. [60 g] extra-fine sugar

Generous ¼ cup [30 g] ground hazelnuts

½ cup *less* 1 Tbsp. [60 g] flour

⅜ tsp. ground cardamom

To bake:

A tart pan with plain rim, 10 inches [26 cm] in diameter and 1 inch [3 cm] deep with removable bottom

The day before, prepare your sweet pastry.

The next day, roll your pastry on a lightly floured work surface into a circle a little less than ⅛ inch [about 2.5 mm] thick and 13 inches [34 cm] in diameter.

Butter your pan and carefully place the pastry in it, pressing it lightly with your fingertips against the bottom and sides. Roll the rolling pin across the top edge of the pan to trim off the small amount of excess pastry. Prick the bottom of the tart with a fork and refrigerate it for 30 minutes, covered with plastic wrap.

Preheat the oven to 350°F [180°C].

Meanwhile, prepare your almond cream. Add the crème fraîche and finely grated orange zest and combine them gently with a wooden spatula. Spread half of the almond cream in the pastry shell. It might be helpful to use a pastry bag with plain tip. Peel the oranges, removing the white pith, and carefully section them. Place the sections on the almond cream. Using a pastry bag with a plain tip, cover the oranges with the remainder of the almond cream. Bake the pastry for about 40 minutes.

Meanwhile, prepare the streusel: Cut the butter into very small cubes. In a bowl, combine the butter, sugar, ground hazelnuts, flour, and cardamom. Work this mixture gently with the fingertips until it has the texture of coarse meal. Rub it together for a few seconds more to obtain a slightly lumpier consistency. When the almond cream is lightly colored and puffed, sprinkle the streusel in little clumps over the tart. Continue baking for about 10 minutes. The edges should be golden and the streusel crunchy and nicely colored. Unmold the tart onto a rack and let it cool.

This tart is delicious with a cardamom-flavored crème anglaise.

Lattice-Topped Tart with Winter Fruit

1 lb. 9 oz. [700 g] semi-puff pastry (*see recipe page 20*)

1 cup *plus* 1 Tbsp. [250 g] almond cream (*see recipe page 27*)

3 Ida Red apples

3 Passe-Crassane pears*

8 dried figs

8 dried apricots

8 prunes

1 cup [100 g] fresh walnuts, broken into pieces

Juice of 2 oranges

1½ oz. [50 g / 5 cl] Grand Marnier

¼ tsp. ground cinnamon

Zest of ½ of an orange, finely grated

For the egg wash:

1 egg

To bake:

A tart pan with plain rim, 10 inches [26 cm] in diameter and 1 inch [3 cm] deep

The day before, prepare your semi-puff pastry. Cut the dry fruit into tiny sticks a little less than ¼ inch [5 mm] long. In a bowl, macerate it with the orange juice, orange zest, cinnamon, and Grand Marnier. Cover the bowl with plastic wrap and set aside.

Passe-Crassane is a French pear resulting from a cross between a pear and a quince. It is an outstanding winter pear because it keeps well. This pear is large and round with thick skin. It has white, slightly granular flesh and is juicy and flavorful. Use a firm Bartlett pear.

The next day, roll 12 ounces [350 g] of pastry on a lightly floured work surface into a circle a little less than ⅛ inch [about 2.5 mm] thick and 13 inches [34 cm] in diameter.

Butter the pan and carefully place the pastry in it, pressing it lightly with the fingertips against the bottom and sides. Roll the rolling pin across the top edge of the pan to trim off the small amount of excess pastry. Prick the bottom of the tart with a fork and refrigerate it for 30 minutes covered with plastic wrap. Now roll the remainder of the dough on a lightly floured work surface to a little more than 1/16 inch [about 2 mm] thick. Roll it around the rolling pin and lift it above the baking sheet covered with parchment paper. Unroll it gently. This allows the pastry to relax and prevents it from shrinking when it is cut. Refrigerate it for 30 minutes covered with plastic wrap.

Preheat the oven to 400°F [200°C].

Bake the pastry shell blind (*see page 14*) for 10 minutes and let it cool.

Meanwhile prepare your almond cream. Peel the apples and pears. Remove the stems, cut them in half, core them, and slice them. Mix the dried fruit with the sliced apples and pears. Fill the pastry shell with an even layer of almond cream. It might be helpful to use a pastry bag with a plain tip. Distribute the fruit mixture on the cream filling.

Cut strips about 1 inch [3 cm] wide and 11 inches [28 cm] long from the refrigerated pastry. Using a pastry brush dipped in cold water, moisten the edges of your tart. Then make an evenly spaced lattice across the surface with the pastry strips. Using a pastry brush, paint the top of the tart with a little beaten egg.

When you are ready to put the tart into the oven, remember to decrease the temperature to 350°F [180°C]. Bake the tart for about 50 minutes. The edges of the tart and the lattice should be nicely browned. Unmold your tart onto a rack and let it cool.

~:~

Serve this tart with thick cream or a cinnamon-flavored crème anglaise.

Apple and Rice Custard Tart

---

    11 oz. [300 g] brioche dough (*see recipe page 23*)

    5 Reine des Reinettes apples*

For the rice custard:

    2 cups 1 oz. [500 g / 50 cl] milk

    Pinch of salt

    1½ Tbsp. [20 g] sugar

    2 Tbsp. / 2 oz. [25 g] butter

    ¼ cup [60 g] short-grain rice

    1 vanilla bean

    2 eggs

    3 egg yolks

    3½ oz. [100 g / 10 cl] whipping cream

For the egg wash:

    1 egg

To decorate:

    3 Tbsp. [25 g] confectioners' sugar

To bake:

    A tart pan with plain rim, 10 inches [26 cm] in diameter and 1 inch [3 cm] deep

The day before, prepare the rice custard: Split the vanilla bean lengthwise. In a heavy-bottomed saucepan, bring the milk, sugar, salt, vanilla bean, and rice to a simmer on low heat, stirring gently with a wooden

---

*Reine des Reinettes are slightly tart, juicy apples, yellow with red color, from southwestern France.

spatula. Cook, continuing to stir, until the rice is soft. It should have absorbed the liquid. Add the butter and mix it in gently. Turn the mixture into a bowl and let it cool.

The next day, prepare your dough. Roll it on a lightly floured work surface into a circle a little more than ¹⁄₁₆ inch [about 2 mm] thick and 13 inches [34 cm] in diameter.

Butter your pan and carefully place the dough in it, pressing it lightly with the fingertips against the bottom and sides. The dough should extend beyond the edge of the pan a little less than ½ inch [1 cm] to make a border. Cover it with a kitchen towel and let it rest at room temperature for 10 minutes. Roll the rolling pin across the top edge of the pan to trim off the small amount of excess dough.

Preheat the oven to 400°F [200°C].

Peel the apples, remove their stems, cut them in half, and core them. Grate the apples using a large-hole grater. Then add the whole eggs, egg yolks, the cream, and grated apples to the rice pudding. Mix gently with a wooden spatula.

Lightly prick the bottom of the tart with a fork. Using a pastry brush, paint the edges with a little beaten egg. Pour the rice and apple filling into the pastry shell.

When you are ready to put the tart into the oven, remember to decrease the temperature to 350°F [180°C]. Bake the tart for about 45 minutes. The edges of the tart will be a pretty golden yellow color and the apple and rice filling colored and puffed. Unmold your tart onto a rack and let it cool. Dust the top lightly with confectioners' sugar.

Semi-Puff Pastry Squares with Shallot Cream

12 oz. [350 g] semi-puff pastry (*see recipe page 20*)

1¾ lbs. [800 g] Charlotte* potatoes, *or* 1½ lbs. [650 g] net

8 thin slices of Bayonne ham**

3½ Tbsp. / 1¾ oz. [50 g] butter

For the shallot cream:

5 shallots

2 Tbsp. / 1 oz. [30 g / 3 cl] peanut oil

2½ oz. [80 g / 8 cl] aged wine vinegar

2 Tbsp. / 1 oz. [30 g] butter

7 oz. [200 g] crème fraîche

2 tsp. [10 g] sugar

Salt

Freshly ground black pepper

To decorate:

1 small bunch of chives

To bake:

A baking sheet covered with parchment paper

The day before, prepare your semi-puff pastry.

*Charlotte potatoes are firm-textured and hold their shape during cooking.
**Bayonne ham is a mildly smoked ham that has been cured in a wine mixture. It is produced near Bayonne.*

The next day, prepare your potatoes: Rinse them in cold water. Put them in a pot with cold water to cover. Salt them, bring them to a boil, and cook them covered on low heat until they are tender all the way through. Drain them and set aside.

Roll your pastry on a lightly floured work surface to a little more than ¹⁄₁₆ inch [about 2 mm] thick. Then roll it around the rolling pin and lift it over the baking sheet covered with parchment paper. Unroll it gently. This allows your pastry to relax and prevents it from shrinking when cut. Cut 10 approximately 4-inch [10-cm] squares. Space them 2 inches [5 cm] apart on the baking sheet so that they bake evenly and don't stick to each other. Prick the squares in the center with a fork. Refrigerate them for 30 minutes, covered with plastic wrap.

Preheat the oven to 400°F [200°C].

Peel the potatoes and cut them into round slices a little more than ⅛ inch [5 mm] thick. Arrange them on the pastry squares, overlapping them slightly. Sprinkle them with chunks of butter, salt, and pepper, and bake for about 15 minutes.

Cut the Bayonne ham into thin strips and set aside.

Meanwhile, prepare the shallot cream: Peel the shallots and slice them. In a skillet, heat the oil and brown the shallots for a few minutes over high heat. Add the sugar and continue cooking, letting them caramelize, for several minutes, stirring constantly. Pour in the vinegar, still stirring, and let it evaporate. Add the crème fraîche, salt, and pepper and let it reduce for a few minutes.

When your pastry squares are lightly browned and the potatoes are crusty, distribute the Bayonne ham over them and coat them with the shallot cream. Continue baking for 5 minutes. Sprinkle the squares with finely snipped chives and serve immediately. Serve with a good green salad.

Paillasson Potato Haystack with Saint-Félicien Cheese and Toasted Hazelnuts

2 Saint-Félicien cheeses*
1¾ lbs. [800 g] Bintje potatoes**, *or* 1½ lbs. [650 g] net
½ cup [50 g] hazelnuts, toasted and finely chopped
5 Tbsp. [75 g / 7.5 cl] hazelnut oil
3½ Tbsp. / 1¾ oz. [50 g] butter
Salt
Freshly ground black pepper

Preheat the oven to 400°F [200°C].

Rinse the potatoes in cold water. Peel them and dry them with a kitchen towel. Grate them using a food processor or box grater. In a nonstick skillet, heat the oil. Add the butter and grated potatoes, pressing them lightly to make a cake. Let them cook on moderate heat for 5 minutes. Turn the potato cake and cook it on the other side for 5 more minutes. Slide it onto a plate. Salt and pepper it. Finish by baking it in the oven for about 10 minutes.

Meanwhile, lightly toast the hazelnuts in the oven, remove their skins by rubbing them between your fingers, and finely chop them. Cut your Saint-Félicien cheese into thin slices.

Now set the oven to broil. Sprinkle the paillasson with hazelnuts and top with the sliced cheese. Let the topping melt and brown under the broiler for a few minutes and serve immediately.

*Saint-Félicien is a soft, mild, nutty goat cheese, with an average weight of 5 or 6 ounces.
** Bintje is a potato that dissolves easily and does not absorb too much oil. It is good, therefore, for making purées and frying.

Pumpkin Clafoutis with Orange Streusel

Scant 2 cups [400 g] pumpkin, grated*

For the flan cream:

1 cup *plus* 1 Tbsp. [250 g / 25 cl] whipping cream

1 cup *plus* 1 Tbsp. [250 g / 25 cl] whole milk

4 eggs

2 egg yolks

½ cup [100 g] granulated sugar

1 vanilla bean

Zest of ½ an orange, finely grated

For the streusel:

4 Tbsp. / 2 oz. [60 g] cold butter

4½ Tbsp. [60 g] extra-fine sugar

Scant ¼ cup [30 g] ground blanched almonds

3 Tbsp. [30 g] flour

¼ cup [30 g] slivered almonds

Zest of ½ an orange, finely grated

To bake:

A ceramic tart pan with fluted rim, 10 inches [26 cm] in diameter and 1½ inches [4 cm] deep

---

* French pumpkins are often smaller and more flavorful than ours. A good substitute is butternut squash.

Preheat the oven to 325°F [160°C].

In a heavy-bottomed saucepan, bring the milk to a boil. Remove from the heat. Add the vanilla bean, split lengthwise. Cover the pan and let the mixture infuse for 10 minutes.

Peel the pumpkin. Remove the seeds. Grate it on the small holes of a grater. Remove the vanilla bean from the milk. Prepare the flan cream: In a bowl, combine the cream, milk, eggs, egg yolks, orange zest, and sugar and beat briefly with a whip. Distribute the pumpkin in the ceramic tart pan. Cover it with this mixture. The flan cream will coat the little pumpkin shreds.

Bake for 35 minutes.

Meanwhile, prepare the streusel: Cut the butter into very small cubes. In a bowl, combine the butter, sugar, ground almonds, flour, slivered almonds, and finely grated orange zest. Work the mixture gently with the fingertips for a few seconds, until it resembles coarse meal. Rub it together a bit longer to obtain a slightly lumpier consistency. When the clafoutis cream is just set and golden yellow, sprinkle the streusel in little clumps over it.

Continue baking for about 10 minutes. The streusel should be crunchy and nicely browned. Serve the clafoutis warm with vanilla ice cream.

Pumpkin Clafoutis with Boule de Siam and Garlic Croutons

¾ lb. [300 g] grated pumpkin* *or* butternut squash

¾ lb. [300 g] rutabaga, grated

For the flan cream:

1 cup *plus* 1 Tbsp. [250 g / 25 cl] whipping cream

1 cup *plus* 1 Tbsp. [250 g / 25 cl] whole milk

5 eggs

Salt

Freshly ground black pepper

For the garlic croutons:

4 slices of firm-textured sandwich bread

4 cloves of garlic crushed

3½ Tbsp. / 1¾ oz. [50 g] softened butter

2 sprigs of parsley, finely chopped

To bake:

A ceramic pan with fluted rim, 10 inches [26 cm] in diameter and 1½ inches [4 cm] deep

Preheat the oven to 325°F [160°C].

Peel the pumpkin. Remove the seeds. Grate it on the large holes of a grater. Peel the rutabaga and grate it on the large holes of a grater.

* French pumpkins are often smaller and more flavorful than ours. A good substitute is butternut squash.

In a saucepan, bring 1 quart [1 liter] of salted water to a boil. Blanch the grated pumpkin for 3 minutes. Remove it with a skimmer and let it drain; then turn it into a bowl and set aside. In another saucepan, bring 1 quart [1 liter] of salted water to a boil and blanch the grated rutabaga for 6 minutes. Remove it with a skimmer, drain it, turn it into a bowl, and set aside.

Prepare the flan cream: In a bowl, combine the cream, milk, eggs, 3 pinches of salt, and 5 grinds of pepper and beat briefly with a whip. Distribute the pumpkin and rutabaga in the ceramic tart pan and cover them with this mixture. The flan cream will coat the vegetables.

Bake the tart for about 40 minutes.

Meanwhile, prepare the garlic croutons: Peel the garlic and crush it well with a mortar and pestle. In a bowl, mix the butter and garlic, then butter the bread slices and cut them into small cubes. Place the cubes on a baking sheet and bake them for about 10 minutes. Turn them occasionally with a wooden spatula.

When the custard is barely set and has a golden yellow color, sprinkle the garlic croutons on the clafoutis. Continue baking for 5 minutes. Sprinkle it with chopped parsley and serve immediately.

Rice Custard Tart with Crunchy Almond Topping

12 oz. [350 g] rich flaky pastry No. 1 (*see recipe page 17*)

1 cup *plus* 1 Tbsp. [250 g] almond cream (*see recipe page 27*)

3½ Tbsp. [50 g] crème fraîche

Zest of ½ orange, finely grated

For the rice custard:

1 quart [1 liter] of milk

Pinch of salt

4 Tbsp. [50 g] sugar

3½ Tbsp. [50 g] butter

½ cup [120 g] short-grain rice

1 vanilla bean

2 eggs

6 egg yolks

4 oz. [120 g] crème fraîche

For the almond crunch:

1 cup [100 g] slivered almonds

½ cup [100 g] confectioners' sugar

2 egg whites

To bake:

A tart pan with plain rim, 10 inches [26 cm] in diameter and 1 inch [3 cm] deep with removable bottom

The day before, prepare your rich flaky pastry and the rice custard: Split the vanilla bean lengthwise. In a heavy-bottomed saucepan, combine the milk with the sugar, salt, vanilla bean, and rice. Bring the mixture to a simmer on low heat, stirring gently with a wooden spatula. Let it cook, stirring constantly, until the rice is tender. It should have absorbed the liquid. Add the whole egg, egg yolks, and 4 ounces [120 g] of crème fraiche. Mix and let cook for a few seconds more. Add the butter and mix in gently. Turn into a bowl and refrigerate.

The next day, roll the pastry on a lightly floured work surface into a circle a little less than ⅛ inch [about 2.5 mm] thick and 13 inches [34 cm] in diameter.

Butter the pan and carefully place the pastry in it, pressing it lightly with the fingertips against the bottom and sides. Roll the rolling pin across the top edge of the pan to trim off the small amount of excess dough. Prick the bottom of the tart with a fork and refrigerate it for 30 minutes covered with plastic wrap.

Preheat the oven to 350°F [180°C].

Meanwhile, prepare the almond cream. Add 2 cups 1 ounce [500 g] of the rice custard, 3½ table-spoons [50 g] of the crème fraîche, and the finely grated orange zest and combine gently with a wooden spatula. Spread an even layer of this mixture in the bottom of the tart shell.

Bake for about 40 minutes.

In a bowl, gently mix the slivered almonds, confectioners' sugar, and egg white with the fingertips. When the almond cream is lightly colored and puffed, sprinkle the coated almonds over it and finish baking. The edges of the tart should be golden and the almonds will form a nice crunchy layer. Unmold your tart onto a rack and let it cool.

∽:∼

This tart is delicious with a cinnamon-flavored crème anglaise or the remaining rice custard mixture that wasn't used in the recipe. You can also serve it with a fresh fruit salad flavored with finely chopped orange or lemon zest.

Rice Custard Tart with Salmon and Dill

11 oz. [300 g] flaky pastry (*see recipe page 15*)

14 oz. [400 g] salmon filet

3½ Tbsp. [50 g] crème fraîche

2 eggs

1 bunch of dill

For the rice custard:

2 cups 1 oz. [500 g / 50 cl] whole milk

¼ cup [60 g] short-grain rice

Scant 2 Tbsp. / 1 oz. [25 g] butter

1 egg

3 egg yolks

4 Tbsp. [60 g] crème fraîche

Salt

Freshly ground black pepper

To bake:

A tart pan with plain rim, 10 inches [26 cm] in diameter and 1 inch [3 cm] deep.

The day before, prepare your flaky pastry and the rice custard: In a heavy-bottomed saucepan, combine the milk, rice, 3 pinches of salt, and 3 grinds of pepper. Bring the mixture to a simmer on low heat, stirring gently with a wooden spatula. Cook, stirring occasionally until the rice is tender. It should have absorbed the liquid. Add the whole egg, egg yolks, and the crème fraîche. Mix and cook for a few seconds more. Add the butter and mix gently. Turn into a bowl, cover with plastic wrap, and refrigerate.

The next day, roll the pastry on a lightly floured work surface into a circle a little more than ¹⁄₁₆ inch [about 2 mm] thick and 13 inches [34 cm] in diameter.

Butter the pan and carefully place the pastry in it, pressing it lightly with the fingertips against the bottom and sides. Roll the rolling pin across the top edge to trim off the small amount of excess dough. Prick the bottom of the tart with a fork and refrigerate it for 30 minutes covered with plastic wrap.

Preheat the oven to 350°F [180°C].

Bake your tart shell blind (*see page 14*) for 15 minutes Then, using a pastry brush, paint the pastry with a little beaten egg. Continue baking for about 5 minutes. The bottom of the tart will be more "moisture-proof"; it will also have a nice golden color and will keep its crunch.

Cut the salmon filets into thin slices. Salt and pepper them and put them into the tart shell. In a bowl, mix the crème fraîche with the eggs, then add the rice custard and finely chopped dill. Pour this filling over the salmon.

Bake the tart for about 40 minutes. The edges of the tart should be browned and the rice custard lightly colored and set. Unmold the tart and serve immediately.

Raised Sugar Tart

11 oz. [300 g] brioche dough (*see recipe page* 23)

1 small egg

2 Tbsp. / 1 oz. [25 g] softened butter

¼ cup [50 g] granulated sugar *or* cassonade sugar*

To decorate:

2 Tbsp. [25 g] granulated sugar

To bake:

A tart pan with plain rim, 10 inches [26 cm] in diameter and 1 inch [3 cm] deep

Prepare your dough. Roll it on a lightly floured work surface into a circle a little more than 1/16 inch [about 2 mm] thick and 13 inches [34 cm] in diameter.

Butter and flour the pan and carefully place the dough in it, pressing it lightly with the fingertips against the bottom and sides. The dough should extend beyond the edge of the pan a little less than ½ inch [1 cm] to make a border. Cover it with a kitchen towel and let it rest at room temperature for 10 minutes.

Preheat the oven to 400°F [200°C].

Meanwhile, beat the egg with a whip. Using a pastry brush dipped in cold water, moisten the edges of your tart. Fold the edges toward the inside, as if making a hem. Cover it with a towel once more and let it rest at room temperature for 10 minutes. Prick the bottom of the tart with a fork. Pour in the beaten egg.

*Cassonade is an orange-red cane sugar from the French Antilles.

Using a pastry brush, paint the edges with a little egg. Distribute the sugar and chunks of butter over the bottom of the tart.

When you are ready to put the tart into the oven, remember to decrease the temperature to 350°F [180°C]. Bake it for about 25 minutes. The edges of the tart will be puffed and nicely golden. The beaten egg and sugar will be lightly caramelized. Unmold the tart onto a rack and let it cool. Dust it generously with granulated sugar before serving. You can also serve it warm.

I love this tart—light and crunchy crust on the outside, incomparably tender on the inside. It is my comfort food.

Tart Flambé

1½ cups [200 g] wheat flour

⅓ of a ⁶⁄₁₀-oz. [17-g] cake of compressed fresh yeast,
   or [5 g] of fresh baker's yeast

1 Tbsp. [20 g / 2 cl] peanut oil

2 pinches of salt

3½ oz. [100 g / 10 cl] warm water

3½ oz. [100 g] crème fraîche

3½ oz. [100 g] salted, smoked pork breast*

1 small onion

To bake:

A baking sheet covered with parchment paper

Prepare your bread dough: Sift the flour, make a hollow, and sprinkle the salt around the edge. Pour the oil and water into the hollow. Gather the flour little by little toward the center and knead the dough for a few minutes. It should turn a lighter color, no longer stick to your fingers, and be very smooth. Cover the dough with a kitchen towel and let it rest in the refrigerator.

Meanwhile, peel the onion, cut it in half and slice it thinly. Cut the smoked salt pork into small lardons. In a saucepan, bring 2 cups [½ liter] of water to a boil. Blanch the onion and lardons for 1 minute. Remove them with a skimmer and drain them. Then turn them into a bowl and set aside.

Preheat the oven to 525°F [270°C].

---

* Use a good double-thick cut bacon.

Roll the pastry on a lightly floured work surface into a thin circle. It should be very thin and translucent, like tracing paper. Roll it around the rolling pin and lift it above the baking sheet covered with parchment paper. Unroll it gently. This allows the dough to relax and prevents it from tearing when it is cut. Using a pastry brush dipped in cold water, moisten a ½-inch [1-cm] border around the pastry rim. Fold this strip toward the inside, as if making a hem. Pinch and mark the doubled edge with the fingertips so that it won't come apart during baking. It should be very narrow and very flat. Prick the bottom of the pastry with a fork.

Pour the crème fraîche over the tart and sprinkle with the onions and lardons. Bake for 3 minutes and serve immediately.

~:~

Tart flambé is a specialty that you have in the winstubs, or taverns, of my area. Traditionally the tart is licked by the flame of a wood fire. The Alsatian word flammekueche literally means "flame tart."

Lemon Tart
(page 237)

*Rich Pastry Hearts
with Sautéed Tropical
Fruits (page 231)*

*Semi-Puff Pastry
Squares with Shallot
Cream (page 265)*

Orange Tart with
Cardamom Streusel
(page 259)

Puréed Chestnut Tart
(page 247)

*Lattice-Covered Tart
with Winter Fruit
(page 261)*

Brioche Tart with
Thick Crème Fraîche
(page 239)

Tart Flambé
(page 278)

Acknowledgments

I couldn't close without thanking everyone who helped in the "confection" of this effort:

- The gourmands of Payot,
- Gilles and Laurence Laurendon,
- Bernhard and Soraya Winkelmann,
- Martine Albertin,
- Fréderick and Pierre Hermé, my friends for as long as I can remember,
- Raymond Émile Waydelich for giving me the inspiration for the Lydia Jacob tart,
- Martine and Jean-Claude Beck, winemakers at Dambach-la-Ville for their Lydia Jacob R.E.W. blue bottle,
- the Écomusée d'Ungersheim that opened its doors to me,
- and finally, the Arts et Collections d'Alsace in Colmar; and the Antiquités Donato in Niedermorschwihr for the lovely articles they let me borrow.

Sources

The elegance and deep flavors of Christine Ferber's tarts stem from the combination of sound culinary technique married with fresh, local fruits and a rich imagination. Ideally, readers who live and cook outside of Alsace will find Christine's recipes not only fascinating and delicious, but inspirational. Local farmers' markets, farm stands, wineries, and other producers are rich sources for the freshest ingredients. Home cooks are encouraged to use their imaginations and seek out the best local ingredients. Particular types of fruits or chocolates are referenced in individual recipes. The following companies and organizations are also good sources for hard-to-find and imported foodstuffs:

Specialty Items, Imported, and Gourmet Foods

- King Arthur Flour, Norwich, VT; tel 800/827-6836; *www.kingarthurflour.com*
- Zingermans, 422 Detroit Street, Ann Arbor, MI 48104; e-mail *toni@zingermans.com*; tel 877/665-3213 or 734/477-5711; fax 734/769-1260; *www.zingermans.com*
- Ethnic Grocer.com; *www.ethnicgrocer.com*
- Dean and Deluca, Attn: Customer Assistance, 2526 East 36th Street North Circle, Wichita, KS 67219; tel 877/826-9246; fax 800/781-4050. New York location: 800/999-0306 ext. 268; *atyourservice@deananddeluca.com*; *www.deananddeluca.com*
- Ideal Cheese, 942 First Avenue (at 52nd Street), New York, NY; tel 212/688-7579; *www.idealcheese.com*
- Vermont Butter & Cheese Company, Websterville, VT 05678; tel 800/884-6287; *www.vtgoats.com*

- Earthy Delights, 1161 E. Clark Road, Suite 260, DeWitt, MI 48820; tel 800/367-4709 or 517/668-2402; fax 517/668-1213; *www.earthy.com*
- National Association of Specialty Food Trade Association; *www.specialty-food.com*
- A Southern Season; tel 800/253 3663; fax 800/646 1118; *www.southernseason.com*
- Harry and David; *www.harry-david.com*
- Sutton Place Gourmet, 3201 New Mexico Ave. NW, Washington, D.C. 20016; tel 202/363-5800; *www.suttongourmet.com*
- Zabar's, 2245 Broadway, New York, NY 10024; tel 800/697-6301; *www.zabars.com*
- Draeger's Gourmet Food and Wine, 222 E. Fourth Street, San Mateo, CA 94401; tel 650/685-3715; e-mail *info@dreagers.com*; *www.draegers.com*
- Cherry Marketing Institute; *www.cherrymkt.org*
- Specialty Produce Market; tel 619/295-1668; *www.specialtyproduce.com*
- Melissa's/World Variety Produce, Inc., Corporate Office, P.O. Box 21127, Los Angeles, CA 90021; tel 800/588-0151; e-mail *Hotline@melissas.com*; *www.melissas.com*
- Frieda's, The Specialty Produce People; *www.friedas.com*
- Sid Wainer & Sons, Specialty Produce, Specialty Foods, 2301 Purchase Street, New Bedford, MA 02746; tel 508/999-6408 or 800/423-8333; fax 508/999-6795; *www.sidwainer.com*
- VegiWorks, Inc.; *www.vegiworks.com*
- Indian River Groves; tel 800/940-3344; *www.floridafruit.com*
- Blackjack Orchards; tel 858/565-0684; fax 858/565-6440; *www.blackjackorchards.com*
- E-Berries, Solimar Farms, Inc., Oxnard, California; tel 877/4BERRIES (877/423-7743); fax 805/986-1178; e-mail *info@e-berries.com*; *www.e-berries.com*
- Pearson Farms Peaches and Pecans; tel 888/423-7374; *www.pearsonfarm.com*
- Diamond Organics; tel 888-ORGANIC (674-2642); fax 888/888-6777; *www.diamondorganics.com*
- Bouquet of Fruits, 2037 W. Bullard, Box 302, Fresno, CA 93711; tel 559/432-9135 or 800/243-7848; fax 559/432-7509; *www.californiatreeripe.com*

For Chocolate
• *www.chocosphere.com*

Teas and Spices
• Seattle Spice, Herbs, and Tea, World Spice Merchants, 1509 Western Avenue, Seattle, WA 98101; tel 206/682-7274; fax 206/622-7564; *www.worldspice.com*
• Penzey's Spice World; tel 800/741-7787; fax 262/785-7678; *www.penzeys.com*

Books and Other Resources
• "The Splendid Table," with Lynne Rossetto Kasper; Minnesota Public Radio; *www.splendidtable.com*
• *The Pie and Pastry Bible*, Ruth Levy Beranbaum. Scribner. A comprehensive resource.
• *Food Finds: America's Best Local Foods and the People Who Produce Them*, Allison Engel and Margaret Engel. HarperCollins, New York
• *The Joy of Cooking*, Irma S. Rombauer and Marion Rombauer Becker. MacMillan, New York
• *http://www.onlineconversion.com/cooking.htm*
• *www.globalgourmet.com*

Index

Fraîche, Served Slightly Warm, 63–64

Brioche Tart with Thick Crème Fraîche, 239–240

in Flan Tart, 243–244

ingredient selection, 9

in Honeycomb Tart with Rhubarb, Orange and
Apple Jam, 89–90

in Raised Sugar Tart, 276–277

recipe, 23–24

Brioche (prepared):

in Kugelhopf Pain Perdu Tart with Black Cherry
Jam (variation), 52

Browned toppings, crème fraîche for, 11

Brown sugar:

in Raised Sugar Tart (substitution), 276–277

Brushes, pastry, 35

Butter, about, 6, 9

C

Cabbage:

Little Cabbage Tarts with Sautéed Salt Pork and
Cabecou Goat Cheese, 65–66

Pumpkin Clafoutis with Boule de Siam and Garlic
Croutons, 270–271

Cabecou goat cheese:

Little Cabbage Tarts with Sautéed Salt Pork and
Cabecou Goat Cheese, 65–66

Cake flour, about, 5

Calvados:

in Flambéed Apple Square, 210–211

Candied citrus peel:

in Florentine Almond Tart, 229–230

in Hazelnut Cream (variation), 28

in Honeycomb Tart with Rhubarb, Orange and
Apple Jam, 89–90

Cantal cheese:

Aligoté Tart with Three Cheeses, 219–220

Caramel:

in Apple Tatin, 212–213

in Apricot Tatin Topped with Dried Fruit and
Gewurztraminer Sabayon, 107–109

Caramel Tartlets with Fresh Walnuts, 189–190

Fig Tart with Caramel, 185–186

Hazelnut Tart with Orange and Caramel, 249–250

Caramelized almonds, in ground praline and praline
paste, 19

Caramelized fruits:

Caramelized Peach Tart with Rosemary, 144–145

in Crunchy Tart with Dried Fruit and Sautéed
Apple Quarters, 216–218

finishing techniques, 31

in Three Pirates Tart, 195–197

Cardamom:

in Black Cherry Jam (variation), 52

Carrot, Orange and Cardamom Jam, 43

in Crème Anglaise (variation), 27

Flaky Pastry Galettes with Carrots, Orange and
Cardamom, 43–44

Mirabelle Plum Tart with Cardamom Sugar,
128–129

Orange Tart with Cardamom Streusel, 259–260

in Sweet Pastry (variation), 16

Chestnuts, glazed:
  Clafoutis with Marrons Glacés, Pears and Fresh
    Walnuts, 187–188
  Puréed Chestnut Tart, 247–248
Chilling of pastry, 13, 14, 33
Chinese cabbage:
  in Pumpkin Clafoutis with Boule de Siam and
    Garlic Croutons (substitution), 270–271
Chives:
  in Baker's Wife's Tart, 81–82
  Chive Cream, 84
  Quiche Lorraine with Brillat-Savarin Cheese and
    Chives, 112–113
  in Semi-Puff Pastry Squares with Shallot Cream,
    265–266
Chocolate:
  Chocolate Tart, 235–236
  in Hazelnut Cream (variation), 28
  Tart with Raspberries and Chocolate, 120–121
  Walnut Tart with Orange and Chocolate, 253–254
  Warm Tart with Pears and Chocolate, 202–203
Christmas cookies, 18. See also Cookies, pastry
Christmas Flavors, Tartlets Tatin with, 241–242
Cinnamon:
  Alsatian Quetsch Plum Tart with Cinnamon Sugar,
    148–149
  in Black Cherry Clafoutis with Fresh Mint (varia-
    tion), 56
  in Black Cherry Jam (variation), 52
  Carrot, Orange and Cinnamon Tart, 41–42
  in Crème Anglaise (variation), 27

Grated Apple Tart with Cinnamon Streusel,
  208–209
in Lydia Jacob Tart, 200–201
in Quetsch Plum Jam, 150–151, 154–155
Rich Flaky Pastry with Cinnamon, 154–155
in Sweet Pastry (variation), 16
in Three Pirates Tart, 195–197
Vineyard Peach Jam Flavored with Pinot Noir and
  Cinnamon, 169–170
Citrus fruits. See specific fruits
Citrus peel, candied:
  in Florentine Almond Tart, 229–230
  in Hazelnut Cream (variation), 28
  in Honeycomb Tart with Rhubarb, Orange and
    Apple Jam, 89–90
Citrus zest. See also Lemon zest; Lime zest; Orange zest
  in Almond Cream (variation), 28
  in Crème Anglaise (variation), 27
  in Flan Cream (variation), 25
  in Hazelnut Cream (variation), 28
  Quince Tart with Slivered Citrus Zest and Spices,
    175–176
  in Rich Flaky Pastry No. 1 (variation), 18
  in Sweet Pastry (variation), 16
Clafoutis:
  Black Cherry Clafoutis with Fresh Mint, 55–56
  Clafoutis with Marrons Glacés, Pears and Fresh
    Walnuts, 187–188
  pans for, 34
  Pumpkin Clafoutis with Boule de Siam and Garlic
    Croutons, 270–271

Croutons, 270–271
Crunchy Tart with Dried Fruit and Sautéed Apple
    Quarters, 216–218
Crusts. *See* Cookie layers; Pastry
Currants:
    Black Currant Jam, 114–115
    in Peak of Freshness Tart with Red and Black Fruit,
        136–137
    in Pierre Hermé's Pineapple Macaroon Tart, 233–234
    Red Currant Jelly, 31
    Red Currant Meringue Tart, 126–127
    Rich Pastry Galettes with Black Currants and
        Raspberries, 114–115
    in Wild Blueberry Meringue Tart (variation), 111
Custard. *See* Creams; Egg Custard; Flan Cream; Rice
    Custard; Sabayon
Custard Cream, 63–64
Custard Tart with Spring Fruits, 77–78
Cutouts, decorating pastry with, 31
Cutting boards, 34

D

Dartois with Morbier Cheese and Tarragon, 179–180
Decorating techniques:
    finishing, 10, 31–32
    glazing, 29–31
Dill:
    Rice Custard Tart with Salmon and Dill, 274–275
Dip and sweep measuring method, 6
Dough. *See* Bread Dough; Brioche Dough; Pastry

Dried beans or rice, blind-baking with, 14, 35
Dried fruit:
    in Apple Strudel, 214–215
    Apricot Tatin Topped with Dried Fruit and
        Gewurztraminer Sabayon, 107–109
    Crunchy Tart with Dried Fruit and Sautéed Apple
        Quarters, 216–218
    finishing techniques, 31
    in Lattice-Topped Tart with Winter Fruit, 261–262
    to make citrus fruit slices, 131

E

Edelzwicker:
    in Sauerkraut and Munster Tart, 173–174
Egg Custard:
    in Alsatian Quiche, 223–224
    in Asparagus and Fennel Tart, 39–40
    in Cauliflower Tart with Mustard Seed, 116–117
    Custard Tart with Spring Fruits, 77–78
    in Leek Tart, 146–147
    in Onion Tart, 257–258
    in Quiche Lorraine with Brillat-Savarin Cheese and
        Chives, 112–113
    in Sauerkraut and Munster Tart, 173–174
    in Spinach Tart with Salmon and Soft Goat Cheese,
        67–68
    in Tartiflette, 221–222
Eggplant:
    Square Tart of Tomato Confit with Eggplant,
        161–163

Eggs:
  about, 10
  Flaky Pastry with Egg, 15–16
Egg wash for finishing tarts, 10, 31
Elderberry flowers:
  Rhubarb Tart with Sautéed Apples and Elderberry
    Flowers, 87–88
Electric mixers, 34
Equipment selection:
  essential items, 33
  pans, 33–34
  scales, 8, 34
  utensils, 34–35
  work surface, 33
Ewe cheeses:
  Little Cabbage Tarts with Sautéed Salt Pork and
    Cabecou Goat Cheese, 65–66
  Tomato Zucchini Puffs with Brin d'Amour Cheese,
    159–160
Extra-fine sugar, about, 6

F

Faisselle:
  about, 7, 8
  in Fromage Blanc Tart, 245–246
  in Leek Tart, 146–147
  in Morello Cherry Tart with Fromage Blanc, 61–62
  in Raspberry Tart with White Munster (variation),
    119
Fennel:

Asparagus and Fennel Tart, 39–40
Figs:
  Fig Tart with Caramel, 185–186
  Fig Tart with Orange and Walnuts, 183–184
  Puff Pastry Pillows with Pears and Figs Sautéed
    with Vanilla, 191–192
Figs, dried:
  in Apricot Tatin Topped with Dried Fruit and
    Gewurztraminer Sabayon, 107–109
  in Crunchy Tart with Dried Fruit and Sautéed
    Apple Quarters, 216–218
  in Lattice-Topped Tart with Winter Fruit, 261–262
Filberts. *See Hazelnuts*
Fillings. *See also specific ingredients*
  ingredient selection, 6, 9, 10
Finishing techniques, 10, 31–32
Flaky Pastry. *See also* Rich flaky pastries; *specific types*
  in Alsatian Apple Tart, 206–207
  in Custard Tart with Spring Fruits, 77–78
  in Fromage Blanc Tart, 245–246
  ingredient selection, 5, 9–11
  in Mirabelle Plum Tart with Cardamom Sugar,
    128–129
  in Morello Cherry Tart with Apple and Lemon
    Zest, 59–60
  in Morello Cherry Tart with Crunchy Almonds,
    57–58
  in Morello Cherry Tart with Fromage Blanc, 61–62
  in My Father's Quince Tart with Raspberries and
    Kirsch, 177–178
  in Peak of Freshness Tart with Red and Black Fruit,

G

Lavender:

    White and Yellow Peach Clafoutis with Lavender, 142–143

Leavening agents, about, 10, 23

Leek Tart, 146–147

Lemon Cream, 237–238

Lemongrass:

    Peach and Raspberry Tart with Lemongrass, 140–141

Lemon Jelly, 255–256

Lemon juice:

    as jelly flavoring, 29

    in Lemon Cream, 237–238

    in Lemon Tart, 237–238

Lemon peel, candied:

    in Florentine Almond Tart, 229–230

    in Hazelnut Cream (variation), 28

Lemon thyme:

    in Tomato Galette with Olives and Grilled Peppers, 164–165

Lemon zest:

    in Almond Cream (variation), 28

    in Crème Anglaise (variation), 27

    in Flan Cream (variation), 25

    in Galette from My Childhood, 251–252

    in Lemon Jelly, 256

    in Lemon Tart, 237–238

    Morello Cherry Tart with Apple and Lemon Zest, 59–60

    Quince Tart with Slivered Citrus Zest and Spices, 175–176

    in Rich Flaky Pastry No. 1 (variation), 18

Lime Jelly, 231–232

Lime zest:

    in Lime Jelly, 232

    in Pierre Hermé's Pineapple Macaroon Tart, 233–234

Linden honey:

    Puff Pastry Square with Mirabelle Plums and Linden Blossom Honey, 130–131

Liqueurs. *See also specific types*

    in Pastry Cream (variation), 25

Liquors. *See also specific types*

    in Pastry Cream (variation), 25

Little Cabbage Tarts with Sautéed Salt Pork and Cabecou Goat Cheese, 65–66

Lydia Jacob Tart, 200–201

M

Macaroon tarts:

    Pierre Hermé's Pineapple Macaroon Tart, 233–234

Mangoes:

    Brioche Tart with Apricots and Diced Mango, 105–106

    in Rich Pastry Hearts with Sautéed Tropical Fruits, 231–232

Mara strawberries:

    Rich Flaky Tartlets with Homegrown and Wild Strawberries, 71–72

Marble work surfaces, 14, 21, 23, 33

Marrons glacés:

N

Normandy butter, about, 9
Nougapricot Tart, 101–102
Nutmeg, fresh:
    in Rhubarb Tart with Spiced Meringue, 85–86
Nuts. *See* Almonds; Chestnuts; Hazelnuts; Pistachios;
    Walnuts

O

Old Bachelor's Tart, 138–139
Old-Fashioned Rich Flaky Pastry Tart with Quetsch
    Plum Jam, 150–151
Olives:
    Tomato Galette with Olives and Grilled Peppers,
      164–165
Onions:
    in Baker's Wife's Tart, 81–82
    Onion Tart, 257–258
    Spring Carrot and Little May Onion Tart, 45–46
    in Tart Flambé, 278–279
Orange blossom, essence of:
    in Almond Cream (variation), 28
Orange juice:
    in Carrot, Orange and Cardamom Jam, 13
    in Carrot, Orange and Cinnamon Tart, 41–42
    in Flaky Pastry Galettes with Carrots, Orange and
      Cardamom, 43–44
    in Lattice-Topped Tart with Winter Fruit, 261–262
    in Vineyard Peach Jam, 169–170
Orange peel, candied:
    in Hazelnut Cream (variation), 28

    in Honeycomb Tart with Rhubarb, Orange and
      Apple Jam, 89–90
Oranges:
    in Custard Tart with Spring Fruits, 77–78
    Fig Tart with Orange and Walnuts, 183–184
    Orange Tart with Cardamom Streusel, 259–260
    Rhubarb, Orange and Apple Jam, 89–90
Orange zest:
    in Almond Cream (variation), 28
    in Flan Cream (variation), 25
    in Hazelnut Cream (variation), 28
    in Hazelnut Tart with Orange and Caramel,
      249–250
    in Pumpkin Clafoutis with Orange Streusel,
      268–269
    Quince Tart with Slivered Citrus Zest and Spices,
      175–176
    in Rich Flaky Pastry No. 1 (variation), 18
    in Walnut Tart with Orange and Chocolate,
      253–254

P

Paillasson Potato Haystack with Saint-Félicien Cheese
    and Toasted Hazelnuts, 267
Pain d'épice:
    in Crème Anglaise (variation), 27
    in Sweet Pastry (variation), 16
Pain perdu:
    Kugelhopf Pain Perdu Tart with Black Cherry Jam,
      51–52

Potatoes:
    in Aligoté Tart with Three Cheeses, 219–220
    in Baker's Wife's Tart, 81–82
    in Bougon Goat Cheese Tartlets, 83–84
    Paillasson Potato Haystack with Saint-Félicien
        Cheese and Toasted Hazelnuts, 267
    in Semi-Puff Pastry Squares with Shallot Cream,
        265–266
    in Tartiflette, 221–222
Praline paste. *See also* Rich Flaky Pastry with Praline
        Paste and Hazelnuts
    about, 19
Produce selection, 8, 11, 30
Prunes:
    in Crunchy Tart with Dried Fruit and Sautéed
        Apple Quarters, 216–218
    in Lattice-Topped Tart with Winter Fruit, 261–262
Puff pastry. *See also specific types*
    ingredient selection, 5, 6, 9
    Semi-Puff Pastry, 20–21
    True Puff Pastry, 21–23
Pumpkin:
    Pumpkin Clafoutis with Boule de Siam and Garlic
        Croutons, 270–271
    Pumpkin Clafoutis with Orange Streusel, 268–269
Puréed Chestnut Tart, 247–248

Q

Quark, as fromage blanc substitute, 8
Quetsch plums:

Alsatian Quetsch Plum Tart with Cinnamon Sugar,
    148–149
Alsatian Tart with Quetsch Plums and Streusel,
    152–153
My Grandmother's Quetsch Tart, 154–156
Old-Fashioned Rich Flaky Pastry Tart with Quetsch
    Plum Jam, 150–151
Quetsch Plum Jam, 150–151, 154–155
Quiche:
    Alsatian Quiche, 223–224
    Quiche Lorraine with Brillat-Savarin Cheese and
        Chives, 112–113
Quinces:
    My Father's Quince Tart with Raspberries and
        Kirsch, 177–178
    Quince Tart with Slivered Citrus Zest and Spices,
        175–176
    in Tartlets Tatin with Christmas Flavors, 241–242

R

Racks, pastry, 35
Raised doughs. *See* Yeast; Yeast doughs
Raisins:
    in Apple Strudel, 214–215
Raspberries:
    in Custard Tart with Spring Fruits, 77–78
    glaze recommendations, 29
    My Father's Quince Tart with Raspberries and
        Kirsch, 177–178
    Peach and Raspberry Tart with Lemongrass, 140–141

Tomato Zucchini Puffs with Brin d'Amour Cheese, 159–160
Turning of pastry, 21
    Type 45 flour, about, 5, 9
    Type 55 flour, about, 5, 6, 9

U

Unbleached flour, about, 5
Utensil selection. *See* Equipment selection

V

Vanilla beans:
    in Apple and Rice Custard Tart, 263–264
    in Caramel Tartlets with Fresh Walnuts, 189–190
    in Clafoutis with Marrons Glacés, Pears and Fresh Walnuts, 187–188
    in Crème Anglaise, 26
    in Fig Tart with Caramel, 185–186
    in Pastry Cream, 25
    Puff Pastry Pillows with Pears and Figs Sautéed with Vanilla, 191–192
    in Pumpkin Clafoutis with Orange Streusel, 268–269
    in Puréed Chestnut Tart, 247–248
    in Rice Custard Tart with Crunchy Almond Topping, 272–273
    in Spiced Pears in Party Dress, 193–194
    in Sunburst Tart, 198–199
    in Three Pirates Tart, 195–197

Vanilla sugar:
    in Flan Tart, 243–244
    as glaze, 31
    to make, 10
    in My Grandmother's Quetsch Tart, 154–156
    Pear and Apple Tart with Vanilla Sugar, 204–205
    in Rich Flaky Pastry No. 1, 17–18
    in Rich Flaky Pastry with Praline Paste and Hazelnuts, 19–20
    in Sweet Pastry, 16–17
Vegetable tarts. *See* Savory tarts; *specific vegetables*
Vermont Butter and Cheese, 7, 8
Victoria pineapple:
    Pierre Hermé's Pineapple Macaroon Tart, 233–234
    in Rich Pastry Hearts with Sautéed Tropical Fruits, 231–232
Vinegar, wine:
    in Lattice-Topped Tart with Cèpes, Chanterelles and Shallots, 171–172
    in Semi-Puff Pastry Squares with Shallot Cream, 265–266
Vineyard peaches:
    Vineyard Peach Jam Flavored with Pinot Noir and Cinnamon, 169–170
Violet, essence of:
    in Black Currant Jam (variation), 115

W

Walnuts:
    in Apple Strudel, 214–215

Gewurztraminer Sabayon, 107–109

Muscat d'Alsace Sabayon, 226

in Sauerkraut and Munster Tart, 173–174

in Vineyard Peach Jam, 169–170

Wine vinegar:

    in Lattice-Topped Tart with Cèpes, Chanterelles and
Shallots, 171–172

    in Semi-Puff Pastry Squares with Shallot Cream,
265–266

Winter Fruit, Lattice-Topped Tart with, 261–262

Wondra flour, about, 5

Wooden board, as work surface, 33

Work surface:

    temperature of, 14, 21, 23, 33

Y

Yeast, about, 10, 23

Yeast doughs. *See also* Bread Dough; Brioche Dough

ingredient selection, 5, 9, 10

Yellow fruits, glaze recommendations, 29. *See also specific
fruits*

Yellow peaches:

    Caramelized Peach Tart with Rosemary, 144–145

    White and Yellow Peach Clafoutis with Lavender,
142–143

Yogurt, as fromage blanc substitute, 8

Z

Zest, citrus. *See* Citrus zest

Zucchini:

    Tomato Zucchini Puffs with Brin d'Amour Cheese,
159–160